The Formative Years
of the
Catholic University of America

Nihil Obstat:

JOHN K. CARTWRIGHT
Censor Deputatus

Imprimatur:

MICHAEL J. CURLEY
Archbishop of Baltimore and Washington

July 3, 1945

For permission to quote from the two works of Schlesinger (pp. 16, 18) thanks
are due to the Macmillan Company; for a similar permission to quote from
the work of Wittke (p. 199) thanks are due to Prentice-Hall, Inc.; for permission to quote from the volume by Cross (p. 19) thanks are due to Yale
University Press.

MURRAY & HEISTER—WASHINGTON, D. C.

PRINTED IN THE UNITED STATES OF AMERICA

 9

JOHN J. KEANE
First Rector of the University, 1887–1896

The Formative Years
of the
Catholic University of America

By JOHN TRACY ELLIS

Associate Professor of American Church History
in the
Catholic University of America

WASHINGTON
AMERICAN CATHOLIC HISTORICAL ASSOCIATION
1946

IN LOVING MEMORY OF MY FATHER
ELMER L. ELLIS
DECEMBER 1, 1879–OCTOBER 26, 1945
WITHOUT WHOSE SACRIFICE AND
GENEROSITY MY UNIVERSITY
EDUCATION WOULD NOT
HAVE BEEN POSSIBLE.

"If then a University is a direct preparation for this world, let it be what it professes. It is not a Convent, it is not a Seminary; it is a place to fit men of the world for the world. We cannot possibly keep them from plunging into the world, with all its ways and principles and maxims, when their time comes; but we can prepare them against what is inevitable; and it is not the way to learn to swim in troubled waters, never to have gone into them." JOHN HENRY NEWMAN, *Idea of a University.*

Contents

Illustrations

ix

Preface

IT IS NOW over six years since the Catholic University of America celebrated its golden jubilee. The festivities of those days of November, 1939, were memorable ones, even though they were somewhat overcast by the shadow of the war which had broken out in Europe less than three months before. When one thinks in terms of Bologna, Paris, Oxford, and the other medieval university foundations, the short term of fifty-six years seems, indeed, as a mere passing moment in the life of a university. Yet despite its youth the Catholic University of America has fulfilled in good measure the hopes of its founders. With a limited endowment which at no time during the years has permitted its administrators to implement all their ideas for the University's advancement, it has, nonetheless, maintained the ideal of a center for graduate study for American Catholics where the best traditions of American and European scholarship have found a friendly atmosphere and a steadily expanding scope. When the Association of American Universities was organized in February, 1900, in Chicago, the Catholic University of America was invited to join as a charter member with thirteen other universities whose principal emphasis was on raising the standards of graduate work. During the forty-six years since that time the University has continued and profited from that membership, and it has endeavored to play its own modest part in the Association's efforts for American higher learning.

It has been thought wise to limit the present study to the formative years of the University's life, in other words, from the post-Civil War days when the bishops first began to think seriously of a university up to the formal opening of the institution in November, 1889. To pursue the subject beyond that time would inevitably involve the historian in problems to which he could scarcely give a satisfactory solution at so early a date. When the time comes for the definitive history of the national Catholic university of the United States to be written the present volume may serve as an introduction. If it succeeds in accomplishing that purpose, as well as throwing some light on the critical problems which marked the University's foundation and the general American reaction thereto as seen through the press, it will have been worth while. In the years which have passed since 1889 the Catholic University of America has won an increasingly strong support from the Catholic people all over the vast expanse of the United States. For this support the University owes much to the American hierarchy and to the general Catholic body of the country, which through its generous response to the annual collection has given the equivalent of a considerable endowment in yearly income. It has enjoyed, too, the loyal support of educators in other Catholic universities, seminaries, and colleges of the nation in carrying out the tasks which it was founded to perform, and among these should specifically be mentioned the members of the many religious orders of men and women who have strengthened the University's life through their professors and students in its classrooms.

No writer can safely undertake a work of this kind entirely on his own. During the period of nearly three years in which the writer has been engaged in this endeavor he has incurred many obligations for assistance in one form or other. If his work possesses value from the point of view of the historian it is by virtue of the fact that it has been done in large measure from archival sources. In his visits to the archival depositories of the Church in the United States he has been treated with singular courtesy and kindness. He wishes especially to thank the Most Reverend Michael J. Curley and his chancellor, the Right Reverend Joseph M. Nelligan, who not only permitted the use of the rich collection of the Baltimore Cathedral Archives, but who gave to the writer the warmest hospitality during those many days. For similar courtesies he is indebted to the Most Reverend Peter L. Ireton, Bishop of Richmond, the Right Reverend John M. A. Fearns, Rector of St. Joseph's Seminary, Dunwoodie, and the Reverends William J. Gauche and Robert Bastian of Mount Saint Mary's Seminary of the West, Cincinnati, Thomas T. McAvoy, C.S.C., of the University of Notre Dame, Robert F. McNamara of St. Bernard's Seminary, Rochester, and Harry C. Koenig of St. Mary of the Lake Seminary, Mundelein. Five kind friends have read the manuscript and by virtue of their criticisms and suggestions it has been immeasurably improved and strengthened. For this generous service the writer is grateful to the Right Reverend John K. Cartwright, Rector of St. Matthew's Cathedral, Washington, the Very Reverend Louis A. Arand, S.S., President of Divinity College at the Catholic University of America, Thomas F. O'Connor, Historiographer of the Archdiocese of New York, Professor Roy J. Deferrari, Secretary-General of the Catholic University of America, and Dr. Martin R. P. McGuire, Dean of the Graduate School of Arts and

Sciences of the Catholic University of America. A number of friends and colleagues in other institutions have been kind enough to make copies of documents and newspaper accounts from the collections in their respective archives and libraries. For this very helpful assistance the writer is indebted to the Reverend Robert H. Lord, pastor of St. Paul's Church, Wellesley, Massachusetts, the Reverend Peter Leo Johnson of St. Francis Seminary, Milwaukee, the Reverend Ambrose G. Wagner of St. Mary's Cathedral, Covington, Sister Agnes Geraldine McGann of Nazareth College, Kentucky, and Sister M. Alphonsine Frawley of Regis College, Weston, Massachusetts. He is likewise grateful to his friend, the Reverend Henry J. Browne of the Archdiocese of New York, for a careful reading of the proofs and to Miss Elsie L. Russell for the exact and conscientious manner in which she carried out the tedious task of compiling the index. To each and every one of these the writer wishes to record his sense of gratitude and obligation, for in their service to him they have gone a long way towards giving the volume whatever worth it may have.

JOHN TRACY ELLIS

Feast of St. John the Evangelist
December 27, 1945

I

The Growth of an Idea

FIVE MONTHS before the Catholic University of America opened its doors to receive its first students there was published in the *North American Review* for June, 1889, a famous essay entitled, "Wealth." Its author, Andrew Carnegie, had already won fame as a dominant figure in the steel industry and his essay caused a stir on both sides of the Atlantic. Carnegie wrote:

This, then, is held to be the duty of the man of Wealth: First, to set an example of modest, unostentatious living, shunning display or extravagance; to provide moderately for the legitimate wants of those dependent upon him; and after doing so to consider all surplus revenues which come to him simply as trust funds, which he is called upon to administer, and strictly bound as a matter of duty to administer in the manner which, in his judgment, is best calculated to produce the most beneficial results for the community—the man of wealth thus becoming the mere agent and trustee for his poorer brethren, bringing to their service his superior wisdom, experience, and ability to administer, doing for them better than they would or could do for themselves . . . Thus is the problem of Rich and

15

Poor to be solved. The laws of accumulation will be left free; the laws of distribution free. Individualism will continue, but the millionaire will be but a trustee for the poor . . .[1]

The essay represented the best expression to date of the philosophy of philanthropy in a period which was characterized by the most lavish outlays of money for cultural advancements on the part of the new industrial barons of the so-called Gilded Age. Much of the wealth assigned by the industrial magnates of the United States in these years for the endowment of cultural pursuits found its way into higher education. "Between 1878 and 1898 private benefaction added no less than one hundred and forty million dollars to the revenues for higher education, affecting all its branches, undergraduate, graduate, professional and technical." [2]

There were many imitators of George Peabody whose amazing success in marketing American securities in London won him a fortune which he liberally dispensed to educational institutions in both the North and South before and after the Civil War. For example, Ezra Cornell's gift of a site and $500,000 enabled Andrew D. White to open Cornell University in the fall of 1868. Cornelius Vanderbilt's gift of one million dollars transformed the old Central University at Nashville into the thriving Vanderbilt University in 1873. Farther north, Baltimore's Quaker bachelor-

[1] Andrew Carnegie, "Wealth," in *North American Review*, CXLVIII (June, 1889), 661–664. Ralph H. Gabriel, *The Course of American Democratic Thought* (New York, 1940), has a good chapter entitled, "The Gospel of Wealth of the Gilded Age," pp. 143–160, which discusses the Carnegie essay.

[2] Arthur Meier Schlesinger, *The Rise of the City, 1878–1898* (New York, 1933), p. 219.

merchant, Johns Hopkins, made his will in 1870 and assigned seven million dollars to be divided equally between the Johns Hopkins University and the hospital of the same name. Daniel Coit Gilman was called from his presidency of the University of California to lead the new university in Baltimore and Johns Hopkins opened in 1876. The railroad magnate, Leland Stanford, by his benefaction of $2,500,000 brought into existence in 1885 Leland Stanford Junior University at Palo Alto. And it was the million dollar gift of the Massachusetts industrialist, Jonas G. Clark, which enabled G. Stanley Hall to implement his ideas on graduate study in heading New England's first exclusively graduate institution in Clark University which opened at Worcester in October, 1889.

Older colleges and universities likewise shared in the benefactions of the philanthropists of these years of the late century. Harvard received many additions to its endowment, and with the inauguration of President Charles W. Eliot in October, 1869, there came as well a new orientation to the oldest university of the United States which led in time to radical departures in a number of phases of American higher education. Eliot's long presidency at Harvard (1869–1909) spanned the period during which American graduate study took firm root. But the most magnificent of all benefactions to higher education in the Gilded Age was yet to come with John D. Rockefeller's millions which gave into the hands of President William Rainey Harper the necessary financial resources to reorganize the old University of Chicago and open it in 1892 as practically a new institution dedicated to the advancement of graduate instruction. In all between 1860 and 1900 over 260 new institutions of college or university

rank were founded in the United States.[3] A number of
these were state institutions, endowed in land through the
provisions of the Morrill Act which was passed by Congress
in 1862. From that date to 1900 this federal aid accounted
for twenty additional state universities, located for the most
part in the Middle West and the Far West.

Although the numerical growth of institutions of higher
learning following the Civil War was, indeed, impressive,
only a very few of these schools made any real contribution
to the advancement of graduate instruction. When the
National Teachers' Association met in 1869 in Trenton
it could report in truth, "We have, as yet, no near approach to a real university in America." [4] To be sure, some
colleges and universities had granted advanced degrees
from a very early date but the degrees were mostly unearned. Harvard had reorganized its academic council in
1872 and had given it charge over the A.M., Ph.D., and
Sc.D. degrees. But only in 1874 was the first master of
arts degree in course conferred at Harvard. Yale University
gave its first master's degree in course in 1876 and Prince-

---

[3] Arthur Meier Schlesinger, *Political and Social Growth of the
American People, 1865–1940,* 3rd ed. (New York, 1941), p. 201.
For a survey of American institutions before this period cf. Donald G.
Tewsksbury, *The Founding of American Colleges and Universities
before the Civil War with Particular Reference to the Religious Influences Bearing on the College Movement* (New York, 1932). The
literature on American institutions of higher learning in general leaves
much to be desired. Samuel Eliot Morison and Henry Steele Com-
mager in *The Growth of the American Republic,* 3rd ed. (New York,
1942), have written: "Practically every college and university has its
'history' but most of them are concerned largely with finances and
athletics, and the character of university histories as of church histories is a major scandal in American scholarship." II, 704.

[4] United States Commissioner of Education, *Annual Report, 1870*
(Washington, 1870), p. 418.

ton followed in 1879.[5] But these, together with some scattered efforts elsewhere, were only feeble beginnings. Others had made earlier attempts, such as President Henry P. Tappan of the University of Michigan where in 1871 Professor Charles K. Adams had introduced from Germany the historical seminar, but their efforts proved in good measure abortive and little substantial gain in graduate instruction came of them. It remained for Daniel Coit Gilman at Johns Hopkins to lead the way in the organization of America's first graduate school after his presidential inauguration at Baltimore on February 22, 1876. That Johns Hopkins did point the way was publicly acknowledged on the occasion of the university's silver jubilee in February, 1902, when President Eliot of Harvard as one of the principal speakers, said:

I want to testify that the graduate school of Harvard University, started feebly in 1870 and in 1871, did not thrive until the example of Johns Hopkins forced our faculty to put their strength into the development of our instruction for graduates. And what was true of Harvard was true of every other university in the land which aspired to create an advanced school of arts and sciences.[6]

[5] Walter C. John, *Graduate Study in Universities and Colleges in the United States* (Washington, 1935), pp. 5–6. In 1732 George Berkeley, the English philosopher and later Anglican bishop, gave his Newport, Rhode Island, farm to Yale College on the stipulation that the rent therefrom be used to maintain three resident students, "during the period of study between their first and second degrees; that is, between their B.A. and M.A. degrees." Wilbur L. Cross, *Connecticut Yankee. An Autobiography* (New Haven, 1943), p. 152. Cross states that a considerable number of students took advanced training on the Berkeley foundation, among them the first presidents of Dartmouth and the College of New Jersey.

[6] *Johns Hopkins University Celebration of the Twenty-Fifth Anni-*

From the outset the emphasis at Baltimore was on a university rather than a college. It was Gilman's idea that the assembling of a group of trained specialists with a small but carefully selected number of students who had already finished their collegiate training, would do more for the advancement of learning in America than would the founding of just another college. John J. Keane, first rector of the Catholic University of America, who became a close student of educational trends at Hopkins in the years that the Washington university was taking shape, appreciated Gilman's position. Almost two years before the university opened at Washington he wrote:

Very recently, President Gilman has found it necessary to impress upon the public mind again and again that the Johns Hopkins University, which he is so ably organizing, was not meant to be an addition to the number of colleges or technical schools, for these are both numerous and excellent enough; that young men were to enter the university after having received a college education, or its equivalent, in order to find there that higher learning which the fullest intellectual development calls for, and which colleges and technical schools are inadequate to bestow.[7]

For this reason Gilman and his colleagues laid stress on

---

versary of the Founding of the University (Baltimore, 1902), p. 105. For a survey of early graduate schools cf. W. Carson Ryan, *Studies in Early Graduate Education* (New York, 1939). This monograph which was published as Bulletin Number Thirty of the Carnegie Foundation for the Advancement of Teaching, confines itself largely to three pioneer graduate schools: Johns Hopkins, Clark, and Chicago. No mention whatever is made by Ryan of the Catholic University of America, although it was founded as exclusively a graduate institution the same year as Clark and three years before the University of Chicago.

[7] John J. Keane, "The Catholic University of Louvain," in *Catholic World*, XLVI (Jan. 1888), 530–531.

quality, offering promising graduate students free scholarships to pursue their studies; the familiar keying of energies and resources to the construction of buildings was expressly relegated to second place by the terms of the Hopkins grant. The trustees of the university prepared themselves for the task of launching this educational experiment by wide travel and observation. They visited in a body Yale, Michigan, Cornell, Pennsylvania, Harvard, Virginia, and other universities, taking counsel with men like Eliot, White, and James G. Angell at Ann Arbor. It was this same studied effort to have the best that caused them to choose the president of the University of California as a man possessing sufficient vision to head the Baltimore institution. One of Johns Hopkins' early professors, G. Stanley Hall, who had been German-trained at Bonn and Leipzig, followed a similar course when he set off in 1888 on a pedagogical tour before assuming active duty as president of the new Clark University in the fall of 1889. Likewise, Bishop Keane spent a good part of two years following his appointment in 1886 touring Europe and America to familiarize himself with the latest methods of university administration and instruction. The response to these initial efforts at graduate work in the United States was not impressive from the point of view of numbers. The academic year 1871–72 found only 198 graduate students throughout the country, a figure which had risen by the year 1888–89, when the new university opened in Washington, to 1,343.[8] The next year, however, 1889–90, showed a total of 2,382 graduate students and the rise thereafter was steady.[9] But

[8] John, *op. cit.*, p. 12.
[9] United States Office of Education, *Biennial Survey of Education, 1928–1930* (Washington, 1932), p. 339.

graduate study was yet in its infancy and the remarkable
growth of our own day was still far in the distance.

With such a condition obtaining generally it is not
strange to find that little or nothing had been done among
American Catholics for the advancement of graduate instruction up to the 1880's. There were numerous institutions with collegiate charters which were conducted under
Catholic auspices, although many of them were hardly
more than secondary schools. By 1866, the year when the
American bishops assembled in Baltimore for the Second
Plenary Council, there were sixty Catholic colleges and
seven institutions which bore the name of universities. By
1875 this number had risen to seventy-four.[10] As early as
January, 1805, the Maryland legislature had granted a
university charter to St. Mary's Seminary in Baltimore and
on March 1, 1815, a university charter was conferred by
Congress on Georgetown College. St. Louis University,
which was formally opened by the Jesuits as a college on
November 2, 1829, won its university charter from the
Missouri legislature in 1832.[11] On December 19, 1844, the

---

[10] Brother Agatho Zimmer, F.S.C., *Changing Concepts of Higher
Education in America Since 1700* (Washington, 1938), p. 96. All
these institutions under Catholic auspices were for men since the
first Catholic college for women was not opened until 1895, the College of Notre Dame of Maryland in Baltimore. For sketches of these
early Catholic colleges for men, cf. Francis P. Cassidy, *Catholic College Foundations and Development in the United States, 1667–1850*
(Washington, 1924) and Sebastian A. Erbacher, O.F.M., *Catholic
Higher Education for Men in the United States, 1850–1866* (Washington, 1931).

[11] For the early history of St. Mary's, cf. Joseph W. Ruane, *The
Beginnings of the Society of St. Sulpice in the United States, 1791–
1829* (Washington, 1935), pp. 37–94, 187–215; and for Georgetown,
John Gilmary Shea, *Memorial of the First Centenary of Georgetown*

legislature of Illinois granted a university charter to the University of St. Mary of the Lake in Chicago, founded by Bishop William Quarter, and the same year marked a similar grant from the Indiana legislature to the University of Notre Dame.[12] But of these early Catholic institutions bearing the name of university or enjoying a charter for such, only St. Louis granted advanced degrees with anything approaching regularity. The first master of arts degree was conferred at St. Louis in 1834. The Civil War played havoc with the university, situated as it was in a border state and drawing a good percentage of its students from the South. The master of arts degree continued to be granted to alumni who had given two years to some literary pursuit after having received the bachelor of arts degree. The annual catalogue for 1861–62 announced that this same degree might be earned "by devoting a second year to the study of Philosophy in the Institution, or two years to a learned profession." In October, 1879, a formal graduate course was inaugurated at St. Louis but here, strangely enough, the emphasis was upon the bachelor of philosophy degree rather than the master of arts. It was not until 1883 that St. Louis University gave its first doctor of philosophy degree.[13]

College, D. C. Comprising a History of Georgetown University (Washington, 1891). For St. Louis University, cf. the extensive treatment given by Gilbert J. Garraghan, S.J., in his chapter, "The Beginnings of St. Louis University," in The Jesuits of the Middle United States (New York, 1938), I, 269–308.

[12] For the University of St. Mary of the Lake cf. Gilbert J. Garraghan, S.J., The Catholic Church in Chicago, 1673–1871 (Chicago, 1921), pp. 112 ff., and for Notre Dame the work of Arthur J. Hope, C.S.C., Notre Dame. One Hundred Years (Notre Dame, 1942).

[13] The development of early graduate work among American Catholics is sketched in broad outline by Roy J. Deferrari in the

In the case of St. Mary's in Baltimore, the Sulpician administration, thinking in terms of their principal purpose of training young men for the priesthood, laid little emphasis on degrees, even though they enjoyed the right from the State of Maryland and the Holy See to grant such. Pope Pius VII had on April 18, 1822, given to St. Mary's the privileges usually accorded to pontifical universities and in pursuance of this right the doctorate of divinity was conferred on January 25, 1824, on James Whitfield, Louis R. Deluol, and Edward Damphoux.[14] But since at the time Whitfield was vicar general of the Archdiocese of Baltimore, Deluol a professor in the seminary, and Damphoux the president of St. Mary's College, obviously these degrees were not earned in course. Moreover, St. Mary's Seminary availed itself little for the balance of the nineteenth century of its right to grant advanced degrees. The Sulpicians also maintained in Baltimore an undergraduate institution for laymen called St. Mary's College. It granted the master of arts degree but not for work done in course. For example, we read in one of the early issues of the *Catholic Almanac* that this degree would be conferred, "on students of the College, who, two years, at least, after having received that of Bachelor of Arts, will apply for it to the President of the Faculty, provided they can prove, that from the

---

volume which he edited under the title of *Essays on Catholic Education in the United States* (Washington, 1942), in a chapter entitled, "The Origin and Development of Graduate Studies under Catholic Auspices," pp. 195–215.

[14] Ruane, *op. cit.*, pp. 210–213. Gabriel Bruté was offered the degree but declined. Sister Mary Salesia Godecker, *Simon Bruté de Rémur, First Bishop of Vincennes* (St. Meinrad, Indiana, 1931), p. 116.

time they left the College, they have been engaged in
literary or scientific pursuits, and can produce certificates
of moral deportment." [15] It was in this college that many
of the prominent men of Maryland were trained in the
first half of the century. In a farewell address given in
1902 when he was leaving office as president of the Johns
Hopkins University after a tenure of a quarter century,
Gilman spoke of higher education in Maryland as it existed
in 1876 and he said:

The Catholic Church had established within the borders
of the State a large number of important schools of learning. One of them, St. Mary's College, under the cultivated
fathers of St. Sulpice, had been the training place of some
of the original promoters of the Johns Hopkins University. [16]

Considering the very faltering steps which had been taken
up to the last quarter of the century by American educators
generally in the matter of graduate studies, one can appreciate the justice of the statement of the Bishop of Wilmington written in 1876: "There is not *to-day*, in the entire
country, a single institution, Catholic, Protestant (of any

---

[15] *Catholic Almanac; or, Laity's Directory, for the Year 1833*
(Baltimore, n.d.), p. 56. In 1822 the degree of master of arts was
conferred in this fashion on Edward Kavanagh, a former student and
a future Governor of Maine. Cf. William L. Lucey, "Letters from
Some Friends of Edward Kavanagh," in *Catholic Historical Review,*
XXIX (Apr. 1943), 53–59. *The United States Catholic Almanac;
or, Laity's Directory for the Year 1834* (Baltimore, n.d.), mentioned
the undergraduate course for students and then added: "If he remains longer, and study the higher branches of Mathematics and
Natural Philosophy, he may take the degree of Master of Arts." p. 66.

[16] Daniel Coit Gilman, *The Launching of a University* (New
York, 1906), p. 128.

shade) or non-descriptive, entitled to the name of *university* in the European sense of the word." [17]

Actually few Americans understood anything about the development of university education in Europe in these years. While it is true that Edward Everett went to the University of Göttingen as early as 1816 and that George Ticknor, George Bancroft, and Joseph Green Cogswell were also training in German universities about the same time, yet the number of European-trained Americans remained comparatively small. Not until the last decades of the century did the influences of German university scholarship and administration begin to make themselves felt on American higher education. As for the Catholics, a considerable number of American young men received their training for the priesthood in the College of the Propaganda in Rome and after 1857 at the American College in Louvain. Many others, born in Ireland, took their training at Maynooth and at All Hallows College, Dublin, and then came out to the United States to exercise their ministry. Likewise, quite a number of German-born priests were trained in the Catholic faculties of the German state universities and later worked in the United States. But only at Louvain were the young American Catholics who studied abroad put in touch with real university traditions as they were taking shape at the mid-century and the years that followed.

That the concept of a university was changing in Europe in these years was evident to all who followed the trends in higher education. At a time when the Sorbonne still enjoyed international prestige as the leading Catholic

---

[17] T. A. Becker, "Shall We Have a University," in *American Catholic Quarterly Review*, I (Apr. 1876), 232.

theological school of Europe, there arose in the German world new universities which initiated novel methods of instruction in which one can trace the dim beginnings of modern university procedure. The University of Halle, founded in 1690, and the University of Göttingen, begun in 1733, were two institutions which marked a break with the past. Halle became a famous center of Lutheran thought and Göttingen developed a school of history which presaged the later accomplishments of Ranke at Berlin. The distinguishing feature of these German universities was the freedom of research which characterized their professors and students, the substitution of the systematic lecture for the exposition of texts, the gradual supplanting of the disputation by the seminar, the friendly attitude shown towards pure science, and the use of German instead of Latin as the medium of expression in the classroom. While these developments grew in Germany, the Sorbonne declined when its faculty of theology continued to hold stubbornly to the doctrines of Gallicanism and the teaching of the Four Articles of Louis XIV.

During the seventeenth and early eighteenth centuries the number of learned academies and societies continued to multiply in all the leading countries of Europe and in these bodies the principal part of the original research of the period was conducted.[18] But with the introduction of the features mentioned above by the newer German universities, the line of demarcation between the learned academy and the university grew less sharp and more and

---

[18] For a good discussion of the learned academies and their part in the advancement of scientific research cf. Martha Orstein, *The Rôle of the Scientific Societies in the Seventeenth Century* (Chicago, 1928).

more did the university absorb the research function of the academy in the German world. Meanwhile Oxford, Cambridge, the Sorbonne, and the universities of both the Church and the State in countries like Italy, Spain, and the Spanish dominions in the new world, continued on the models of the older foundations with the traditional faculties of arts, medicine, law, and theology employing the disputation, the exposition of authoritative texts, and the Latin language. There were, of course, exceptions, but in the main these universities followed the older models. In 1809 there was opened the University of Berlin where original research and investigation on the part of both professors and students, especially in the fields of philosophy, philology, and history were stated as a goal from the outset. Berlin made a deep impression in the learned world and it soon found imitators at other German universities. The old bachelor of arts degree gradually disappeared as time went on and the master of arts was merged with the doctor of philosophy which was given in many branches of learning. In this German movement the Catholics played little part. Catholic faculties of theology were maintained at Bonn, Breslau, Freiburg, Munich, Münster, Strassburg, Tübingen, and Würzburg, although the general atmosphere of these universities was often quite unfriendly to Catholic thought. But the maintenance of a corps of Catholic professors at the German state universities was believed to be preferable to yielding place entirely in the university world and the Church in Germany continued this system all through the century and down to the Nazi regime.

With the radical reform of Napoleon I in 1808 in erecting the University of France as an over-all state agency for the supervision of French education, much of the spontaneity and freedom of learning disappeared from French institutions. In England the decline which had begun in the eighteenth century at Oxford and Cambridge was not arrested until these two traditional centers of English university life reformed themselves by widening the range of studies, substituting written examinations for the *viva voce* ceremonies of the eighteenth century, and ultimately throwing open their fellowships to students on the basis of merit. Cambridge's tripos examination of the eighteenth century had brought it distinction in mathematics and in 1824 the new classics tripos was introduced. In 1871 Parliament abolished all religious tests at both universities and in 1877 further reforms were enacted which gave encouragement to the natural sciences. The student bodies in both universities rose steadily after these years. Oxford and Cambridge acted in part because of the competition which threatened in the opening of the University of London in 1825 which was followed by universities at Durham, Manchester, and other large English cities. As the century advanced the English universities showed an ever friendlier feeling towards the natural sciences, and the vogue of science accounted in part for the introduction of research in place of the previously exclusive function of teaching. This was, as well, a reflection of the change that had been brought about in the German universities where by the middle of the nineteenth century research had been firmly established as a university function.

When John Henry Newman published his famous *Idea of a University* in 1852 he showed clearly his Oxford background and his preference for the university as a center for the diffusion of knowledge rather than for its original discovery. Speaking of his view of a university, Newman said:

. . . it is a place of *teaching* universal *knowledge*. This implies that its object is, on the one hand, intellectual, not moral; and, on the other, that it is the diffusion and extension of knowledge rather than the advancement. If its object were scientific and philosophical discovery, I do not see why a University should have students . . .[19]

Newman accepted the eighteenth-century distinction between the academies as centers of research and the universities as disseminators of knowledge. As to the reason why the Church concerned herself with universities, Newman maintained:

. . . when the Church founds a University, she is not cherishing talent, genius, or knowledge, for their own sake, but for the sake of her children, with a view to their spiritual welfare and their religious influence and usefulness, with the object of training them to fill their respective posts in life better, and of making them more intelligent, capable, active members of society.[20]

It would be interesting to know just how much Newman's views influenced the minds of the American bishops who in the late nineteenth century made the founding of a university their business. But it is not possible to be precise in speaking of this influence. That men like Bishops Becker, Spalding, and Keane did read Newman there is no doubt, for we see it in their not infrequent quotations from his work, but aside from Spalding's insistence on "cultivation of mind," to which Newman devoted considerable attention, and Keane's citing the English cardinal on the place

---

[19] John Henry Newman, *The Idea of a University,* new impression, (New York, 1923), p. ix.

[20] *Ibid.,* p. xii.

of theology in the university curriculum, it is not clear from the writings of the American churchmen that they had worked out the Newman idea in its fulness and made it their own.

In America, of course, as we have seen, there was no such thing as a university, properly speaking, at the time Newman wrote his famous work. The American colleges, beginning with Harvard in 1636 and William and Mary in 1693, had evolved through the eighteenth century along the pattern of the English colleges and the early nineteenth century saw little substantial change in function and method, although the number of institutions increased considerably. It was only after the mid-century with the addition here and there of graduate studies to undergraduate instruction that it was possible to detect the first steps towards university status. But these efforts were so scattered and irregular that there emerged no American type of university. Only with the opening of Johns Hopkins in 1876 could there be said to be a model university after which American institutions took their direction. A month before the opening in Baltimore, Daniel Coit Gilman issued in the name of the trustees a statement of principles upon which the new university would be based. It read in part:

. . . the institution now taking shape should forever be free from the influences of ecclesiasticism and partisanship, as the terms are used in narrow and controversial senses; that all departments of learning,—mathematical, scientific, literary, historical, philosophical,—should be promoted, as far as the funds at command will permit, the new departments of research receiving full attention, while the traditional are not slighted.[21]

---

[21] Gilman, *op. cit.*, p. 41.

The all-embracing character of instruction to be offered was clear from this statement, and the aim of cultivating research as well as imparting knowledge was evident from Gilman's remarks on the selection of a faculty:

In selecting a staff of teachers, the Trustees have determined to consider especially the devotion of the candidate to some particular line of study and the certainty of his eminence in that specialty; the power to pursue independent and original investigation, and to inspire youth with enthusiasm for study and research . . .[22]

The influence of the recent German university trends was obvious in the emphasis at Johns Hopkins on research together with teaching and on the effort expended at Baltimore on the natural sciences. After 1876 there was no single American institution which influenced university development in the United States more than Johns Hopkins, and by the end of the century the German seminar, specialized research on the part of both professors and students, well-equipped science laboratories, and an ever-expanding curriculum of subjects offered for instruction characterized all the leading American universities.[23]

Any initiative, of course, for a real university among the Catholics of the United States would most naturally come

---

[22] *Ibid.*, p. 43.

[23] The literature on the history of universities in general is a vast one. For the universities of the period since the sixteenth century down to around 1860, cf. Stephen d'Irsay, *Histoire des Universités,* Vol. II (Paris, 1935); "Universities," by Edward A. Pace in *Catholic Encyclopedia,* XV, 188–198; "Universities," by various contributors in *Encyclopaedia Britannica,* 14th ed., XXII, 862–879; "Universities and Colleges," by Stephen d'Irsay in *Encyclopaedia of the Social Sciences,* XV, 181–186.

from the bishops, and although a scattered mention can be found here and there concerning such an idea in the early years of the century, it was not until after the Civil War that the matter was broached with real seriousness. When the American hierarchy looked to the university efforts of their European colleagues the prospect was not encouraging. Only the University of Louvain, reopened in November, 1834, after a thirty-seven year interval of suppression caused by the French revolutionary forces in the Low Countries, showed a genuine university character. The Belgian bishops might well be proud of the success of their university in the learned world, for Louvain embraced practically all the faculties commonly associated with a university and by the mid-century it was offering instruction superior to that found in any Catholic institution in Europe. Even its instruction in canon law seemed, in the opinion of John Lancaster Spalding, beyond that offered in the schools of Rome. Young Spalding, who had completed his theology at Louvain, wrote from Rome on November 15, 1864, to his uncle, Archbishop Martin J. Spalding of Baltimore: "I have already seen a good deal of Canon Law at Louvain where it is undoubtedly better and more profoundly taught than here in Rome." [24] When John J. Keane visited Louvain on his tour in 1887 two things especially impressed him, first, that the institution was directed from the outset to university education, not merely collegiate or seminary training. Keane wrote:

. . . when reorganized in the nineteenth century, it took

---

[24] John Tracy Ellis (Ed.) "Some Student Letters of John Lancaster Spalding," in *Catholic Historical Review*, XXIX (Jan. 1944), 530.

at once the shape neither of school, nor of college, nor of seminary, but of university; because institutions of those lower grades already existed in sufficient number, and so the university was free to simply supplement their work and confine itself to the higher learning which alone it was meant to impart.[25]

The second characteristic which Keane stressed in his report on Louvain was that it made prompt provision for the other faculties besides theology and for the admittance of laymen. Speaking of Louvain opening with the school of theology in 1834 and the next year adding another faculty, he remarked, "And it is noteworthy that this faculty was not that of Law or Medicine, but the faculty of Philosophy and Letters. Such was also the method of the Johns Hopkins University." [26]

But Louvain was almost alone of the Catholic universities of Europe. In Ireland the state-endowed Maynooth College which had been founded in 1795 did give graduate courses in theology. For students who had distinguished themselves in the ordinary seminary course the so-called Dunboyne Establishment at Maynooth maintained a certain number of scholarships for further study, but these were confined to theological studies. The Catholic University of Ireland opened in Dublin in November, 1854, with John Henry Newman as its first rector. The long and difficult negotiations with Archbishop Cullen and the Irish bishops which began in 1851 had been brought to an issue in the formal opening, but the Irish Catholic university did not prosper as its well-wishing founders hoped

---

[25] Keane, "Louvain," in *Catholic World,* XLVI, 530.
[26] *Ibid.,* p. 531.

and in 1858 Newman withdrew.[27] In England a failure
of even a more dismal character than Dublin occurred a
few years later. At the Fourth Provincial Council of Westminster held at St. Edmund's College in 1873, the project
of a Catholic university was discussed by the bishops under
the presidency of Archbishop Henry Edward Manning and
it was decided to make a beginning, as well as to pass dis-
ciplinary regulations against Catholics attending the secular
universities. With undue haste the University College at
Kensington was opened in October, 1874, with sixteen students, but because of lack of support from the Catholics
themselves, Manning's refusal of the proffered co-operation
of the Jesuits, and the unhappy choice of Monsignor T. J.
Capel as first rector the institution failed badly.[28]

---

[27] Wilfred Ward, *The Life of John Henry Cardinal Newman* (New
York, 1912), I, 305–416. The American bishops assembled in the
First Plenary Council of Baltimore in May, 1852, took notice in their
pastoral letter of the plans for the Irish university. Speaking of their
efforts for Catholic schools the bishops said: "We are following the
example of the Irish Hierarchy, who are courageously opposing the
introduction of a system based on the principle which we condemn,
and who are now endeavoring to unite religious with secular instruction of the highest order, by the institution of a Catholic University,
—an undertaking in the success of which we necessarily feel a deep
interest, and which, as having been suggested by the Sovereign Pontiff, powerfully appeals to the sympathies of the whole Catholic
world." Peter Guilday (Ed.) *National Pastorals of the American
Hierarchy (1792–1919)* (Washington, 1923), p. 191.

[28] Edmund Sheridan Purcell, *Life of Cardinal Manning* (New
York, 1896), II, 492–505. The lack of a Catholic university for England is still regretted by many. Reporting on the work of the Newman Association in the *Sword of the Spirit* (Feb. 3, 1944), Mary
Tew stated that the Association's survey "focuses attention on the
element which is missing from Catholic education in this country:
the idea of a Catholic University," p. 9. The Irish and English
Catholic universities were discussed in an article by Brother Azarias,
"The Catholic University Question in Ireland and England," in

In the German world matters were not much better. Repeatedly the question of a Catholic university arose at the various meetings of the Catholic societies held during the 1850's and 1860's. But faced by unfriendly governments, the German Catholics were inclined to continue the unsatisfactory arrangement of the Catholic faculties in the state universities lest in abandoning this medium for higher education in the sacred sciences they should lose everything. That the arrangement was unsatisfactory we learn from young John Lancaster Spalding who, on his way to Rome from Louvain, spent some weeks visiting in Germany in 1864. He attended the lectures of several professors at the University of Freiburg for three weeks, becoming quite well acquainted with Johann Alzog, the church historian, and the theologian, Alban Stolz. Spalding at twenty-four caught the trend in German university circles. Writing to Archbishop Spalding from Venice on September 19, 1864, he said: "In Germany even in the Catholic universities the lay professors have often no religion. The natural consequence of this is that the greater part of those who receive an university education do so at the expense of their religion and in Europe all who wish to become lawyers, doctors, notaries, apothecaries etc. must study at the University." [29] True, certain bolder spirits kept agitating the question of a separate Catholic university at the annual Catholic congresses, and at Würzburg in 1848 the approval

---

American Catholic Quarterly Review, III (Oct. 1878), 577–594. However, the writer's account of the Kensington experiment is quite superficial and unrealistic, due, in part perhaps, to the fact that written four years after its opening, the full extent of the failure of the University College had not yet become known on this side of the Atlantic.

[29] Ellis, *op. cit.*, p. 528.

of a number of bishops had been given to the idea. At Aix-la-Chapelle the Catholic congress heard an enthusiastic report of Louvain's progress in a paper read by Professor Möller of that university. From it resulted the appointment of a committee to begin the collecting of funds for a German Catholic university. By the time the Catholic Congress assembled again in Würzburg in 1864 about $30,000 had been collected, but that sum was, of course, far from enough to launch so ambitious a project. Although the matter of a Catholic university continued to be discussed, nothing came of it, and with the unification of the German states under Prussia in 1871 and the subsequent outbreak of the *Kulturkampf* begun against the Catholic Church by the government of Bismarck in 1873, all hope of success faded away.[30] When Keane was in Europe in 1887 visiting universities in the interest of the Washington foundation he quite naturally wished to see one or more of the German universities in operation, for as he said, "No one who desires to profit by the educational experience of the world can afford to overlook the universities of the German Empire."[31] He was well aware that the general atmos-

---

[30] Concerning the efforts to establish a German Catholic university, cf. the article of Andrew Niedermasser, "Malines and Würzburg," in *Catholic World*, II (Dec. 1865), 332–347. A committee of German Catholics headed by Count Clement de Brandis issued a printed appeal from Stuttgart on January 9, 1863, for assistance in founding a university, a copy of which was sent to Archbishop Kenrick of Baltimore. Baltimore Cathedral Archives, 32B–J–1. It was followed by a second appeal in May, 1863, from the same committee, BCA, 32B–J–2. These appeals were written in Latin and apparently circulated among persons who, it was hoped, would be of help to the cause. Hereafter these archives will be designated as BCA.

[31] John J. Keane, "The University of Strassburg," in *Catholic World*, XLVI (Feb. 1888), 643.

phere of these universities was not friendly to the Catholic philosophy of education since rationalism in religion and positivism in philosophy had permeated their curriculum so thoroughly. Time prevented him from seeing more than the University of Strassburg but what impressed him most there was the *Lehrfreiheit* of the professors and the *Lernfreiheit* of the students. He felt the Germans carried the idea too far, but he conceded their insistence that this spirit of freedom in education produced more mature and highly-developed university education had something in it. America, it had to be admitted, did not produce the "manliness" that the German university world showed and the bishop concluded: "Unquestionably, further training and of another kind is necessary, and the university, in seeking to bestow it, has much to learn from the German universities." [32]

During the years of the nineteenth century up to 1870 French higher education had been kept under close state regulation with the laws of Napoleon I for the most part remaining in force. However, with the fall of the Second Empire in 1870 a change was introduced and on July 12, 1875, the National Assembly passed a law giving freedom of higher education to all who cared to avail themselves of it. The French bishops lost no time and in a preliminary meeting in Paris on August 11 of the same year plans were drawn up for beginning a number of Catholic universities. Actually by January 1, 1877, five such institutions were in operation. Lille opened with courses in law in 1874 with other faculties inaugurated in January, 1877; Lyons was decreed by a group of the bishops of southeastern France

---

[32] *Ibid.*, p. 650.

in August, 1875; Paris opened with faculties of letters and law in November, 1875, with other schools added during the next five years; Angers was begun largely through the initiative of Bishop Freppel about the same time, and Toulouse was founded by Archbishop Desprez in 1877 with the theological faculty added in 1879.[33]

Time proved, however, that these French Catholic universities had been begun in too much haste and that their number was too great to insure solid success. Bishop Keane included these five French institutions on his European tour. He said he found three of the five languishing, with Lille the best equipped and supported of the five. The mistake of the French bishops in beginning five universities almost at once was borne in on Keane. He wrote:

Again and again the moral of this lesson was urged upon us, both in France and in Rome. The observant eyes of Cardinal Czacki, of the Propaganda, and especially of the Holy Father, took in the situation fully, and repeatedly they impressed upon us that, while the immense extent of our country will assuredly call for several Catholic universities eventually, we must so advance as to make certain the success of one before starting another. Unite, they said, all the energies of your country in perfectly organizing first your central and national university, and then you can safely follow the expansion of the church by establishment

---

33 J. Calvert, "Catholic University Education in France," in *Catholic University Bulletin*, XIII (Apr. 1907), 191–210. Cf. also Alfred Baudrillart, *Les Universités catholiques de France et de l'Étranger* (Paris, 1909), where the reader will find a discussion of the vicissitudes of the French Catholic institutions (pp. 68–120) as well as a rather dismal and unsympathetic picture of the Catholic University of America (pp. 43–48) as seen by the rector of the Catholic Institute of Paris at that time.

of others. And they were glad to learn that such is precisely the determination of the Hierarchy of our country.[34]

The qualified success experienced by the Catholic universities of France was due, however, to more than their excessive number and their hasty beginning. Hardly had they opened their doors than the government of the Third Republic embarked on the policy of strident anti-clericalism which marked virtually its entire life. So obstructive was this policy that, according to the law of 1880, the Catholic universities were not even permitted to assume the name of universities but were compelled to call themselves simply institutes, nor were they allowed to confer degrees. When one views the policy of the French government after 1875 towards the Church it is small wonder that the French Catholic effort in university education did not show more brilliant results; the wonder is that it was able to do anything.

The evil from which French Catholic higher education suffered was not confined to France. The years after 1870 were tense ones for the Church in Italy, too. The once thriving state of Rome's ecclesiastical universities had long since declined. They had not been, of course, universities in the sense of giving instruction in all branches of learning. The Roman schools under the patronage of the Church had been pointed towards the preparation of ecclesiastics for their special walk of life, but there was a day when the University of Rome, or the Sapienza as it was called, did give superior training in many branches of learning. In 1870 confiscation by the Italian government was its lot.

---

[34] John J. Keane, "The Catholic Universities of France," in *Catholic World*, XLVII (June, 1888), 293.

The Roman schools were affected for many years by the struggle between the Church and the State so that when Keane visited the Eternal City in 1887 it was to study its theology schools in the main, for with Newman he wished theology to be the center of the intellectual disciplines.[35]

Aside from Louvain, therefore, the Catholic bishops of the United States might well hesitate before embarking on a university foundation if they were inclined to be guided by the experiences of their European brothers. A more encouraging example could be found, however, in the new world, for since 1852 the Canadian Catholics had a university when Laval was organized in that year out of the nucleus of the old Seminary of Quebec. Laval University made slow but steady progress and on April 15, 1876, Pius IX by the bull *Inter varias sollicitudines,* granted a pontifical status to the Quebec university. The once thriving Catholic universities of Latin America which had a splendid record for scholarship in the late sixteenth and seventeenth centuries, had, for the most part, long since passed under the aegis of the various governments and had been thoroughly secularized.

The earliest suggestion for the establishment of a Catholic university in the United States came from the Irish-born Augustinian, Robert Browne, who had been appointed to the congregation at Atlanta, Georgia, by Archbishop Carroll in 1810. Browne became deeply involved with Simon Gallagher in the trustee troubles in Charleston and around 1819 he wrote an account of the Church in the United States for the Congregation of the Propaganda. In this document, among other subjects, he discussed the

---

[35] John J. Keane, "The Roman Universities," in *Catholic World,* XLVI (Dec. 1887), 313–321.

need for the establishment of a Catholic university in Washington which would be under the direction of the Holy See and presided over by a bishop whose see would be Washington itself. Browne considered Georgetown and St. Mary's in Baltimore as failures because of their adherence to foreign methods and administration in education, and he suggested that a Catholic university of an American character would meet with the approval of American Catholics and could be supported through annual collections. An American seminary taught by Americans for American youths might, according to Browne, be erected near the proposed university.[36] Needless to say nothing came of this

---

[36] Peter Guilday, *The Life and Times of John England* (New York, 1927), I, 288–289. Cf. also "The Founding of the Catholic University of America," by Peter Guilday in *American Ecclesiastical Review*, CIX (Jan. 1944), 2–16, for a general account of the University's early history. When Bishop Dubois of New York was in Europe in 1830 he made contact with Henri-Dominique Lacordaire, O.P., and offered him a place in his diocese. Whether it was to fill the post of vicar general or to be a professor in the seminary which Dubois was soon to open at Nyack, at any rate the story was set forth by F. Duine in his *LaMennais, sa vie, ses idées, ses ouvrages* (Paris, 1922), that Lacordaire was to have a hand in the founding of a Catholic university in America. "Une oeuvre qui correspondait pleinement aux vues de l'auteur des *Progrès de la Revolution* vint s'offrir a La Chesnaie dans les premiers mois de 1830. Comprenant l'importance de la fondation d'une université catholique aux Etats-Unis, l'évêque de New-York fit appel a la *Congrégation de Saint-Pierre*. Et il fut convenue que Lacordaire, qui, en Mai s'était agrégé au Port-Royal nouveau, s'embarquerait dans le courant d'octobre, avec trois autres Menaisiens pour travailler a l'institution projetée. *Dis aliter visum.*" p. 135. B. Chocarne, *Le R. P. H.-D. Lacordaire* (Paris, 1873), speaks of Lacordaire as visiting La Chesnaie in the spring of 1830, having already decided to go to the United States as a missionary. He met Dubois who offered him the vicar generalship of New York. The revolution of 1830 broke out some months later but he still persisted and set out for Bourgogne to say farewell to his family and

suggestion, due to the unpreparedness of the American Church at the time and also to Browne's personal troubles which cast a shadow over his reputation.

Among the most forward-looking legislation passed by the American bishops in the years of the mid-century was that of the various councils of the Province of Cincinnati. When Archbishop John B. Purcell presided at the opening session of the First Provincial Council in his see city in May, 1855, Mount Saint Mary's Seminary of the West was nearly four years old, having opened in October, 1851.[37] At this council the bishops of the province determined on making this seminary a provincial one with a board of five bishops appointed for the administration. But the Cincinnati bishops went beyond this when they petitioned Rome to erect Mount Saint Mary's of the West into a pontifical institution with the right to confer the doctorate in philosophy and theology. The doctorate in philosophy in this instance, of course, was meant to be confined to the field of philosophy alone. To this petition from Cincinnati in 1855, however, Cardinal Barnabò, Prefect of the Congregation of Propaganda, answered Purcell on February 16, 1857, that the matter should be deferred.[38]

friends. There he received a letter from Abbé Gerbet announcing the founding of *L'Avenir* and saying La Mennais wanted his help. This changed Lacordaire's mind about going to the United States, I, 91, 95. R. P. Lecanuet, *Montalembert* (Paris, 1898), I, 136, also speaks of Lacordaire about to depart for America to become vicar general of New York.

[37] For the history of this seminary, cf. Michael J. Kelly and James M. Kirwin, *History of Mt. St. Mary's Seminary of the West, Cincinnati, Ohio* (Cincinnati, 1894).

[38] John H. Lamott, *History of the Archdiocese of Cincinnati, 1821–1921* (New York, 1921), pp. 214–215; *Concilium Cincinnatense Provinciale I Habitum Anno 1855* (Cincinnati, 1855), Decretum VII.

Precisely what kind of institution the bishops had in mind it is impossible to say from the evidence at hand, although one is warranted in believing that their intention was the erection in Cincinnati of a pontifical seminary with power to grant the degrees for which they petitioned, rather than a real university. At any rate, what might have developed into a university of the Church in the West at this early time was postponed by the action of Rome.

It was just nine years after the council in Cincinnati that the man who played a leading role in that assembly as promoter and author of the pastoral letter—having meanwhile served in the same capacity for the councils of 1858 and 1861—was removed from the Province of Cincinnati and promoted in June, 1864, to the Archdiocese of Baltimore. Martin J. Spalding was named by Rome to succeed the distinguished theologian, Francis P. Kenrick, who had died at Baltimore on July 8, 1863.[39] As Bishop of Louisville since 1850 he had shown a keen interest in the advancement of Catholic educational facilities, not only in his assistance to the various teaching orders which were conducting secondary schools, but in his efforts to have the Jesuits staff St. Mary's College, Lebanon, St. Joseph's College, Bardstown, and the short-lived St. Aloysius College in Louisville.[40] Moreover, it was Spalding and Peter P. Lefevre, Coadjutor Bishop of Detroit, to whom was owed in the main the opening of the American College at Louvain in March, 1857.[41] It is not surprising, therefore, to

[39] For the life of Archbishop Spalding, cf. J. L. Spalding, *The Life of the Most Rev. M. J. Spalding, D.D.* (New York, 1873).

[40] On these Kentucky colleges and their relations to the Jesuits and to Spalding, cf. Garraghan's two chapters in *The Jesuits of the Middle United States*, III, 253–348.

[41] For this college, cf. J. Van der Heyden, *The Louvain American College, 1857–1907* (Louvain, 1909).

learn that as Archbishop of Baltimore, he continued his interest in higher education and that to him must be given credit for advancing the idea of a Catholic university among the American bishops.

One of the first great tasks to which Spalding set his hand after his installation in Baltimore was the convoking of a plenary council. It was twelve years since the bishops of the United States had met in council under Archbishop Kenrick and the need of further legislation for the growing Church was evident. Likewise, the close of the Civil War in April, 1865, confronted the Catholic Church with a number of pressing problems on which joint consultation seemed necessary, among them the question of what action to take in regard to the recently freed slaves. As usual with Spalding, he made careful preparations for the council, requesting his nephew, John Lancaster Spalding, then a priest-student in Rome, to procure for him copies of the legislation of recent councils held in Europe so that he and the other bishops might be guided in drawing up their decrees.[42] Over a year before the Second Plenary Council assembled in October, 1866, the Archbishop of Baltimore had broached the subject of a Catholic university in a letter to Bishop John Timon of Buffalo. Writing him on August 23, 1865, he spoke of having received word from Bishop Wood of Philadelphia that Cardinal Barnabò had approved the idea of a plenary council, and he added: "The intelligence is favorable to our project, from which I anticipate much good to flow. Why should we not have a Catholic University? It would be a great thing, if we could

---

[42] Ellis, *op. cit.*, p. 537. John Lancaster Spalding told the archbishop he would try to secure copies of these European councils in a letter from Rome on March 13, 1865.

only agree as to the location & arrangement." [43] The reply
of the Bishop of Buffalo to this suggestion was favorable
if not very clear. Timon wrote: "I agree with you as to
a Catholic University. I further said to almost all our
Bishops of this quarter, that as the Ecclesiastical functions
have long and legally been established in Balto. there should
other functions congregate. And then when we perfect the
first, we can think of a second." [44]

Spalding likewise sought guidance in these months before
the council on the subject of a university from Archbishop
Paul Cullen of Dublin. He wrote Cullen to make inquiries
concerning the sponsors for confirmation in Ireland and to
request information on other points of church law and he
added:

Finally if Yr Grace has any document showing in brief the
organization & government of the Catholic University, I
would be much indebted if you would send me a copy. We
expect to hold a Plenary Council next year, though the
matter is not yet definitely settled, & in this case, all these
points & others will come up. [45]

Five months later he again addressed Cullen asking "for any
document or practical hints in regard to a Catholic University." [46] In the meanwhile Spalding had intensified his

---

[43] BCA, Copybook of Archbishop Spalding, p. 150.

[44] BCA, 36–F–16, John Timon to Martin J. Spalding, Buffalo,
August 27, 1865.

[45] BCA, Copybook of Archbishop Spalding, p. 722, December 14,
1865.

[46] *Ibid.*, p. 734, May 7, 1866. The Baltimore Cathedral Archives
contain eighteen letters from Cullen to Spalding, 33–O–1 to 14;
26A–E–17 to 20, dated between August 20, 1864, and October 24,
1870, but the contents is largely devoted to the problem of the
Fenians with whom the Archbishop of Dublin was at that time much

efforts with the leaders of the American hierarchy to get them to assist in planning for the general assembly of bishops. One of those on whom he was depending for assistance was Archbishop John McCloskey of New York. On May 11, 1866, Spalding wrote McCloskey:

Many thanks for your prompt & able attention to my request. You are not the last, two Metropolitans—of St. Louis & N. Orleans remain to be heard from.

Your conciliatory exposition is, like yourself, neat & eloquent, & quite satisfactory so far as it goes. But peccat per duplicem defectum: 1. Besides being rather short, though terse enough, it fails to embody, & "dove-tail" in, the Balt. Decrees, which were in accordance with our plan. This deficiency I may be able to supply, but Your Grace could have done it more *gracefully*. 2. It fails to pronounce on, & suggest the form of a decree in the matter of the University, & of Newspapers relate ad Ordinarios, & of the Catechism:—the very points on which I most desired your explicit & detailed opinion, in the shape of decrees which you think should be adopted by the Council. I trust you will do this yet, at yr early convenience. We both know enough about Councils to understand that if nothing definite be prepared, there will be nothing done, but all will end in talk . . .[47]

The reply from New York was not too encouraging, although McCloskey did not rule out the idea of a university. He wrote:

I did not submit a decree or statute on the subject of the University, for the reason that I presumed there would

---

concerned. There is nothing in the letters in answer to Spalding's inquiries concerning the Catholic University of Ireland.

[47] New York Archdiocesan Archives, A–35. Hereafter these archives will be designated as NYAA.

be considerable diversity of opinion; 1st. on the question of the University itself, 2nd. on the spot to be chosen, or the institution already existing to be adopted. The decrees will of course be presented as emanating from Your Grace, as Apostolic Delegate, and it seemed to me it would be best consulting for the dignity of your office to let the matter first come up in the form of a *question,* which would elicit the views and opinions of the assembled Prelates, and lead perhaps to the proposing of an appropriate decree, rather than put it in the form which might subject Your Grace to the risk of an apparent defeat. Would it be well to introduce a *degree* [sic] without having all the probabilities in favor of its acceptance? The same train of thought and feeling operated also in the case of "Relation of Bishops to Newspapers," and the Catechism of Dr. McCaffrey. I calculated to be prepared with a degree [sic] to be introduced after hearing the opinion of the Bishops, which would insure its being previously put in an acceptable shape. The newspaper question is a difficult as well as an important one. It was considered in one of our New York Provincial Councils, but nothing definite was arrived at. Of course Your Grace will decide the matter according to your better judgement, and frame such form of degree [sic] as may have already suggested itself to you.[48]

The Second Plenary Council opened in Baltimore on Sunday, October 7, 1866, with the first formal session held that day in the cathedral. During the two weeks they were in session the bishops framed three chapters of legislation pertaining to education, the first on the need for parochial schools and the moral obligations of parents to send their children to these schools, the second on industrial schools, and the third chapter on what was entitled, "De Univer-

---

[48] BCA, 35–E–10, John McCloskey to Martin J. Spalding, New York, May 14, 1866.

sitate Literarum Fundanda." After paying tribute to the colleges already founded and to the service they were rendering in preparing men for the ministry, the bishops spoke especially of the American College in Rome, the American College in Louvain, and All Hallows College near Dublin as having won the gratitude of the American Church for the training they had given to so many of its priests. The final paragraph of this chapter signaled the postponement of the project of a national Catholic university in the United States, although the hope for such had not been abandoned. It read:

Would that in this region it were permissible to have a great college or university which would embrace the advantages and the usefulness of all these colleges whether domestic or foreign; in which, namely, all the letters and sciences, both sacred and profane, could be taught! Whether or not the time for founding such a university has arrived, we leave it to the judgment of the Fathers, that they may examine the whole matter more maturely hereafter.[49]

Who precisely framed the language of this paragraph of the council's legislation it is not possible to say, but it is not unlikely that Archbishop Spalding himself was responsible for it. Certainly whoever did the writing gave

---

[49] *Concilii Plenarii Baltimorensis II., in Ecclesia Metropolitana Baltimorensi . . . Decreta* (Baltimore, 1868), p. 228. The original Latin of the decree was as follows: Atque utinam in hac regione Collegium unum maximum, sive Universitatem habere liceret, quod Collegiorum horum omnium, sive domesticorum sive exterorum, commoda atque utilitates complecteretur; in quo, scilicet, literae et scientiae omnes, tam sacrae quam profanae, traderentur! Utrum vero Universitatis hujusmodi constituendae tempus advenerit, necne, Patrum judicio, rem totam maturius posthac perpendentibus, relinquimus.

evidence of understanding what a university ought to be;
its all-inclusive character as compared with a seminary is
obvious in the language employed to distinguish the institution from the American and European colleges of
which the decree had spoken immediately before. The
American hierarchy had not yet advanced to the point
where they could feel assured of all the essentials of a university of which the Johns Hopkins president once wrote:
"Before a university can be launched there are six requi-
sites: An idea; capital to make the idea feasible; a definite
plan; an able staff of coadjutors; books and apparatus;
students." [50] One of the most important reasons for the
bishops delaying action on a university in 1866 was the
crippled financial condition of the American College in
Rome. For some time that institution had been in an in-
secure way financially. Four years before the Baltimore
council the rector, William G. McCloskey, had written
Archbishop Kenrick telling of his troubles and saying,
"owing to circumstances beyond my control the pension of
the students does not now equal the expenses of the College." [51] The American hierarchy felt a responsibility for
this institution which had opened in December, 1859, and
for that reason the prospect of its grave financial state contributed a good deal to lessen enthusiasm for a university.

But once the idea had been discussed among the bishops
and entered into the conciliar decrees of 1866 it would not
down. Two years later in an unsigned article in the *Cath-*

---

[50] Gilman, *op. cit.*, p. 9.

[51] BCA, 30–P–9, William G. McCloskey to Francis P. Kenrick,
Rome, September 6, 1862. Again on November 25, 1862, McCloskey
addressed Kenrick concerning the unsound finances of the college,
BCA, 30–P–10.

olic World the question was raised in a discussion of the value which a Catholic congress would have for the American Church.

Then there is the project of a Catholic University. Every day we read of wealthy gentlemen leaving donations of thousands of dollars to educational establishments belonging to the state or to religious denominations other than Catholic. In Europe this is also a common custom. We have read of Mr. Peabody's donation to Yale College. Girard, an infidel, founded the institution in Philadelphia which bears his name. Our Catholic millionaires of New York and other cities, we are sure, only need to be asked to show their generosity in the founding of a Catholic university. Several of the petty German states have theirs. Even impoverished Ireland has had the courage to originate one. Will not rich America follow her example? What is wanting? Not the money; not the patronage; not the ability to conduct it; but simply that there is no united, powerful body of Catholics to undertake it. Give us a congress, and we can have this union; a congress of the brain, good sense, and faith of the American church.[52]

Nor were there lacking voices from the West in behalf of a university in the years after the Second Plenary Council. At a time when Father John Lancaster Spalding was serv-

---

[52] "Shall We Have a Catholic Congress?" in *Catholic World,* VIII (Nov. 1868), 227. The author of this article was probably Isaac Hecker, editor of the journal. Father Hecker was a strong promoter of the university idea. At the time of the opening of the new St. Paul's College at the University in 1916 the sermon was preached by Charles F. Aiken, professor of apologetics in the University, who said: "When the project of setting up the Catholic University was broached at the Second Plenary Council, one of its most enthusiastic supporters was Father Hecker." Paulist Fathers Archives, 48, p. 14. The writer is indebted to Richard Walsh, C.S.P., for this reference.

ing as secretary to Bishop William McCloskey in Louisville and writing frequently for the *Catholic Advocate,* the weekly paper of that diocese, there appeared an editorial on the subject which more than likely was written by Spalding.

If we recall to mind the various works, written in this country, in defense of Catholicism, we shall be struck by the fact that, for the most part, their authors have been brought up and educated outside of the church.

We may say that we scarcely have an American Catholic literature, and that there are fewer able writers in the church in this country today than there were twenty years ago. How many Catholic books of the least merit have been written in the United States since the close of the war? If we except a few biographical compilations, which can at most have but a passing interest, we know of none.

It would seem that there is not sufficient literary talent in the church of the United States to sustain a first class magazine; or, shall we say, even to get up a respectable newspaper.

But how shall the works be written when we have no men who are able to write them?

The lantern of Diogenes would be of no service to us.

Humiliating as the confession may be, it will be good for the soul to make it candidly. There is in the church of this country a deplorable dearth of intellectual men.

We are, moreover, inclined to think that at present few Catholic youth of talent and promise turn their thoughts to the priesthood and that therefore, if this state of things is to continue, we are not to expect to find, in the future, much ability even in the clerical body. Various opinions and theories are adduced to account for these facts; whilst some may possibly deny that they exist at all.

We, at present, wish simply to call attention to what we consider a chief defect in Catholic education in this country. We have no university—no central seat of learning encircled by the halo of great names, to which the eyes of Catholics from every part of the land might turn with pride and reverence. The passion for learning and literary excellence, like the other passions, grows by contact with that which stimulates it. Many a mute, inglorious Milton dies unwept, unhonored and unsung, because he had never felt the magnetic influence of a living mind, enamored of high excellence.

The universities of England, Germany, France and Belgium are not only the great seats of learning in those countries, but they are also centers of literary taste and culture.

The youths of those countries whilst drinking in the words of men who have achieved fame in the various departments of knowledge and literature, feel their hearts fired with a noble ambition, which tames them down to patient labor and thus prepares them to become champions in the intellectual arena of the world.

Even in this country the universities of Yale and Harvard are the great foci whence the rays of literary taste and culture have been diffused throughout the land.

The Catholics of the United States, it is true, have certain rudimentary Greek and Latin Grammar schools, kept by Jesuits and others, which in sheer mockery of the name, are called universities. But these titles deceive no one, and provoke no comment, out of respect to the spirit of humbug which is so prevalent with us. If a young man, upon leaving one of these institutions, has sufficient education to enable him to construe words grammatically, we must be satisfied.

The young men, who graduate from our colleges, if we may believe the writer of an article on Catholic literature, in a recent number of the Catholic World, not only have no literary culture or passion for intellectual pursuits, but have not even a taste for reading.

We know that candidates for the priesthood, who have more than ordinary talent, may be sent to some of the Catholic universities of Europe.

Men of great wisdom and experience, however, make

very serious objections to the practice of educating the future priests of this country in the various schools of theology of Europe. But we do not care for the present to refer to this phase of the subject.

Whatever the advantages of an European education may be, they in no way affect the very great good which the Catholics of this country would derive from an university of their own.

There can be no real obstacle to the founding of a Catholic university in the United States similar to that of Dublin or Louvain. We have perfect freedom and abundant wealth for the purpose, and, we feel confident that the laity would eagerly engage in an enterprise, in which they have such great interests, both as Catholics and American citizens. It would be easier to raise two million dollars to endow an American university, than half a million to establish a foreign college.

The existence of a first class university, by creating a demand for talent, would call it forth. What is there to prevent us from having an university?

Surely local and personal prejudices are not sufficiently strong to prevent the realization of a project which is of such vital importance to the highest interests of the church in the United States.[53]

This strong indictment of Catholic higher education as it existed in 1871 naturally provoked others. Two months later the *Catholic World* carried an article, "On the Higher Education," in the March and April issues. It was unsigned but it is obvious from the context that it was written by Father Isaac T. Hecker, C.S.P., editor of the journal and founder of the Paulist Fathers. After stating that his article was prompted by some essays on the same subject which recently appeared in the *Civiltà Cattolica*, the writer went

---

[53] *Catholic Advocate,* January 28, 1871.

on to say that philosophy must be made the basis of university education and, among other points, he maintained that the Latin textbooks in philosophy then in use should be replaced by texts in English. He defined higher education as that which "obviously included all that belongs to every kind of institute of learning above common schools." [54] That Hecker had not in mind another Catholic college was clear, for, as he expressed it, "a well-conducted college for undergraduates is not a university, though it is often dignified with that name; but is merely one of the principal constituent parts of a university." [55] The writer mentioned the efforts of European Catholics in the direction of university education and he alluded to the recent editorial in the *Catholic Advocate* of Louisville. He sketched what he believed would be an ideal university, "as it lies in our own imagination, and of the possible method of making it a reality." [56] This plan called for one or more undergraduate colleges, schools of all the professional studies, and a school of the "higher and more profound studies in every department of literature and science." [57] Moreover, the writer spoke of the need for a vast library, museums, laboratories with full scientific equipment, a botanical garden, art gallery, collegiate church, publishing house, and periodical reviews and magazines. Just how all this was to be done the writer did not say, although he stated that the work would necessarily be slow. "The first thing to be done, then,

---

[54] "On the Higher Education," in *Catholic World*, XII (Mar. 1871), 721–731; XIII (Apr. 1871), 115–124. The quoted passage is contained in XIII, 115.

[55] *Ibid.*, p. 118.

[56] *Ibid.*, p. 119.

[57] *Ibid.*, p. 120.

is to select some already existing colleges, or to establish a new one, as the nucleus of the future university." [58]

Besides the features outlined, Hecker would have also a minor and major seminary connected with the university, and he scoffed at the notion that a university atmosphere would contaminate the seminarians. "We have never heard that Louvain is considered in that light by the clergy of Belgium, and the glimpse we had of a large body of the Louvain students at Malines during the session of the Congress of 1867, gave us the most favorable impression of their virtuous character." [59] Religious orders and congregations should be invited to co-operate and share in the enterprise and wealthy Catholic laity might be stimulated to give by the recent benefactions of men like Peabody and Cornell. None of the existing Catholic colleges and seminaries of the United States needed to have anything to fear from such a university. The writer concluded: "So far as we can see, every reason and consideration cries out imperatively for the speedy foundation of a Catholic University in the United States." [60]

The first installment of this article, which was largely devoted to an analysis of the place of philosophy in Catholic education, did not meet with the approval of the *Catholic Advocate* which characterized it as "stale, flat and unprofitable in the extreme." [61] The Louisville writer did not wait for the second installment which discussed the need of a university before saying: "A course of philosophy in one of our Catholic colleges is not likely, unless things

---

[58] *Ibid.*
[59] *Ibid.*, p. 122.
[60] *Ibid.*, p. 124.
[61] *Catholic Advocate*, March 11, 1871.

have greatly changed, since we were a boy, to develop principles of any kind, good or bad. . . . Assuredly, if we wish to have a higher education at all, in the proper sense of the word, we must first establish a Catholic university. But of this—the great want of the church in our country—no word is spoken in this article." [62] Three weeks later, however, the *Catholic Advocate* revised a little its previous harsh estimate of the *Catholic World* writer when the second installment in the latter had been seen. The Louisville paper conceded that here "we have some desultory, but highly interesting remarks and suggestions concerning what is the great want of the church in this country—an American Catholic university, on the plan of that of Louvain." [63] Through these years of the 1870's one of the most persistent advocates of a university was Father Hecker and it was his belief that the organization of a Catholic congress or union somewhat along the lines of the German Catholics' model, might be the medium for the university. Writing to Orestes Brownson he mentioned the possibilities of this Catholic union for a Catholic daily newspaper, and he added: "Other important subjects are before it, such as a University, Catholic Congresses, etc. I confess confidence in the movement." [64]

It was in 1876, the year which marked the opening of the Johns Hopkins University, that the proposal for a national Catholic university received one of its strongest expressions. In 1868 the convert, Thomas A. Becker, had become first Bishop of Wilmington. There was nothing in

---

[62] *Ibid.*

[63] *Ibid.*, April 1, 1871.

[64] Paulist Fathers Archives, 98, Isaac Hecker to Orestes Brownson, New York, January 8, 1872.

Becker's early training that might seem to have especially qualified him to speak on the subject of university education. He spent a brief time at the University of Virginia, being received into the Church in 1853 at Charlottesville and the next year he enrolled in the College of the Propaganda in Rome. He took the doctorate in theology there and was ordained in June, 1859. Nonetheless, Becker was a keen critic of higher education and he had a clear conception of what it should constitute. In April, 1876, he published an article, "Shall We Have a University?" in the *American Catholic Quarterly Review* in which he defined his idea of a university.

A university . . . is properly an institution of learning, in which the whole round of letters, arts, and sciences (*universitas scientiarum*) is taught by special professors for each branch; which confers degrees in each or all, in which (besides the academic studies) law, medicine, and theology are taught by their respective faculties, and which may consist of an agglomeration of colleges, as in England, or of a sole corporation, as is usually the case on the continent of Europe.[65]

[65] Becker, *op. cit.*, p. 232. Just how much influence educational trends at the University of Virginia had on Becker during his brief stay there it is impossible to say. The University did give the master of arts degree to a considerable number of students but the requirements for such were not those commonly exacted in graduate schools of a later period. Around Becker's time the requirement of two modern languages was enacted which, during the year 1859–1860 was specified as French and German. German-trained scholars were on the Virginia faculty, e.g., Maximilian Rudolph Schele de Vere in modern languages and Basil L. Gildersleeve in the classics. Both these men had been trained at Bonn and Berlin. Whether the influence of these professors made an impression on the young mind of Becker we have, unfortunately, no way of knowing. For educational developments at Charlottesville in these years cf. Philip Alex-

The Bishop of Wilmington criticized Catholic colleges in the United States for following the lead of non-Catholic institutions and he added, "that we have followed their lead in this matter of multiplying small, feeble, helpless institutions, magniloquently calling them colleges, conferring degrees in course and honorary by means of their charters, and in all respects enacting annual solemn farces at their *commencements*, is too patent a fact to be denied." [66] Becker felt Catholic institutions were in no way superior to non-Catholic colleges, "except in the single matter of classics." But the bishop made allowance for the backwardness of the Catholic institutions of higher learning in taking into account the poverty of the Catholic people, the persecution of the Nativists and Know-Nothings, the secret societies, and the Civil War. He felt the project of a Catholic university was such as to warrant the most careful preparation. "It is not a work into which, in any case, we should dash at haphazard," he wrote.[67]

Becker was aware of the lack of understanding in America of a true university at the time he wrote, but he was at pains to make it clear that he did not have in mind another college. As he put it:

. . . we think that the great points that contradistinguish the two systems (those, namely, of the *college* and *university*), are the extent and thoroughness of the latter as compared with the former—the greater variety of studies, the higher standard of attainment, the more frequent and

---

ander Bruce, *History of the University of Virginia, 1819–1919* (New York, 1921), III, 62–63, 81–87, gives information on the requirements for degrees and on the faculty of the 1850's.

[66] *Ibid.*, p. 234.
[67] *Ibid.*, p. 236.

rigorous examinations, the greater number and skill of professors, the greater completeness of library, philosophical and chemical appliances, to say nothing of the appurtenances in astronomy and other studies, by which they can be acquired not merely theoretically but practically.[68]

While there is a recognition here of the difference between a university and a college there is no mention specifically of graduate work as such. To Becker there were many reasons for insisting on a university besides the duty of the Church to provide higher education as well as elementary and secondary instruction. He instanced the present number of Catholics and the prospects of their increase, the gain for souls in a university with it providing as well a medium through which losses could be checked by answering the attacks of the new school of scientism, the inadequacy of college faculties to cope with men like Buckle, Huxley, Darwin, and Mill, and the need that Catholic professors and students had for a stimulus such as a university would provide. He anticipated opposition among Catholics, realizing that there were those "whose constant cry is *"quieta non movere,"* and they translate it into "let well enough alone." [69] He foresaw, too, opposition from some of the existing colleges whose faculties might misunderstand the intent of a university, but most of all from the young men since it was their idea to get established in their professions as soon as possible. He felt that the most serious difficulty for some time to come would be finding a sufficient number of young men "whose preparation has been of such a nature, and whose attainments are such, as to enable them to profit by a grade of instruction which must

[68] *Ibid.,* p. 239.
[69] *Ibid.,* p. 244.

be imparted in a university at all worthy of the name, and we do not advocate the establishment of any other." [70]

Yet Bishop Becker was for going ahead and in this he revealed an optimism which was not altogether in keeping with the facts.

The feasibility is made out then (1), by the fact that Catholic means are abundant and Catholic charity ample to furnish the initial funds necessary to a fair inauguration of the enterprise; (2), because, once in operation, it will be frequently advanced in capacity of usefulness by donations, bequests, and foundations; (3), because we can readily secure competent professors, and shall only need to exercise care in excluding those who would be likely rather to injure than to benefit the institution . . ."[71]

Six months later he followed up this article with another in the same journal in which he outlined a plan for a university. He conceded that at first standards of scholarship could not be made too high, otherwise "it would be simply impossible to find students." [72] Becker would have the university governed by a board of corporators at least eighteen in number; professors appointed by this board would elect a rector every year, and for the time being the archbishops of the country should fill the vacancies among the corporators. As for endowment, he felt $500,000 would be enough to begin, with $100,000 allotted for land and buildings, $50,000 for equipment, and $350,000 to be invested for a steady income for the university. As for salaries of professors, the bishop remarked:

[70] *Ibid.*, p. 250.

[71] *Ibid.*, p. 253.

[72] T. A. Becker, "A Plan for the Proposed Catholic University," in *American Catholic Quarterly Review*, I (Oct. 1876), 655.

It is very plain that for some few years the salaries would have to be comparatively small; nor, to say truth, should we consider this a great hardship, since, with our notion of what a Catholic university should be, the prominent idea in the mind of the professor or other official likely to do credit to the institution, should be, not the amount of salary to be pocketed but the opportunity of doing most good . . .[73]

In designating the ranks of the teaching staff, he consciously followed the German system with professors *ordinarii*, professors *extraordinarii*, and *privatim docentes*. "To our view this portion of the German system is a most valuable one." [74] Each professor would have to pass a rigid examination in his specialty before appointment and no man might be appointed simply because of his reputation "for such may be based on a myth which has grown by being repeated "like the snowball or the 'Fama' of Virgil." [75] As for student entrance examinations, Becker again turned to the German system, "the constant aim should be to approximate until we finally reach the high standard which the Germans have set us." [76] He would have four faculties of theology, law, medicine, and literature or academic studies, as he termed the humanities. In the first three of these faculties no degree was to be conferred except that of doctor and in the humanities two degrees were to be granted, doctor of philology and doctor of science. Under no circumstances were honorary degrees to be conferred by the university. Athletics were to be deliberately avoided: "At the establishment we have in view the students do not

[73] *Ibid.*, p. 661.
[74] *Ibid.*, p. 669.
[75] *Ibid.*, p. 670.
[76] *Ibid.*, p. 672.

come together to boat, box, practice baseball, or in any way to cultivate mere muscularity." [77] He made a strong appeal to American Catholics for support of the enterprise and he urged that a beginning be made at once. "Now is the time to make it. We shall never begin younger as a nation." In closing Bishop Becker remarked:

Certainly we do not overrate the importance of the subject in saying that no proposal has, in this century, been laid before American Catholics the consideration of which is of more consequence and a just decision on which is fraught with results of such magnitude to the Church of these States and to the Faithful as a body.[78]

Becker's two articles in the *American Catholic Quarterly Review* were the most thorough and reasoned which had appeared up to this time on the subject of a Catholic university. They found a response in a number of circles and the *Catholic Mirror,* weekly paper of the Archdiocese of Baltimore, championed the Bishop of Wilmington in an editorial of November 11, 1876, entitled, "A Catholic University." The editor quoted Becker's arguments and urged his readers to support the bishop in his campaign for a university.

But who will make the beginning? Assuredly the bishops of the country are the proper persons to break the ground. Right Reverend Bishop Becker, of Wilmington, has begun the agitation, and, from the two articles that he has already written, it is evident that he has given time and thought to the subject. He has already proposed a plan, demonstrated its feasibility, and made valuable suggestions. He may make

[77] *Ibid.,* p. 678.
[78] *Ibid.,* p. 679.

further suggestions, such as the place where the university should be situated, which place we think should be at Washington, New York, or St. Louis. Now, let the other bishops of the land unite with him in settling the preliminaries, call upon the generous Catholics to found this noble, necessary, and beneficent seat of learning, and we shall soon see the Catholic National University, not as an idea, but as an established fact.

This was followed by a second editorial on November 18 in which they questioned mildly Becker's severe judgment of the existing colleges but agreed that their standards were presently low, and, therefore, a university would help to lift these Catholic colleges to a higher level of scholarship. Three weeks later the *Catholic Mirror* returned to the subject in again editorializing on the services rendered to the Church by the Catholic universities in Belgium, Canada, and Ireland. "If, then, the Catholics of Ireland and Canada can establish and maintain universities, Catholic Yankees cannot fail in the same undertaking." [79] In fact, the Baltimore paper kept up a fairly steady campaign for a university and in its editorial of January 6, 1877, outlining the tasks ahead for the Church of the United States in the new year, it called attention to the university as one of the chief works of the year just opening, this time suggesting Becker as the man properly fit to be chosen as first rector since, "His Eminence Cardinal McCloskey, his Grace Archbishop Bayley, and the other Archbishops have not the strength for new burdens, and there is no one more conversant with the subject than Bishop Becker." [80]

---

[79] *Catholic Mirror,* December 9, 1876.
[80] *Ibid.,* editorial entitled "What Should be Done Next Year," January 6, 1877.

In its issue of St. Patrick's Day, 1877, the *Catholic Mirror* carried among its editorial comments the remark of Donn Piatt (1819–1891), editor of the weekly *Capital* of Washington, a non-partisan paper which was severely critical of the dishonesty uncovered during the Grant administration. Piatt had said, "There is no disguising the fact,—this nation is rapidly outgrowing religion." To which the *Catholic Mirror* added:

This is the deliberate opinion of one of the most observant editors in the United States. If the nation be rapidly outgrowing religion, the greater and more urgent is the necessity of establishing a National Catholic University, which will turn out men armed at all points to resist the tendency of the age, and to meet and defeat those who have already yielded to its baneful materialism. When will a beginning be made? [81]

In the fall of that year an article in the *Catholic World* on "College Education" had hazarded the opinion that, "We cannot have a university for the present, and therefore it is all important that the one essential thing a university can give—a higher mental training—should be given to our young Catholic men." [82] This lack of logic angered the *Catholic Mirror's* editor who retorted:

Of course "we cannot have a university for the present," in first-class running order, with a full head of steam on, the wheels all oiled, a smooth road-bed stretching out into the limitless distance, a crowd aboard, and the whole in charge of experienced engineers. But unless a beginning is

---

[81] *Ibid.*, March 17, 1877.
[82] "College Education," in *Catholic World*, XXV (Sept. 1877), 824.

made, we never shall have, and the sooner a beginning is made the sooner shall we be able to point to the American National Catholic University.[83]

In the spring of 1879 the Catholic historian, John Gilmary Shea, always interested in anything that would advance Catholic intellectual standards, contributed an article on the rising threat of socialism to the *American Catholic Quarterly Review*. Shea was genuinely alarmed at the growing manifestations of social unrest, particularly as it might affect the thousands of Catholic poor whose living was gained in the great industrial cities and whose environment of the tenement house was so calculated to produce a way of life conducive to a loss of religion. He suggested the building of more churches and the strengthening of the Society of St. Vincent de Paul in all parishes, and he called Catholics of wealth to a sense of their obligation in the crisis which he foresaw. He wrote:

Not only must we have more and plainer churches, with ragged schools, if you like, societies to aid the tenement-house poor in obtaining a livelihood in country parts, more extended associations to support establishments, a great Catholic University that will give us what we lack, a class of thoroughly educated and truly Catholic young men, who will inspire Catholic life in the upper class and by example and influence act on the lower class. Unless the Catholics more favored by fortune do not show more of Christian life, and exert a wider and more general influence than they have yet done, they will be swept away in the general irreligion around them, and so far from preserving or reclaiming their poorer brethren, will have to be brought to

[83] *Catholic Mirror*, September 8, 1877, editorial entitled "A National Catholic University."

higher and better thoughts by the examples furnished among their humbler brethren. On them rests a grave and a great responsibility. They are called upon by every motive to give time, influence, and exertions to avert the evils which menace us.[84]

Aside from Bishop Becker of Wilmington, whose efforts we have already seen, the member of the hierarchy who was giving the most serious and continuous thought to the need of higher education for the American clergy in these years was John Lancaster Spalding, first Bishop of Peoria. Spalding had shown from his student days in Cincinnati, Louvain, and Rome an uncommon interest in intellectual pursuits. Moreover, as a young priest he had done considerable writing, contributing articles and editorials to the *Catholic Advocate* of Louisville, publishing in 1873 an able biography of his uncle, the Archbishop of Baltimore, and three years later a volume entitled, *Essays and Reviews*. It was not strange, therefore, that when the Holy See erected the Diocese of Peoria on February 12, 1875, this promising priest of only thirty-six years of age should be chosen its first bishop. As a bishop, Spalding continued his keen interest in writing, lecturing, and broad reading. When the panic of 1873 dragged on for a number of years it carried with it to ruin not only banks and business corporations but a number of church projects as well. Late in 1878 disaster overtook Father Edward Purcell, brother of the Archbishop of Cincinnati, who for over forty years had taken in the deposits of many of Cincinnati's Catholic poor when they felt the banks were unsafe. Although in the long

---

[84] John Gilmary Shea, "The Rapid Increase of the Dangerous Classes in the United States," in *American Catholic Quarterly Review*, IV (Apr. 1879), 268.

and painful trials which ensued both the archbishop and his brother were cleared of any personal guilt in the loss of the deposits, the failure of Purcell did bring a financial crisis to the Archdiocese of Cincinnati the effects of which were felt for a quarter century. Among the losses was the once thriving Mount Saint Mary's Seminary of the West which had to be closed until 1887.[85]

It was the Cincinnati disaster which awakened in Spalding the hope that out of it might come the realization of his cherished hope for a Catholic university. In January, 1880, Bishop William H. Elder of Natchez was named Coadjutor Archbishop of Cincinnati to assist the aging Purcell in the calamity that had befallen his old age. In a letter of August 29, 1880, to Elder the Bishop of Peoria broached the subject that was uppermost in his mind.

I have been thinking of late that possibly the troubles in the finances of Cin. might offer an opportunity to make a beginning towards founding a Catholic University; and I hope you will pardon me for inquiring whether you will be forced to sell your Seminary Property. If so, might not the Bishops of the U. S. buy it in and start there a Theological High School for the best students among those who have already made the three years course of theology in the different seminaries of the country. In this high school they would go through what is called the profound course of theology. I see no other way by which we can hope to raise the standard of Clerical Education and you know better than I how difficult it is to find priests who have the learning which bishops ought to have; and as our dioceses are becoming so numerous it seems to me to be necessary to set about doing something in earnest by which we may raise up a class of men in the priesthood who will

[85] For the story of this financial disaster to the Church in Cincinnati, cf. Lamott, *op. cit.*, pp. 189–207.

become the ornament and the strength of our holy faith. If you think there is any thing in this suggestion, I should be glad to cooperate in order to help carry out some such plan.[86]

The personal correspondence of Bishop Spalding having, unfortunately, been lost or destroyed, we are unable to know the exact answer which Elder gave to this communication. However, it was favorable in general as we learn from Spalding himself who about a week later wrote Elder again.

I felt sure that you would gladly cooperate in any feasible plan to raise the standard of Clerical Education. All the Bishops of this country, I suppose, agree in admitting the urgency of our need; but what is everybody's business receives the earnest attention of no one. Several bishops have urged me to take a special interest in this matter, and since no one else seems at present to think of the work, it can surely do no harm to try to get at the real thought of some of the leading bishops of the U. S. on this point. To begin, I should think it unwise to entrust such an institution to a religious order. Omne animal generat simile sibi, and secular priests alone can efficiently train secular priests. We might be able to get the services of this or that learned man among the orders for a time, to act as professor. There will I think be little difficulty in finding suitable Professors; and Father Vandenhende, the first President of Troy seminary, and one of the most experienced and able priests in Belgium, would I have reason to believe, be willing to accept the direction. The great difficulty is that of deciding on a location, and unless some preponderant reason determine the point, there is danger here. It is for this reason

---

[86] Archives of the Archdiocese of Cincinnati, 612–b. J. L. Spalding to William H. Elder, Peoria, August 29, 1880. Hereafter these archives will be referred to as AAC.

that I think of Cin. The diocese is in great trouble. The bishops sympathize with the archbishop and yourself; and by agreeing to locate the theological University there they would add dignity to the See, inspire courage in the People and by buying your Seminary property, help in some slight measure to lighten your financial burden. If you intend to continue the Seminary as a diocesan institution, then of course my suggestion need not be considered; but if you have no such intention, then I feel confident that two or three bishops could be induced to canvass the country to raise funds to found there and endow the Theological University of the U. S. Only those who had finished a three years' course of theology would be admitted to this institution. As many dioceses are now supplied with priests, a considerable number of bishops would be able to allow their best students to continue their course of learning. What is greatly needed and never acquired in foreign seminaries and universities is a thorough knowledge of the English language and of English literature. A competent professor of Sacred Eloquence would give these theologians an insight into this subject. Then we could induce men of ability to give short courses of lectures on special subjects. Bishops and others would be invited to treat special matters. I have not written to the Cardinal or to any one on this subject but yourself. I wish to know before taking any further step whether my ideas with regard to Cin. meet with your approval. I am sorry to trouble you and have only good intentions to offer as an excuse.[87]

About ten days later Spalding again addressed Elder on his proposal, having meanwhile received another favorable response from the Cincinnati bishop. On this occasion Spalding went into more specific details.

Your letter encourages me. I have frequently spoken with

[87] AAC, 612–c, J. L. Spalding to William H. Elder, Peoria, September 7, 1880.

Bp. O'Connor on the subject of a Theological High School. He himself has no hope of being able to do anything either with Philadelphia or Woodstock.[88]

You are perfectly right in saying that if Cincinnati is to be chosen, the impulse and agitation should come from others, not from you. All that my plan contemplates is your consent and cooperation. The institution would have to be under the supreme direction of a Board chosen by the Bishops of the Country and representing their authority. I beg you therefore to mention the subject to the archbishop, as you suggest, and to any others whom you may care to consult. I should also like to get a rough estimate of what you think we ought to pay for the property, together with a statement of the amount of ground and some general description of the buildings. When I have a tangible proposition of this kind I shall try to enlist the Cardinal, the archbishop of Baltimore and others in the work. Bishop of Grace [sic] of St. Paul has begged me to undertake some such work; at least to make the attempt; and as he is a holy man I have thought it might be the will of God. It will be time to discuss many details when influential persons have approved of the general idea. The Holy Father would I am confident be delighted with the progect [sic] and we could rely upon his encouragement.[89]

After having received the approval of his plan from the Coadjutor Archbishop of Cincinnati, Spalding then turned to enlist the support of Cardinal McCloskey, Archbishop of New York. The proposition of a Catholic university was not new to McCloskey, for, as we have seen, Spalding's

---

[88] Bishop James O'Connor (1823–1890) was at the time Vicar Apostolic of Nebraska. He had been connected with St. Michael's Seminary, Pittsburgh, and St. Charles Borromeo Seminary, Overbrook, in the years before he was made a bishop.

[89] AAC, 612–d, J. L. Spalding to William H. Elder, Peoria, September 16, 1880.

uncle fourteen years before had attempted to secure his co-operation in such an enterprise at the time of the Second Plenary Council. Archbishop Spalding's nephew now tried his hand with New York's cardinal, but apparently with no better success than his uncle. On October 23, 1880, Spalding wrote McCloskey as follows:

There is another subject which I beg permission to submit to your consideration. There is, it seems to me, urgent need of a Theological High School in the U. S. Something like the Dunboyne in Ireland or the Theological Faculty of Louvain; where a few of the best students, after finishing the elementary course, could get a more thorough training in philosophy and theology.

This is not given in the Colleges at Rome or Louvain; it will never be given unless we create a home institution. The Seminary property at Cincinnati would be suitable for such a purpose and Bp. Elder with whom I have corresponded on the subject, heartily approves of the idea. The plan would be to have the Bishops of the U. S. purchase this property, for the purpose of a Theological High School for the whole country. It would be under the direction of a Board appointed by themselves. Only the best students, who had finished the ordinary course in the various seminaries would be admitted. Such an institution at Cincinnati would encourage the disheartened Catholics of that diocese; it would heighten the standard of clerical education throughout the country and it would create a body of men who in time would be able to fill our episcopal sees with honor. If Your Eminence and the archbishop would propose such an undertaking, I doubt not but several of the younger Bishops would offer their services to appeal for funds.

For my own part I should be willing to devote my whole life to such a work, for I am persuaded that in no other way shall we be able to meet the demands which the near future will make upon us. Your greater wisdom and experience will enable you to pronounce whether such a project may be entertained. If you do not think favorably of it, I shall at once put it out of mind. Apologizing for this long letter, I am with great respect, your Eminence's humble servant.[90]

The cardinal's reply was not favorable and Spalding apparently did not know just where to turn to win the support he needed. Two weeks after writing McCloskey the Bishop of Peoria wrote Elder again.

I enclose a letter which I have just received from the Cardinal. This, I fear, shows that the progect [sic] in regard to the seminary can not be carried out. Please return the Cardinal's letter to me. Could you suggest anything. I have thought that Mr. Springer [91] might be induced to buy the property and present it to the Bishops of the United States provided that [they] would agree to found there a catholic University.[92]

In spite of the fact that he told Cardinal McCloskey he would drop the question if the latter disapproved, Spalding kept up the agitation. He continued writing Elder in the fall of 1880 and if he had not lost heart entirely it was evident that he was growing provoked at the failure to win a response to his proposal. On November 14 he again wrote Cincinnati's coadjutor.

---

[90] NYAA, A–35, J. L. Spalding to John McCloskey, Peoria, October 23, 1880.

[91] Reuben Springer (1800–1884) was a generous benefactor of the Church in Cincinnati. Cf. *Dictionary of American Biography*, XVII, 482–483.

[92] AAC, 612–e, J. L. Spalding to William H. Elder, Peoria, November 6, 1880.

I most sincerely hope that something may still be done, by which we may establish a Theological High School in Cin. Nothing that I can do shall be omitted. I would be willing even, for a few years, to become a teacher in such an institution. It could be founded, without the smallest shadow of doubt, within a year, if the Bishops of the Country had the will. Nothing else is needed. Those who urged me to stir up the matter are unfortunately, like myself, in new or small dioceses. The impulse must be given by those higher up. When I see the blindness with which we allow opportunities to pass us by, I almost lose heart. What you say of Provincial Seminaries is my own conviction. Those bishops who have no seminaries, will choose the places for their students, and will rarely unite in support of a provincial seminary. A High School would raise the standard of instruction at once in all our Seminaries. It would be well I think if you were to sound the Archbishop of Balt. and others on the progect [sic]. I shall be delighted to beg, work, [?] or do anything as the servant of the bishops if they will but unite in saying let us make the effort. Would it not be well to have the Holy Father get the bishops to meet in some sort of Council? [93]

That Archbishop Elder was well disposed towards the proposal of the Bishop of Peoria we know from a letter written to Archbishop Gibbons a few days after Spalding had made the suggestion outlined above. Elder told Gibbons:

Bp. Spalding wrote to me of a suggestion made to him—of letting our Seminary here be purchased to establish in it a Theological College of a superior course of studies. In that form it would be doubly beneficial to us here. But apart from the selecting of this place, the project of having such an institution I think a most important one, and one

---

[93] AAC, 612–f, J. L. Spalding to William H. Elder, Peoria, November 14, 1880.

that ought not to be delayed a year longer than necessary. His Eminence of N. York seems to think the time is not yet come. But my conviction is that with such exertions as could be made, it might be instituted in a year or two. Even if begun on a small scale it would begin to produce fruit at once, and it would certainly grow larger.

One chief factor of success is to have a person able & willing to work for it. This we have in Bp. Spalding himself, and another time such a person might be hard to find. He himself may be advanced to some position demanding all his attention.

Please consider & consult & use your influence to push it without delay. I wd. very much like that our building be taken for it, but wherever it is, I wd. like to see it begun speedily.[94]

Although Bishop Spalding was aware that his position as Bishop of Peoria did not give him great prominence in the leadership of the Church of the United States, he was unwilling to leave his see. In October, 1880, Michael A. Corrigan, Bishop of Newark, had been named by Rome as Coadjutor Archbishop of New York. To fill the vacancy in Newark the name of Spalding had been advanced. In a note of April 29, 1881, enclosed in a letter from Archbishop Corrigan to Bishop Bernard J. McQuaid of Rochester, the New York prelate wrote: *"Private.* I had a letter from Miss Edes a few days ago in which she says that the names sent from New York—(which she does not know)—do not seem to be *acceptable* to the Propaganda. Bp. Spalding has written absolutely to Card. Simeoni that he would *not* leave Peoria, under any consideration; and

---

[94] BCA, 75–M–9, William H. Elder to James Gibbons, Cincinnati, November 19, 1880.

this seems to have been accepted at headquarters." [95] Mc-
Quaid apparently wanted Spalding in Newark, for a
month later he wrote Corrigan:

What is meant by Spaulding [*sic*] refusing to go to Newark?
Perhaps Miss Edes is only repeating newspaper talk. Such
a rumor went the rounds a short time ago. Is there anything to it? Can some body else be thrusting himself into
the management of the N Y Province? I do not think that
any one Province has been playing a double game? [96]

To which Archbishop Corrigan answered on May 30: "Bp.
Spalding himself told me of his writing to Rome (more
than once) of his absolute reluctance to leave Peoria for
any other field of labor." [97]

But if Spalding chose to pass over the chance for advancement to an eastern see, he did not choose to forget
the project for a university. On June 30, 1881, St. Francis
Seminary in Milwaukee celebrated its silver jubilee and the
Bishop of Peoria was invited to give the sermon at the
jubilee Mass. It afforded Spalding an excellent opportunity
to advance his plea for an institution of higher studies for
priests. After reviewing the role which Christ intended the
priesthood to play in the Church with the glories which
Massillon, Bossuet, and others had described concerning
the Catholic priesthood's part in the history of the Church,
the bishop insisted on the supreme importance to be attached to the best possible education for priests. In this he
reviewed the work of St. Charles Borromeo, Cardinal Pole,

---

[95] Rochester Diocesan Archives. Hereafter these archives will be
referred to as RDA.

[96] RDA, May 27, 1881, copy.

[97] RDA.

St. Francis de Sales, St. Vincent de Paul, Jacques Olier,
and that of the followers of St. Ignatius in the German
College in Rome. He paid tribute to the seminaries of the
United States for their accomplishments in stating: "Our
theological seminaries are at present, if I may express an
opinion, not in any essential point inferior to those of
Europe, and the worthy and enlightened men who control
them manifest an earnest desire to reach yet higher standards of excellence." [98]

Having expressed his admiration for the work of the
seminaries, Spalding then proceeded to distinguish between
seminaries as professional schools and higher institutions of
learning. "You will not, therefore, . . . misunderstand me
when I affirm that it is not possible that seminaries such as
these are and must remain, here and elsewhere, should give
the highest intellectual education. They are elementary
schools of theology, and to deprive them of this character
would not only be a departure from the end for which they
were instituted, but would render them useless." [99] Spalding
outlined what he regarded as the functions of a seminary,
insisting that a seminary could not give the "best intellectual culture." The United States had only such elementary seminaries and in that category the bishop included the American colleges in Rome and Louvain. He
made an exception for the Jesuits' new Woodstock College,
but, as he said, that institution was only for their own men.
At this point in his sermon Spalding outlined what he had

[98] John L. Spalding, *Lectures and Discourses* (New York, 1882),
p. 151. The sermon was published as an essay in this volume under
the title of "The Catholic Priesthood."
[99] *Ibid.,* p. 151.

in mind by way of remedy and it is odd to find him saying that he did not intend a university.

I am not speaking of a university, but of something far simpler, less expensive, and, in my opinion, better fitted to supply the most pressing want of American Catholics. The institution of which I am thinking might be called a High-School of Philosophy and Theology.[100]

It is quite evident from this and other references made to the proposed institution that Bishop Spalding had not in mind a university as commonly conceived today. As he had said to McCloskey the previous fall, he thought in terms of the Dunboyne Establishment at Maynooth and the theological faculty of Louvain.[101] In this his conception was far less expansive and far less specific than the plan outlined by Bishop Becker five years before. At Milwaukee in 1881 Spalding maintained that only one such institution as he had in mind should be founded for the entire country and that its location was a matter of indifference. "Some secluded spot, hallowed by memories of true men who have departed, like the Old Mountain near Emmitsburg, would be more favorable to high thinking and undisturbed meditation than the suburbs of a great city." [102] While no one would deny the signal services rendered the Church by Mount Saint Mary's College in Emmitsburg, it could hardly be thought of seriously as the seat of a university, but since Spalding specifically said he did not have a university in mind, the point, of course, should not be stressed. He thought five or six men would be enough to

---

[100] *Ibid.*, p. 154.
[101] Cf. p. 72 of this study.
[102] *Ibid.*, p. 155.

form a faculty with forty or fifty gifted young priests as the first student body. The aim of "such a college would not be to make profound theologians, learned exegetes, or skilful metaphysicians, or specialists of whatever kind, but rather it would teach theology as a subject of contemplation. It would seek to impart not professional skill but cultivation of mind." [103] For this venture the Bishop of Peoria believed that a half million dollars would be sufficient, and for those who might plead inopportuneness he answered:

. . . to those who say to me that the time has not come, that it is not possible now to found a high school of philosophy and theology such as is here contemplated, I make answer that it is possible to try . . . Ambitious men may fear failure, but good men need not be subject to this weakness.[104]

Spalding's sermon at the Milwaukee jubilee of 1881 did have the effect of arousing enthusiasm for some kind of institution of higher learning beyond the seminary. But that it was a clear outline of a Catholic university or its function is obviously not true. The bishop's very terminology was vague, calling his prospective institution "high school of theology" and "college" and deliberately excluding a university from consideration. His use of the term "high school" was doubtless a reflection of his observation of the German *Hochschule* and would not, of course, imply a high school in the American sense. But the sermon did have importance in the evolution of the university idea in that it focused the attention of the bishops and clergy on the need for some kind of training beyond the

[103] *Ibid.*, p. 156.
[104] *Ibid.*, p. 157.

elementary seminary course. Spalding published his Milwaukee sermon as an essay in a volume which appeared
early in the year 1882. He sent a copy of it to Archbishop
James Gibbons of Baltimore who wrote commending him
on the work. In reply Spalding said:

Please accept my sincere thanks for your very kind words
in reference to my "Lectures and Discourses." It is very
difficult to write any thing worthwhile in the midst of the
labors and cares in which a missionary bishop finds himself. If we could only begin a University college for the
higher education of priests, it would be my greatest happi-
ness to go into it and devote the rest of my life to this work,
which, I am convinced, is of all others the most important
and the most urgent.[105]

Later in the summer in which Spalding gave the Milwaukee address Elder of Cincinnati spoke of the university
project in a letter to Gibbons in which he asked: "Would
it not be practicable to arrange with the Jesuits of Woodstock for giving a longer or higher course of Philosophy &
Theology to some secular students who might be thought
capable of profiting by it? That would be a simple beginning, capable of growing into a great institution & forming
the first & most needed faculty of a university." [106]

The university having definitely entered the discussion
stage on a national scale by 1882 there were few more alert
observers of the various opinions expressed than the Bishop
of Rochester. In a pastoral letter of August 20, 1882, which

[105] BCA, 76–A–8, J. L. Spalding to James Gibbons, Peoria, July 18,
1882.

[106] BCA, 76–B–2, William H. Elder to James Gibbons, Cincinnati,
August 8, 1881.

accompanied his report on the diocese for the year 1881, McQuaid made reference to the question.

It is at this time that some are calling aloud for the establishment of a grand Catholic University, and of a Theological Seminary for extended and higher studies. An essential condition preparatory to the founding of such a University is to know that there are young men willing and ready to take advantage of its facilities for a university course of study. A second condition lies in the getting together of a large sum of money sufficient to place the University on a solid financial basis. A University, in a rich country like America, cannot go a begging among the poor, and rich; Catholics show no inclination to rival non-Catholics by endowing educational institutions. We must wait and pray for a change in both respects before the dream of a Catholic University, except in name, can be realized.

The founding of a Theological School for higher studies is more feasible, and is nearer at hand than that of the University. It may lead the way to the University. But antecedent to the founding of this Theological University will be the establishing of Diocesan Seminaries to answer the ordinary and usual wants of a Diocese, and to serve as feeders to the higher school. This is the primary necessity, and is according to the mind of the church and the instructions of Rome.[107]

At this time Bishop McQuaid was making preliminary plans for the beginning of St. Bernard's Seminary at Rochester which was finally completed and dedicated in

---

[107] RDA, Bernard J. McQuaid's pastoral letter, August 20, 1882. The pertinent passages of McQuaid's pastorals were kindly copied for the writer by the Reverend Robert F. McNamara, professor of church history in St. Bernard's Seminary, from the collection of pastorals kept in the Rochester Diocesan Archives.

August, 1893. He, therefore, was quick to sense a project
which might draw off support from his diocesan seminary
and in the ensuing years the Catholic University of America
did not have a stronger and more unrelenting foe than the
Bishop of Rochester, as we shall have occasion to see later.
That many were dissatisfied with the condition of Catholic
higher education in the United States at this time is obvious
to anyone who examines the literature of the period. The
July, 1882, issue of the *American Catholic Quarterly Review* published an anonymous article entitled "What is the
Outlook for Our Colleges?" [108] The writer confined himself to the Catholic institutions of collegiate rank and did
not mention a university. He set forth certain ideas which
he thought might help to bring an improvement, among
them a greater supply of improved textbooks for class use.
Three months later the same journal carried another article
on the Catholic colleges by Augustus J. Thébaud, S.J., a
professor at St. Francis Xavier College, New York, and
former rector of St. John's College, Fordham. Thébaud
discussed the weaknesses of the existing colleges and he conceded that the most thorough study of the highest branches
of knowledge would mean that "a well-organized university would be absolutely required," but he ruled a university out of consideration as being impossible of attainment at that time. "A complete university would be still
more desirable; but is this now possible?" Thébaud seemed
to think it was not.[109]

---

[108] "What is the Outlook for Our Colleges?" in *American Catholic
Quarterly Review,* VII (July, 1882), 385–407.

[109] Augustus J. Thébaud, S.J., "Superior Instruction in Our Colleges," in *American Catholic Quarterly Review,* VII (Oct. 1882),
691, 696.

McQuaid's pastoral won the warm admiration of James McMaster, editor of the *Freeman's Journal* of New York. He commended it to his readers in an editorial of October 21, 1882, and in agreement with the Bishop of Rochester on a university, McMaster wrote:

On the subject of the "grand Catholic seminary" for which some of us are calling, Bishop McQuaid's remarks are sound and to the point.

It is so easy to make a grand seminary in imagination— so easy to write a promising prospectus—that men who think in print neglect the lesson of plain, hard facts. If some of the small schools, chartered as colleges, were consolidated in one, we might have the nucleus of a university, which might begin to "fill a long-felt want" some time about the year 2082. But at present the need of a Catholic university is much less than the need of good parochial schools and, as Bishop McQuaid suggests, the founding of a theological school for higher studies. A thoroughly trained priesthood is the wedge which must gradually convert the American people from unbelief to Faith.

But all were not of the mind of McQuaid and McMaster. Three weeks after the editorial quoted above appeared the same paper carried a lengthy communication signed "A Priest" and entitled, "The Higher Theological School." It was in the form of an open letter to the editor of the *Freeman's Journal*. The writer invited further consideration of Bishop Spalding's idea, stating, "apart from the magnanimity of the offer made by one of the greatest ornaments of the American Episcopacy to lay aside the mitre and crosier and become a simple professor in the proposed institution, the matter itself is of vast importance." The writer instanced the examples of Louvain and Maynooth

and made a strong plea for such an institution in the
United States, giving it as his belief that an advanced theological school might well serve as a ready instrument to
check the serious leakage from the Church which had occurred in America. Again, as to opportuneness, "we are
weary of hearing such objections in ecclesiastical matters.
The time is not yet ripe, it is said, for the introduction of
the regular Canon Law into this country, though what
degree of maturity is required has never yet been stated."
As for the objection that money was lacking, "such a question is an insult to the generosity of American Catholics."
The writer mentioned Spalding's willingness to procure
the money for the buildings and he saw no reason why the
6,000 priests in the United States could not each give $10
a year and with this annual $60,000 a beginning could be
made. "What, then, is wanting? The light arose in the West,
and, so far, it appears to have dawned only on the Rt. Rev.
Bishop of Rochester, who, as may be seen from his recent
pastoral, fully understands the situation." He believed that
after a few years the institution could easily supply professors for its various chairs, conceding that it might be difficult at first, although the American Church was capable
of producing "a galaxy of professors equal to Dr. Corcoran
—rare genius though he be . . ." [110]

---

[110] A Priest, "The Higher Theological School," in *Freeman's Journal,* November 11, 1882. The theologian to which the writer made
reference was James A. Corcoran (1820–1889) who figured in the
Eighth (1855) and Ninth (1858) Provincial Councils of Baltimore,
was secretary-in-chief of the Second Plenary Council of Baltimore
in 1866, and the choice of the American hierarchy on the preparatory
commission for the Vatican Council in 1868. Corcoran was a professor
at St. Charles Borromeo Seminary, Overbrook, for many years, and
was secretary to the American archbishops for the preparatory ses-

Although this lengthy communication to the *Freeman's Journal* did not outline clearly a university plan, the general emphasis on advanced study in theology and philosophy would indicate that the writer had in mind a graduate school for those two disciplines. In a letter of November 10, 1882, to Bishop McQuaid the writer was identified by Father Patrick Hennessy, pastor of St. Patrick's Church in Jersey City, as being John Larkin, Irish-born, who became a professor of theology at Mount Saint Mary's, Emmitsburg, in October, 1881, and in 1882 was given the Ph.D. degree by that institution.[111] Hennessy was anxious that McQuaid should take up the matter in the Catholic papers. He wrote:

I send you this week's Freeman containing an article on the Theological High School by my friend Rev. Dr. Larkin, professor of Dogma & Moral at Emmitsburg—a young Maynooth man whom I believe you saw here last June a year ago. Bishop Spalding told me the other day that he intended to bring the subject of the High School of theology to the notice of the Holy Father. I think a few letters from you in the Freeman, or Catholic Review on the subject would contribute much toward the bringing of it before the American people . . .[112]

---

sions in Rome for the Third Plenary Council of 1884. He had also had considerable experience in journalism, having been a co-editor of the *United States Catholic Miscellany* from 1846 to 1861, co-editor of the *Works* of Bishop England in the 1849 edition, and editor-in-chief of the *American Catholic Quarterly Review* after 1876. *Dictionary of American Biography,* IV, 439.

[111] Mary M. Meline and Edward F. X. McSweeny, *The Story of the Mountain. Mount St. Mary's College and Seminary* (Emmitsburg, 1911), II, 197, 450.

[112] RDA, P. Hennessy to Bernard J. McQuaid, Jersey City, November 10, 1882.

Spalding did go to Rome that winter and word reached the Bishop of Rochester that the Peoria prelate was pushing his university idea at the Holy See. Writing to his friend, Bishop Richard Gilmour of Cleveland, on February 27, 1883, McQuaid said:

How does Bishop Spalding stand in regard to the question of an Agent? He is now in Rome. He will be able to present his view of a case and make it appear the right one. His practical experience as a working priest has been *nil*. I am afraid he will not help our cause, being too much taken up with the University scheme.

Just after writing the above I received a letter from a priest of my diocese who is staying in Rome to prosecute his studies in Canon Law, etc. He writes: "Bishop Spalding has left for the East. He is to be absent three months in Palestine, etc. His pet-work, the American University, has fallen through completely, it seems, sic erat expectandum. I have heard many reasons why; but I can say nothing for certain. Now they say he is working for a national council." [113]

If the report in this letter was true, and there is no reason to believe that it was not, the Holy See was made aware of the need for an American Catholic university or a higher school of theology well in advance of the Third Plenary Council, as Bishop McQuaid's correspondent suggests. In any case, no serious steps were taken to implement Spalding's plan until the American bishops had assembled in the autumn of 1884 for their plenary gathering at Baltimore.

---

[113] RDA, Bernard J. McQuaid to Richard Gilmour, Rochester, February 27, 1883, copy.

THIRD PLENARY COUNCIL, NOVEMBER–DECEMBER, 1884
St. Mary's Seminary, Baltimore

II

The Council and Some Preliminary Steps

AN INTERVAL of eighteen years transpired between the Second Plenary Council in 1866, when the subject of a university first entered into the conciliar pronouncements of the bishops, and the Third Plenary Council in 1884, when the establishment of a university was definitely determined upon. They were eventful years for the Church of the United States. The quarter century between 1860 and 1885 witnessed a continuing flow of immigration to American shores from Ireland and the German world as well as from other countries of western Europe. Thousands of these Irish and Germans who had begun coming to the United States in increasing numbers after the 1830's were Catholics. In the years following the Civil War the first sizable groups from Italy and Austria-Hungary swelled the numbers of new members for the Catholic Church in the United States. From an estimated Catholic population of 3,103,000 in 1860 the total number of Catholics had increased by 1880 to 6,259,000 and by the beginning of the last decade of the century the Church had approximately

8,909,000 members in the United States.[1] This phenomenal growth, of course, brought with it serious problems of social and economic adjustment to their new environment for these European Catholics. Yet if the immigrant Catholics created at times acute tension by their needs and demands upon the Church, they also constituted a great strength. Few of the serious questions which arose for settlement among the bishops in the last two decades of the century were unrelated to the immigrant and his status.

As a clear reflection of the growth of the American Church in the years between 1866 and 1884, one may instance the fact that during that time twenty-two new dioceses and five vicariates apostolic were erected by the Holy See. At the same time five new provinces were created, bringing the number of archbishops in the country by 1884 to twelve. During these years, too, new leaders appeared in the hierarchy who were to leave a deep impression upon the Catholic life of their day. Of the six archbishops at the council of 1866 only two were still living in 1884, Peter R. Kenrick of St. Louis and Cardinal McCloskey of New York, and the latter was too feeble to take part in the Third Plenary Council. James Gibbons had become Archbishop of Baltimore in October, 1877, on the death of James Roosevelt Bayley and John Ireland succeeded to the See of St. Paul in July, 1884, on the resignation of Bishop Grace. By the time of the council of 1884 John Lancaster Spalding had been seven years Bishop of Peoria, Bernard J. McQuaid sixteen years Bishop of Rochester, and Richard Gilmour twelve years Bishop of Cleveland. The year 1880 was marked by four notable changes

---

[1] Gerald Shaughnessy, *Has the Immigrant Kept the Faith?* (New York, 1925), pp. 145, 161, and 166.

in the leadership of the American Church when William
H. Elder, Bishop of Natchez, was named Coadjutor Archbishop of Cincinnati, Michael Heiss of LaCrosse appointed
Coadjutor Archbishop of Milwaukee, Bishop Michael A.
Corrigan of Newark promoted as Coadjutor Archbishop
of New York, and Patrick A. Feehan of Nashville was made
first Archbishop of Chicago. John J. Williams had been
the ordinary of Boston since 1866, and just four months
before the opening of the council Patrick J. Ryan of St.
Louis was named Archbishop of Philadelphia. The prelates
whose names are so closely identified with the turbulent
years of the 1880's and 1890's in American Catholic history
had, therefore, all taken their posts before the Third
Plenary Council convened.

As we have seen, in the years between the councils the
idea of a Catholic university gained ground. Some of the
Catholic reviews and newspapers emphasized the need
which the Church had of an institution which would give
more advanced instruction than the colleges and seminaries
then existing. This publicity helped to prepare the way for
more effective action in the council of 1884. Through the
articles of Becker, Spalding, and Hecker and the agitation
of such papers as the *Catholic Advocate* of Louisville and
the *Catholic Mirror* of Baltimore an increasingly large
number of American Catholics were made aware of the
services which a university might render to the Church of
the nation.

When the question of holding another plenary council
of the American hierarchy was first raised there were a
number of the bishops who at first demurred. As early as
November, 1880, Spalding had suggested a council in a

letter to Archbishop Elder.[2] But certain of the leading eastern bishops were not enthusiastic. On January 4, 1882, Archbishop Gibbons confided to his diary that Cardinal McCloskey had asked the New York coadjutor to call on him regarding this question, and the Baltimore prelate wrote:

I gave as my opinion that it would not be expedient to hold a council for some time to come; but as a preliminary step, provincial councils might be held, or the Bishops of each province might assemble informally and consider what subjects might be discussed in the plenary council. The Bishops of the West seem to favor a national council, as some of them have intimated to me.[3]

It was at the instance of Giovanni Cardinal Simeoni, Prefect of the Congregation of the Propaganda from 1878 to 1892, that these inquiries were made. About three weeks after Gibbons' entry in his diary Archbishop Williams of Boston wrote Corrigan on this point. He said:

We had a meeting of the Bishops of this province yesterday. All were present except the Bp. of Providence who is down South. All agreed that the holding of the plenary Council was not desirable. The reasons given in your letter seemd [sic] to us all very forcible.[4]

Despite these adverse views, the sentiment for the council grew among the bishops during the next year and a half, doubtless prompted in good measure by the fact that Rome

---

[2] Cf. p. 74 of this study.
[3] Baltimore Cathedral Archives, Cardinal Gibbons' Diary, p. 158.
[4] New York Archdiocesan Archives, C–17, John J. Williams to Michael A. Corrigan, Boston, January 27, 1882.

seemed to favor holding a council. At length Pope Leo
XIII summoned the American archbishops to the Holy
See to confer with him and the officials of the Propaganda
about the details for the assembly. All the twelve metropolitans of the United States were present either in person or
through a representative, except Archbishop Joseph S.
Alemany of San Francisco. From November 13 to December 13, 1883, the American prelates met in eleven sessions at
the College of the Propaganda with Simeoni, Franzelin,
Jacobini, and other curial officials and during these weeks
the groundwork was laid for the council. Their deliberations
were summarized in a Latin document and, although it contained a chapter entitled, "De Clericorum educatione et
instructione," it made no mention of a university, nor are
the minutes of the archbishops' conferences more enlightening on the subject.[5]

After the council had finally been decided upon and
Archbishop Gibbons had been named apostolic delegate to
preside over the gathering, his time and energies were
naturally very much given to immediate preparations upon

-----

[5] This document was entitled, *Capita proposita et examinata in
collationibus, quas coram nonnullis Emis Cardinalibus Sacrae Con-
gregationis de Propaganda Fide ad praeparandum futurum Concilium plenarium habuerunt Rmi Archiepiscopi et Episcopi foedera-
torum Statuum Americae Septemtrionalis* [sic] *Romae congregati.*
BCA (uncatalogued). These same archives contain the minutes of
the archbishops' conferences in Rome in a document of fifty-three
pages in Latin, 77–L–20. There is nothing in the minutes on the
university. The closest approach to the subject is contained in a
statement issuing from the session of November 13 which read as
follows: "Dictum etiam est, in concilio commendandum esse ut Episcopi quosdam ex suis Clericis mittant ad ea Seminaria, in quibus
instructio superior et magis ampla confertur. In specie commendandum esse Collegium Americanum Urbis et Louvaniense." p. 5.

his return to Baltimore from Rome in March, 1884. We are interested in the Third Plenary Council here only insofar as it related to the project of a university.[6] One of the first tasks facing Gibbons was to assign different subjects for special study to members of the hierarchy who seemed particularly qualified for the work. Two weeks after his return he wrote Bishop Becker of Wilmington, asking him to make a study of the first chapter of the schema which had to do with seminaries. Becker, by reason of the articles he had published on university education some eight years before, might well have seemed the proper person to be asked. However, he did not welcome the assignment and he wrote Gibbons that he was not the person since he had no seminary in his own diocese and had had little experience, but the archbishop's request was "equivalent to a command" and he would do his best. Becker suggested that Gibbons in his role as apostolic delegate assume authority for a set of questions to all the bishops which would demand categorical answers. He ended his letter by saying:

The subject is one fraught with immense consequences, for on it depends, in a great degree, the character of the

6 The literature on the history of the council is not very extensive. Peter Guilday, *A History of the Councils of Baltimore (1791–1884)* (New York, 1932), devotes a fairly lengthy chapter to it, pp. 221–249. There is the *Memorial Volume. A History of the Third Plenary Council of Baltimore, November 9–December 7, 1884* (Baltimore, 1885), which contains something of the external aspects of the council with the texts of the sermons preached. There are, as well, the *Acta et Decreta* (Baltimore, 1884) which was an edition printed immediately after the close of the council and intended for private use; it contained the minutes of the private congregations. Finally, the *Acta et Decreta* (Baltimore, 1886) was the volume issued for public use and giving the actual legislation as confirmed by the Holy See.

future laborers in the vineyard of Christ. How to sail safely between the Scylla of condemnation of the many weak affairs called Diocesan, or College Seminaries, and the Charybdis of costly and ill-controlled Provincial institutions actually existing is, to speak frankly, more than I now see.[7]

It is an odd fact that in the council itself Becker played little or no part in the question of a university. On November 11 he preached one of the sermons in the cathedral on the subject of "The Church and Science," the text of which was carried by the *Catholic Mirror* in its issue of December 6, but the sermon contained not so much as a mention of a university. Nearly three years later when the university had been assured, Father Benjamin J. Keiley, who had served Becker as theologian in the council and was at this time pastor of the Church of the Immaculate Conception in Atlanta, Georgia, wrote the Archbishop of Baltimore a letter which throws some light on Becker's attitude towards the university's founding. He wrote:

I arrived home a few days ago and have been very busy putting things straight. Since my return I have thought over our conversation regarding the University question, and fear I may have done injustice to Bp. Becker in my statements. As I said, I am not aware of his views on the question, but I feel confident his position in regard to it is, that he considers it impracticable *now;* that, even if matters were ripe, he does not believe the choice of a Rector was a wise one; that he never considered either Mgrs. Spalding or Keane as sufficiently *prudent* men to give a *fair* start to the ground work. I know that he favored Cor-

---

[7] BCA, 77–R–7, Thomas A. Becker to James Gibbons, Wilmington, March 31, 1884.

coran for the position.[8] Now, with these and other like
convictions, I can readily understand why he was indifferent to the *site*.

I only write these lines to Your Eminence fearing I may
have led you to an inaccurate judgement of the Bp's
position.[9]

Whatever the reason, Bishop Becker, who in March, 1886,
was transferred to the Diocese of Savannah, played no part
in the actual founding of the university which he had so
strongly and intelligently urged in 1876.

In the months preceding the council Archbishop Gibbons received varied reactions from the bishops on the
question of a university. On April 6, 1884, Bishop Gilmour
of Cleveland wrote, in a letter dealing with matters of the
council, "I hope something will be done to establish a seminary in our midst for higher education, as I once suggested to you & also to the Propaganda when I was
there." [10] Spalding, as ever, was active and, although he
pleaded that he had a great deal of work facing him during
the summer and autumn of 1884 and would prefer that
Gibbons assign the sermon he had in mind for him to some
other bishop, he nonetheless wrote, "I do not wish to put
his Grace to inconvenience, and if he should find difficulty

---

[8] For Corcoran cf. N. 110, p. 84 of this study.

[9] BCA, 83–H–2, Benjamin J. Keiley to James Gibbons, Atlanta,
August 18, 1887. The writer read through forty-five letters from
Becker in the Baltimore Cathedral Archives, dated between November 20, 1861, and December 18, 1889. They revealed the most cordial
relations between the bishop and Archbishops Spalding, Bayley, and
Gibbons, but there was not a single allusion to a Catholic university
in any of these letters.

[10] BCA, 77–T–6, Richard Gilmour to James Gibbons, Cleveland,
April 6, 1884.

in getting some one else to speak on the subject he has chosen for me, he may rely upon my doing the best I can." [11] It was this sermon of Spalding's which was destined to be one of the most forceful pronouncements spoken during the council on the need for a university. Archbishop Heiss of Milwaukee reported an unfavorable reaction to a university from the meeting of the bishops of his province that spring. When he transmitted to Gibbons their opinions on other questions confronting the council, Heiss said:

The proposition for a "Catholic University" or rather for a higher "Seminary for Philosophy and Theology" has been made by Rt. Rev. Bishop Grace, without having much support from the majority of the Bishops; the most of them are of the opinion, all what [sic] can be done now, would be to improve the studies of our larger or Provincial Seminaries. [12]

But by the early autumn of 1884 a more encouraging aspect was given to the university question when it was

---

[11] BCA, 77–Y–9, John Lancaster Spalding to "Rev. and Dear Doctor," Peoria, April 29, 1884. Spalding was probably writing to John S. Foley, one of the two chancellors of the council. Just at this time Spalding was being considered for another eastern see as we learn from a letter of Archbishop Williams to Archbishop Corrigan. Writing the New York prelate on April 21, 1884, he said: "This morning I received a letter from the Propaganda asking if I thought Bp. Spalding or Bp. Chatard a good choice for Philadelphia. I should like to have your opinion on this matter. If we agree, it will make our answer stronger. I know Bp. Chatard pretty well, and think him scarcely large enough for the place. I know Bp. Spalding less, but he seems to me a strong man. You must know him well. Have you any other name to recommend? " NYAA, C–17.

[12] BCA, 78–C–6, Michael Heiss to James Gibbons, Milwaukee, May 17, 1884.

learned that Miss Mary Gwendoline Caldwell, a wealthy young heiress of New York City, was disposed to give a large sum of money to get the project under way. Miss Caldwell and her sister, Lina, were the sole heirs of a large fortune left to them by their father, William Shakespeare Caldwell, formerly of Kentucky. The Caldwell family had been friends of the Spaldings in Kentucky and it was through the Bishop of Peoria that Miss Caldwell was made aware of the work in which her generous impulse for the Church's welfare might best be employed. Two weeks before the council opened in Baltimore, Spalding wrote Gibbons.

Miss Mary Caldwell has informed me that she intends to be present at the opening of the Council and as she is disposed to be very generous in aid of the project of founding *Unum Seminarium Principale,* I am anxious she should have a good seat in the Cathedral. She will I suppose be accompanied by one or two friends. May I ask your assistance in this matter? I expect to arrive in Balto with Bps Ireland and Grace on the evening of Nov. 6th. My discourse on the higher education will I fear be long, and hence it will probably be better to give me some evening, as I doubt whether I could make it fit in at the High Mass.[13]

The formal opening of the Third Plenary Council took place on Sunday, November 9, in the Cathedral of the Assumption with Archbishop Kenrick of St. Louis celebrating the Mass and Archbishop Ryan of Philadelphia preaching on "The Church in Her Councils." Four days after the opening of the council Miss Caldwell, who was in

---

[13] BCA, 78–S–11, J. L. Spalding to James Gibbons, Peoria, October 26, 1884.

Baltimore for the occasion, wrote out a statement of her intention to give a grant of money with the conditions attached. The letter was as follows:

I hereby offer the sum of three hundred thousand dollars ($300,000) to the Bishops of the Third Plenary Council, for the purpose of founding a National Catholic School of Philosophy and Theology. This offer is made subject to the following conditions: 1st. This school is to be established in the United States. 2nd. It is to be under the control of a committee of Bishops representing the Catholic Episcopate of the United States. 3rd. It is to be a separate institution, and not affiliated to any other institution. 4th. Only ecclesiastics who have completed their elementary course of Philosophy and Theology are to be received into this institution. 5th. This institution is never to be under the control of any religious order, and its chairs are to be filled in preference by professors chosen from the secular clergy and laity. 6th. Other faculties may be affiliated to this institution with a view to form a Catholic University. 7th. This fund shall never be diverted from the purpose for which it is given, and the site once chosen shall not be changed without the greatest reasons. 8th. In consideration of this donation I am to be considered the founder of this institution. Mary Gwendoline Caldwell. Baltimore, Nov. 13, 1884.[14]

On November 10 the New York *Herald* had carried a story about the Caldwell gift, stating the amount as $300,-000 and that the news of the benefaction "was the chief topic of conversation in Catholic circles yesterday." The *Herald* quoted at length Eugene Kelly, one of the executors of William Shakespeare Caldwell's estate, concerning the need for a Catholic university, and "a distinguished doctor

---

[14] BCA, 78-T-6.

of the Church" told a *Herald* reporter that the Caldwell gift would stimulate others to contribute. The "distinguished doctor" thought the new institution would "turn out to be a training school for those who propose to become priests," rather than an institution for priests. Asked if he thought the proposed university would "in some degree take the place of the American College," he replied, "Naturally, because there is no reason why students should go abroad for instruction if they can obtain it at home." The doctor, however, was careful to say that "none of the details in regard to the work have yet been made public, and . . . my remarks are based on the supposition that the intention of Miss Caldwell and her friends is to provide America with a university similar to those in Europe." This account in the *Herald* was only the first of a series of reports in the secular and Catholic press during the ensuing weeks and, since no details had been determined on by the bishops themselves, it is not strange to find a great deal of inaccurate and faulty reporting in these stories. We shall have occasion to notice more of them later on.

It was at the evening service in the cathedral on Sunday, November 16, that Bishop Spalding preached his sermon on "The Higher Education of the Priesthood." [15] The Baltimore *Sun* in its report of the council's progress remarked upon the sermon in its issue of November 17 and said: "Bishop Spalding has given this subject a great deal of attention. It is his favorite theme, and his sermon last night is regarded as a powerful one." Spalding's sermon was devoted in the first part to the services rendered the

---

[15] The text of Spalding's sermon was published in a volume entitled, *Means and Ends of Education* (Chicago, 1895) as "The Higher Education," pp. 181–232.

Church through the ages by her trained clergy, and he developed the idea of the value to be attached to intellectual discipline. "The narrower the range of our mental vision, the greater the obstinacy with which we cling to our opinions . . . He who possesses a disciplined mind, and is familiar with the best thoughts that live in the great literatures, will be the last to attach undue importance to his own thinking." [16] In broad strokes Spalding traced the great intellectual currents in the western world since the Middle Ages, and in speaking of the nineteenth century's advance in science and loss of supernatural faith, he said:

. . . the continuance and the progress of doubt, and consequently of indifference, is, to some extent at least, to be ascribed also to the fact that the most earnest believers in God and in Christianity have, for now more than a century, been less eager to acquire the best philosophic and literary cultivation of mind that others who, having lost faith in the supernatural, seek for compensation in a wider and deeper knowledge of nature, and in the mental culture which enables them to enjoy more keenly the high thoughts and fair images which live in literature and art. [17]

He returned to a favorite theme of his in deploring the narrowness of purely professional training. Applying it to priests, he maintained that if they were to be free from "this narrowness and onesidedness, this lack of openness to light and freedom of mental play, the education of the priest must be more than a professional education; and he must be sent to a school higher and broader than the ecclesiastical seminary, which is simply a training college for the practical work of the ministry." He paid tribute, as

---

[16] *Ibid.*, p. 191.
[17] *Ibid.*, p. 207.

he had done at Milwaukee three years before, to the work of the American seminaries, but he insisted:

> . . . the ecclesiastical seminary is not a school of intellectual culture, either here in America or elsewhere, and to imagine that it can become the instrument of intellectual culture is to cherish a delusion . . . its methods are not such as one would choose who desires to open the mind, to give it breadth, flexibility, strength, refinement, and grace. Its text-books are written often in a barbarous style, the subjects are discussed in a dry and mechanical way, and the professor, wholly intent upon giving instruction, is frequently indifferent as to the manner in which it is imparted; or else not possessing himself a really cultivated intellect, he holds in slight esteem expansion and refinement of mind, looking upon it as at the best a mere ornament. I am not offering a criticism upon the ecclesiastical seminary, but am simply pointing to the plain fact that it is not a school of intellectual culture, and consequently, if its course were lengthened to five, to six, to eight, to ten years, its students would go forth to their work with a more thorough professional training, but not with more really cultivated minds.[18]

Since, therefore, seminaries could not give the kind of instruction of which Spalding was speaking, it was apparent to the bishop that only a university could do so. "It is only in a university that all the sciences are brought together, their relations adjusted, their provinces assigned." [19] Speaking of the need the Church had for the best possible training in her clergy to keep abreast of modern educational developments, Spalding saw no possibility for this training outside the founding of a university. ". . . so long as we

[18] *Ibid.,* pp. 212–213.
[19] *Ibid.,* p. 216.

look rather to the multiplying of schools and seminaries than to the creation of a real university, our progress will be slow and uncertain, because a university is the great ordinary means to the best cultivation of mind." And to the Bishop of Peoria there was no place more inviting for a Catholic university than the United States. "Here, almost for the first time in her history, the Church is really free." Without a university no hope was foreseen that American Catholics might enter as a "determining force" in the controversies of the age, Catholics of wealth would continue to send their sons to universities where their faith would be undermined, and the effort for reforms in public life and for the rights of the Catholic citizens will "lack the wisdom of best counsel and the courage which skilful leaders inspire." While making a fervent plea for the university to be begun, Spalding recognized that there would be real difficulties, but he felt they could be overcome. The beginning would have to be modest and it might well be confined to courses in philosophy and theology as was the case with Paris in the twelfth century and Louvain when it first reopened in 1834. But this "national school of philosophy and theology, which will form the central faculty of a complete educational program," would be only the beginning, for "around this, the other faculties will take their places, in due course of time." [20]

This sermon of Spalding in November, 1884, went considerably beyond his pronouncement at Milwaukee in June, 1881, insofar as it specifically spoke of a university rather than a "high school of theology." It would appear that in the interval the Bishop of Peoria had become clearer in his

---

[20] *Ibid.*, p. 231.

own mind as to the institution which ought to be established. At least his insistence on a university rather than a glorified seminary would indicate a closer proximity to the concept which Bishop Becker entertained in his articles of 1876. Doubtless the knowledge of Miss Caldwell's willingness to give a very substantial sum of money made Spalding feel that there was now a real possibility of going beyond an advanced course of theology in the new institution, and the fact that he specifically stated the theological faculty would be but the beginning of the enterprise and "around this, the other faculties will take their places, in due course of time," pointed clearly to a university in the proper sense of the term.

Spalding's sermon was preached about ten days in advance of the detailed discussion of the university question in the full sessions of the council. There had been considerable private exchange of views among the bishops from the outset, but only in the last week of November did the formal treatment of this topic enter the business of the council. In the fifth public congregation held on November 25 the subject, "De Seminario Principali," which composed the third chapter of Title V of the council's agenda, came up for discussion. Different opinions were expressed by the bishops present and, as the minutes stated:

The debate centered especially around Title V, c. III, *On the Principal Seminary*. Although many of the speakers favored the proposal of the Schema, some thought it best that there should be given a longer and more perfect course of studies in theological seminaries, for there could not be obtained a supply of money and persons for founding the principal seminary.[21]

---

[21] *Acta et Decreta Concilii Plenarii Baltimorensis Tertii* . . . (Bal-

It is regrettable that the minutes of the private congregations do not give us more information concerning the arguments advanced for and against the proposed university. It is noteworthy, however, that the language employed was a "principal seminary" rather than a university. On November 30, in the fourth solemn session the same title on clerical education and instruction was read, but the minutes are no more enlightening than before on the turn which the discussion took.

That there was considerable opposition within the council to the bishops' acting positively in this matter we know from later developments. As late as 1917, Thomas S. Byrne, Bishop of Nashville, who was at Baltimore in 1884 in the capacity of theologian to the Archbishop of Cincinnati, wrote an account of some aspects of the university question to Sister Mary Agnes McCann of the Sisters of Charity of Cincinnati.

Monday, Dec. 3rd, 1917.

My dearest Sister:

Thanks for your letter—this is not going to be a scold. How long is your residence at the University going to last? What an institution it is getting to be! On what straws do great undertakings turn! I think I told you that in all probability the University would not have been a reality it might be [sic] up to the present, had it not been for my courage in replying to a speech of Fr. Fulton's, S.J.[22] In

timore, 1884), p. lvii. All citations to the legislation on the university in the council are to this edition containing the minutes of the private congregations unless otherwise noted.

[22] Robert Fulton, S.J. (1826–1895), was provincial of the New York-Maryland Province of the Society of Jesus. Shortly after his death in California in September, 1895, there appeared an anonymous appreciation of Fulton entitled, "Father Robert Fulton. A Sketch,"

fact the Bishops had agreed to allow the subject of the University [to] go over until the summoning of another Plenary Council, and none has yet been held. Fortunately, Fr. F., who did not know this, made a violent attack on the paragraph of the Schema of subjects for discussion, beginning—Hoc Magnum Opus, heaping ridicule upon the idea of setting up a University, saying it was foolish to attempt to do so; that universities were not created, but grew out of small beginnings; that if the Diocesan Clergy wanted degrees they could obtain them as they were obtained in London, from a Board established by the government for the purpose of granting them to those making a satisfactory examination; that the Diocesan Clergy were not intended to be an educated Clergy or at least a learned and erudite body; that they were ordained to do the ordinary work of a parish and that the proper custodians, cultivators, and representatives of learning in the Church were the Religious Orders to whom alone Universities should be entrusted. He interspersed his entire remarks with biting sarcasm and scoffing and ridicule—at one point holding

in *Woodstock Letters,* XXV (1896), 90–112, which gave principal space to his career as president of Boston College. The author paid high tribute to Fulton's industry, energy, and kindness of heart, but he did note that, "Father Fulton was not an ordinary man. Like many such men he had his own way of doing things, which it were unwise for the rank and file to imitate . . ." p. 112. The writer wishes to thank Joseph G. Causey, S.J., archivist of the Georgetown University Archives, for permitting him to use the *Woodstock Letters,* as well as to read several dozen letters of Robert Fulton in those archives. An effort to locate further material on Fulton and the university question in archives of the Society of Jesus was not successful. Edward A. Ryan, S.J., archivist of the Woodstock College Archives, informed the writer in a letter of December 17, 1945, that although these archives contained Fulton correspondence, "there appears to be nothing on the subject of Catholic University." Similarly, Robert I. Gannon, S.J., in a letter of December 18, 1945, wrote that at Fordham University, "we have no material in our archives touching on the point you raise . . ."

up the Schema and blowing upon the page which contained the paragraph, and saying contemptuously—Hoc Magnum Opus!!

When he came down from the rostrum, I said to myself, I will not let that go by—if no one else replies to him, I shall.

Cardinal Gibbons, who was presiding, waited a few moments evidently waiting for some one to answer him. Finally, he said—If no one else wishes to speak on this subject, we shall take up other business. At this point I rose and asked leave to say a word in reply to the Rev'd Gentleman. Leave was promptly granted and I ascended the rostrum and took up his speech point by point and proved in a matter of fact historically [sic], he was incorrect in nearly every statement and certainly in every essential one; that it was not historically true that universities were not created by the Church, by civil governments, and by eminent ecclesiastics, that it was not true that the diocesan clergy had not been in the past and were not in the present, an erudite body as Theiner had proven in his Life of Clement XIV; that it was unfair and ungenerous for him to wish to deny to Diocesan Clergy advantages which Religious Orders enjoyed; that his suggestion of a Board of Examiners was not practical, and if it were, it would be degrading to the Diocesan Clergy; that he virtually wished to make them ecclesiastical hewers of wood and haulers of water and the Religious Orders the aristocracy of the Clergy; and that it was to say the least unbecoming in a son of St. Ignatius to hold up to scorn and contempt a project which had been sanctioned and introduced into the Schema by Archbishops and Bishops of the United States with the knowledge and consent of the Pope and the Cardinals in Rome where the Schema was prepared and printed. I also showed how it was feasible to begin a University at once and called upon the Fathers of the Council there assembled to take work in hand. I fear I was quite as scornful and contemptuous in my remarks as he was and I knew I

had the better of the argument. When I came down from
the rostrum the old Archbishop of St. Paul, Abp. Grace,
met me at the foot of the steps; took me by the hand,
almost embraced me, saying, That's the kind of a speech
we want—that will make the University. When I was
leaving the hall, Fr. Piccarelli, [*sic*] S.J., superior of Woodstock, stopped me and said—"Dr. Byrne, you must not believe that the statements made by Fr. Fulton express the
sentiments of the Jesuits. It is just such foolish speeches as
his that do the Jesuits more harm than the active opposition
of twenty Bishops." This was offset by what Fr. Sabatti
[*sic*] told me the next day on our way to Woodstock where
a public disputation was to take place. We sat in the same
seat and naturally the row of the day before came up in
our conversation and I told him what Piccarelli [*sic*] had
said to me. His prompt reply was—"Don't you believe it
—the Jesuits are opposed to the University and they will
kill it if they can. They did the same thing in Naples when
I was a young man (he had been a secular and a lawyer,
I think). The King of Naples founded a University and
admitted into it two students on competitive examination
from every Diocese in Italy—the Jesuits at once started to
fight it and they never ceased fighting it until they killed it,
and simply because the young men of the University put
their young men in the sack."—These were his very words
—I related the incident, but not his name, while he lived,
to many Jesuits. The way of the whole story is this.
When I went up to a room in the Cardinal's to change my
clothes, I found there the present Bp. of Richmond, the
present Abp. of Milwaukee, and His Eminence, the Cardinal of New York,[23] and all of them attacked me directly
by saying emphatically that Fr. Fulton was right. My only
answer was—Gentlemen, had you defended his position in
the Council Hall, I might have had something to say in

---

[23] The three men mentioned by Byrne in his letter were, in 1917,
Bishop Denis J. O'Connell of Richmond, Archbishop Sebastian G.
Messmer of Milwaukee, and John Cardinal Farley of New York.

answer, but this is not the place to continue the discussion. Subsequently, these gentlemen were, and may be yet the fiercest upholders of the University, and it has been intimated, fortunately, I believe, from keeping me from having anything to do with its management. This is the first time I have ever said a word of this story; but I got started somehow, and am carried forward to the end. Pardon me sending it to you . . . P.S. I cannot muster courage to read this over. If you find any lacunae note them, and I may be able to fill them out.[24]

This is one of the very few detailed accounts extant on the conciliar discussions on the university. Since Byrne wrote his letter over thirty years after the event he may not have remembered accurately all the details. That there was opposition from some American Jesuits to the university is true, but it is likewise true that there were members of the Society of Jesus who were friendly to the university idea as we know from the letter of Father Leopold Buchart, S.J., Provincial of the Missouri Province, to Gibbons. Buchart was one of the six Jesuit provincials present at the council. He wrote Gibbons on November 26 from Loyola College in Baltimore as follows:

I called last night to see your Grace but you were out. Today all the Superiors have been invited by the students of philosophy in Woodstock who celebrate the feast of their Patron Saint and I do not wish to disappoint them; hence I shall state in a few words the reason which induced me to seek an interview with your Grace.

From my own impression and from the remarks made by the Rev. gentlemen who spoke last night, I fear that

---

[24] Thomas S. Byrne to Sister Mary Agnes McCann, December 3, 1917. A copy of this letter was kindly loaned to the writer by Peter Guilday who had it made from the original.

the words of F. Fulton may have made an unfavorable
impression on the Most Rev. and Rt. Rev. Fathers of the
council as well as on the Rev. Clergy. I wish to state to
your Grace, that Father Fulton has expressed his own
private opinion and by no means the opinion of the Fathers
of our Society as far as I have been able to ascertain. We
are not opposed to the higher education of the Clergy, on
the contrary we favor it and we shall do all in our power
to promote it. Any measure the Most Rev. and Rt. Rev.
Fathers may adopt to reach this object will meet with the
most cordial approval of our Society.[25]

At any rate, on the morning of November 26 in the seventeenth private congregation the deputation of twelve professional theologians chosen to examine subjects under
Title V on clerical education, made their report. It was
their view that the entire subject of the university should
be referred to a special committee. Bishop Tobias Mullen of
Erie moved to have the entire chapter on a university ex-
punged or referred to the next plenary council. This motion was seconded by Archbishop Kenrick of St. Louis,
accepted by Archbishop Ryan of Philadelphia, and joined
in by twenty other bishops. However, the motion lost with
only twenty-three votes mustered in its favor.[26] Thereupon

---

[25] BCA, 78–T–11, L. Buchart, S.J., to James Gibbons, Baltimore,
November 26, 1884.

[26] The rought draft of the minutes of the council written in both
Latin and English are kept in the Baltimore Cathedral Archives. They
contain this information concerning the voting. The minutes are not
indexed in the archives' general catalog. A little additional information on the debates in the council concerning the university was
found in the Collected Hyvernat Papers and Correspondence, Institute for Christian Oriental Research, Catholic University of
America. These personal papers of Professor Hyvernat contain considerable material on the early years of the university; it was collected by him and incorporated into a memorial on the university

the apostolic delegate appointed the committee to consist of Corrigan, Kenrick, Alemany, Ryan, and Spalding. Bishop Keane was appointed to the committee but excused himself.[27] Shortly thereafter Archbishop Corrigan wrote Cardinal McCloskey, speaking of other conciliar business and adding:

Concerning the University . . . a special Committee (Abp. Kenrick, Alemany, Ryan, Bp. Spalding and myself) will report favorably, recommending the acceptance of

which he submitted to John Cardinal Bonzano, December 8, 1922. Among the papers in the Hyvernat collection are some rough copies of notes taken during the sessions of the council by Sebastian G. Messmer, one of the secretaries of the assembly. Under date of October 19, 1917, when Messmer had become Archbishop of Milwaukee he sent copies of these notes, based on the minutes of James A. Corcoran, a certain "McManus" (there were two of that name at the council), and himself, to Professor Hyvernat at the latter's request. They do not add a great deal to what we already knew from other sources, although they do mention that in the debate on November 25 among the theologians Charles Goldsmith, Henry A. Brann, and Robert Fulton, S.J., spoke against the university while Sebastian B. Smith, Thomas S. Byrne, and William J. Wiseman spoke in its favor. The collection contains extensive notes written in pencil by Hyvernat himself on the university in the council. In one of these we find the statement: "The Council broke up without having made clear in its decisions exactly what kind of university it wanted." In another place, speaking of the school of theology, he wrote: "There is no doubt that originally that school was to be nothing more than a seminary of a higher order, i.e., with fuller programs and better trained instructors; hence its name of seminarium principale which appears for the first time in the schema of the Third Council of Baltimore and clung to the new foundation throughout its evolution." The writer wishes to thank Theodore C. Petersen, C.S.P., for putting the Hyvernat Papers at his disposal.

[27] *Acta et Decreta,* p. lx.

Miss Caldwell's gift, and the beginning of a nucleus of a future University.[28]

In the meantime Archbishop Gibbons had requested Miss Caldwell to state the names of those whom she wished to have on the university committee. In answer to the apostolic delegate Miss Caldwell said:

In accordance with your request, I hereby present you a list of the Archbishops and bishops, whom I wish to see appointed as the permanent committee, for the management and control of the University. Most Rev. Archbishop Gibbons, Archbishop Corrigan, Bishop Spalding, Bishop Ireland, Archbishop Ryan, Archbishop Williams, and Archbishop Heiss. I would also suggest the names of the following laymen—Mr. Eugene Kelly, Mr. Reuben Springer and Mr. Drexel of Philadelphia. In case a priest is appointed I suggest the name of Mgr. Farley.[29]

In the twenty-third private session of the council on December 2 the committee appointed the previous week made its report. The minutes read as follows:

1. A Seminary is to be erected like the Dunboyne in Ireland or Louvain in Belgium, from which as from a seed the University is to grow. 2. It is to be erected near a large and populous city. 3. A very respectable lady has promised that she will give $300,000 for the erection and endowment of the Seminary. 4. A commission is to be formed of five or seven prelates and some laymen to whom is to be given the care of erecting and administering the Seminary.

Bishop James A. Healy of Portland suggested that priests

---

[28] NYAA, A–22, M. A. Corrigan to John McCloskey, Baltimore. This letter is not dated more specifically than "Nov. 1884."

[29] BCA, 78–U–3, M. G. Caldwell to James Gibbons, New York, December 5, 1884.

likewise be admitted to the membership of the committee and Bishop John Hennessy of Dubuque further suggested that the number of bishops should be greater than the number of priests and laymen combined on the committee. These two suggestions, together with the report of the committee, were accepted by the council.[30] The day before the close of the council in the thirtieth private congregation on Saturday, December 6, the letter of Miss Caldwell offering $300,000 for the beginning of a university was read. The bishops in council approved Miss Caldwell's selection of names with the proviso that other priests and laymen might be added to the committee later if the bishops so desired.

It remained, therefore, only to frame the decree by which the council espoused the plan for a Catholic university in the United States. As finally worded Chapter III of Title V of the *Acta et Decreta* on this subject read as follows:

So great is the breadth and depth of Philosophy and Theology that the established course of studies as taught in Major Seminaries is not at all adequate to ferret out the hidden treasures of these sciences. Yet, it is of the greatest importance that the Church militant in these regions be never wanting in men well versed in these disciplines, who may be able to protect the cause of truth zealously and courageously against all kinds of monstrous errors and insane doctrines which, in our age especially, spring forth daily from the lurking places of a mad philosophy; so that those who teach in our seminaries may be useful in the development of learning; or that they may also be able to render useful help in handling ecclesiastical cases. For this reason it is highly to be desired that in these States there should exist a distinguished center of learn-

---

[30] *Acta et Decreta*, p. lxxix.

ing where youths excelling in talent and virtue, after finishing the usual course of studies, may be able to devote three or four years to theological disciplines, or canon law, or philosophy along with the natural and other sciences which are becoming to clergymen of our day, so that, once such a seminary were started, there would be a nucleus or seed from which, God's grace favoring, there would blossom forth in its time a perfect university of studies.

After mature deliberation the Fathers agreed that the time had come when this work should be undertaken. In order to expedite this work more vigorously the Council thought it best to appoint a Committee whose duty it will be to endeavor, after due consultation, to bring about, as soon as possible, the erection of a Principal Seminary for the United States of North America, near some well known and populous city, to which from everywhere clerics of superior talent, after having completed their ordinary course of studies, and also the priest, may be able to come to acquire a more profound learning. Such a Seminary will be entirely subject to the jurisdiction, direction, and administration of the Bishops of these States, who, through a committee named by them, will define the program of studies, will appoint Professors and other Officials, and will ordain all other things which concern the right governing of a Seminary. The Committee will consist of Bishops, priests and some laymen chosen from a distinguished number, with the condition that the bishops together outnumber all the others.

In order to bring this undertaking more quickly and more safely to a happy issue let not the Bishops be ashamed, if we may use the words of Pope Pius IX., of blessed memory, to exhort and ask the outstanding clergymen of their dioceses and also those laymen of great wealth who are clearly enthusiastic about Catholicism to follow their noble example and freely to contribute some money to a work so useful for the good of the Church and the salvation of the people. (Apostolic Letter to the Archbishops and Bishops of the Austrian Empire, March 17, 1856.)

In the meantime let the Bishops see to it that they send their students who show more hope of greater success than others to the existing American College of Rome or Louvain, or even Innsbruck.[31]

This decree was sent to Rome for approval along with the others enacted during the council. Certain changes were made in the language of the decree by the officials of the Propaganda. For example, the final sentence in the second paragraph was omitted and in its place there was substituted:

Quoniam de facultate theologica et philosophica juxta normam Universitatis Catholicae agitur, leges regiminis et disciplinae ac rationis studiorum, postquam de iis inter Archiepiscopos et Episcopos deliberatum erit, examini et approbationi S. Sedis subjicientur, nec nisi hac approbatione obtenta vigorem habebunt.[32]

This change had the effect of safeguarding the Holy See's right of approving the constitution and program of studies for Catholic universities before papal approval was given to their establishment. The only other substantial change was by way of an additional sentence to the final paragraph which read:

Quae commendatio non minus etiam pro futuro tempore valet, quando Seminarium Principale jam fuerit institutum, cum hoc pro iis qui studia sua theologica jam absolverint, sit destinatum.[33]

This sentence had in mind the future welfare of the ec-

---

[31] *Ibid.*, pp. 54–55.
[32] *Acta et Decreta* (1886 edition), p. 94.
[33] *Ibid.*

clesiastical colleges at Rome and Louvain maintained or patronized in part by the American bishops, and it was apparently intended to protect the patronage which these institutions had hitherto enjoyed from the Church of the United States.

In the decree of the council as finally framed in Baltimore and approved in Rome, it will be noticed that the term "principal seminary" is employed throughout, although it is stated that from such a seminary it was to be hoped a "perfect university of studies" would eventually evolve. Likewise the decree made mention of the fact that the students would spend three or four years not only in theology, canon law, and philosophy but in "the natural and other sciences," which would indicate something beyond the scope of a seminary curriculum. Moreover, that the institution was to be a graduate school is clear from the fact that the students were to be those who had finished "the usual course of studies." Attention is called to the language of the decree on these points, for in the years after the council there developed considerable discussion on the part of those opposed to the university concerning the precise character of the institution voted on at Baltimore. It would be urged more than once that the plan approved in 1884 called for only a higher seminary, not a university. If the historian had at his command an outline of what the leading bishops had in mind by their use of these different terms it would help him in delineating more sharply their ideas on the projected institution. It seems safe to say that none of the bishops except Becker, Spalding, and McQuaid had given the subject thorough study. By the time action was taken in 1884 Becker had dropped out of the picture, Spalding had preached his sermon in the council which made it evident he had in mind a university, and the Bishop of Rochester was of the opinion that only a higher seminary was meant, not a university. Of the others, no one bishop gave evidence of having thought through the distinction between a higher seminary and a university, and from this point on the working out of the whole plan was left in good measure to the committee appointed during the council, with the opposition conducting a fairly lively campaign against the project in private correspondence and in the Catholic press.

The university received a good deal of attention in the Catholic and secular press in the weeks following the close of the council. In its issue of December 6, 1884, the day before the formal close of the assembly in Baltimore, the Boston *Pilot* carried a lengthy quotation from Spalding's sermon on the need for a Catholic university and stated that the "remarkable address" had been published in pamphlet form by the John Murphy Company of Baltimore. The Baltimore *Sun,* which had reported the business of the council fully since its opening on November 9, said in its issue of December 6:

No decree has yet been passed by the Plenary Council providing for the higher education of the clergy, and it is understood none was formulated in the schema, but the subject is regarded as one of the most important that could engage the attention of the members of the council, and if not put in the form of a decree the subject as well as that of the general education of Catholic children, will be treated upon in the pastoral letter which is now in preparation, and will be issued soon after the adjournment of the council. From members of that great assembly it is learned that it has long been apparent that some special provision will be an absolute necessity of the church in the future in this country for the sufficient endowment and the establishment of a thoroughly equipped college or seminary, as schools for the education of priests are generally entitled in the United States. The need is recognized of a school upon a solid and wealthy foundation, which the rulers of the church here hope to see started in a few years, which will turn out an erudite and polished body of divines, equipped at all points to meet and overthrow the learned, brilliant and dexterous disciples of the agnostic school and the prominent scientists who reject revelation . . . It is therefore considered a very vital question for the Catholic Church, that of the higher education of the clergy, and one which must secure attention, to be followed before long by action. The current of opinion amongst members of the council seems to turn in favor of a college on a proper foundation for the instruction of a special body of clergymen, from which will spring skillful logicians, polished orators and deep thinkers, writers for the Catholic press and authors of books defending their faith.

Action was taken in council the very day the *Sun's* article appeared. The New York *Sun* of December 10 carried the story of an interview with Miss Caldwell in which she was quoted as telling the reporter that "it is my own notion," and that she had been thinking of her gift for two or three years. Her benefaction of $300,000 would be only the nucleus around which in time would grow a great institution. Miss Caldwell was reported to have said: "It is not determined where the university will be founded, but it will be near a large Northern city. Personally I should have preferred to see it in a Southern State, but, on the whole, it is best to establish it in the North." The next day the same paper commented on the Caldwell gift: "The Roman Catholic Church has now no great educational institution in this country which fitly represents its dignity and power. Its colleges are well conducted, and deserve higher reputation than they now have among Protestants, but none of them can be put on the same plane with Harvard and Yale, for instance; and hitherto Roman Catholics have made no attempt to compete with these leading universities, to which the sons of Catholic families are sent without regard to the religious influences which prevail in them." The *Sun* then spoke of the increasing secularization of education in schools like Harvard, Yale, Princeton, and Columbia, and remarked how at variance their current philosophy of education was with that of the Catholic Church. "The Roman Catholic theory of education, however, puts religious training in the foreground as the most essential of all . . . Miss Caldwell, accordingly, is only concerned to found a distinctively Catholic university, whose object shall, first of all, be the glory of the Roman Church . . . Viewed from the point of observation of Protestantism, it will be nothing more than a college for the teaching of Roman Catholic theology, but according to the educational theory of the Roman Church, it will provide the only sort of higher training which belongs to the Church specifically to offer and preside over. Undoubtedly, too, Roman Catholics feel the need of better attainments in the priesthood. Their Church has grown so rapidly in this country that they have had to accept priests who were not always up to the standards of education and cultivation they desired." [34]

The Third Plenary Council closed on Sunday, December 7, and Bishop Spalding was again the preacher. He reviewed the work which had been done by the bishops

---

[34] New York *Sun*, December 11, 1884.

during their four weeks in Baltimore and, regarding the university, he said:

We have laid the foundation of an institution which, under God's providence, is destined to grow into an American Catholic University, the measure of whose usefulness, the grandeur of whose scope, and the fruitful blessings of which cannot be forecast by the mind.[35]

But if Spalding was optimistic, an editorial writer on the New York *Times* was not. The *Times* of December 13 carried a lengthy editorial on the university which is worth quoting in full.

Now that it appears that we are about to have a great Roman Catholic university the question naturally arises, What will the university teach?

It is evidently not meant to be merely a theological school. The Roman Church has already in this country a sufficient number of theological seminaries to educate all the candidates for its priesthood, and there is no complaint that in these seminaries Roman Catholic theology is not sufficiently well taught. Although the new university will naturally have its own theological school, we may be very sure that it will be something more than that.

As a scientific school a Roman Catholic university would hardly be successful. The Church of Rome is generally regarded as hostile to modern science. It is true that eminent Roman Catholics, such as Father Secchi—to mention no other name—have been ardent and admirable disciples of science, but the church has repeatedly shown that it regards science as dangerous. The Roman Church is bound to uphold the infallibility of the Bible, and although on matters not affecting doctrine and concerning which the church has made no formal decision the Roman Catholics may to

---

[35] *Catholic Mirror,* December 13, 1884.

some extent doubt the literal accuracy of Biblical statements, all Roman theologians would earnestly oppose any
scientific teaching which would tend to overthrow the
chronology of Moses, or to cast doubt on the Mosaic account of the creation of man. The hypothesis of evolution
would find no countenance in a Roman Catholic university,
and its pupils would feel that in many fields they must
practically ignore much of the work of the most eminent
scientific men of the century.

Latin and Greek could, of course, be thoroughly taught
at the proposed university, but there can be no question
that these studies have lost much of the importance that
was formerly theirs. Medicine and law could also find a
place in any Roman Catholic university, but with medicine
and law religion has no necessary connection, and there is
no reason why a Roman Catholic university should be
founded in order to teach purely secular branches of study.
It would be like establishing a Presbyterian school of mines
or a Methodist agricultural college.

The great universities of Italy, which were naturally
under the control of the priesthood in the days when the
priests were the only educated men, have long since become secularized, for the obvious reason that it is not the
province of any church to teach science, law, and medicine. There does not seem to be any need here of a university of the kind that is found necessary in Italy, and
though our Roman Catholic friends might take a natural
pride in a great Roman Catholic university, it is not certain
that in founding and maintaining it they would spend their
money wisely.

The rather patronizing editorial in the New York *Times*
aroused the ire of the editor of the *Catholic Herald* of
Philadelphia who answered the charge that the Church
was unfriendly to science and he remarked:

Let the *Times* rest satisfied. When the Catholic University

of America becomes a fact its teachings, scientific and
otherwise, will be broad enough, deep enough, and of
such a universal character as to make the *Times* wonder
—at itself.[36]

Speculation was rife in the press from the outset on where
the new university would be located. The Boston *Pilot* of
December 13 quoted a Baltimore dispatch to the effect it
would be located "in New York City or its vicinity." The
Catholic Mirror of Baltimore on the same day said the
idea was current that it would be somewhere near New
York, although, "Emmitsburg had its advocates as the
proper location, but it was thought to be somewhat un-
suitable for the university . . ." In the same issue of the
Mirror appeared an editorial summing up the work of the
council and stating concerning the university, "Had the
council determined on nothing else, this important result
would be a worthy fruit of its assemblage." In a long editorial of December 14, 1884, the *Sunday Democrat* welcomed the idea of a Catholic university as an instrument to
offset the growing secularization of life. "The Darwins and
Ingersolls warn us that profane science cut off from religion
is religion's deadliest foe. The revival of paganism makes
the establishment of a Catholic University timely." The
Boston *Pilot* was friendly to the project from the beginning
and in its issue of December 20 expressed the hope that
the Catholics of the United States would raise Miss Caldwell's $300,000 to a million dollars "so that the founda-
tions of an institution shall be laid as deep and wide as
the future of American Catholicity demands."

In the pastoral letter which was published by the bishops

---

[36] Quoted in *Ave Maria*, XXI (Feb. 28, 1885), 176.

at the close of the Third Plenary Council major attention was devoted to the needs and problems of Catholic
education, and Catholics of wealth were exhorted to be
generous to educational foundations conducted under the
Church's auspices. However, nothing specific was said
concerning the university.[37] The church historian, John
Gilmary Shea, wrote an analysis of this document for the
American Catholic Quarterly Review in which he appealed
for financial assistance from wealthy Catholics for the university, instancing the generosity of Edmund B. O'Calla-
ghan and his wife to St. Joseph's Seminary, Troy, and to
the Jesuits, as well as the benefactions of Reuben R.
Springer of Cincinnati to Mount Saint Mary's Seminary
of the West. Shea took up the bishops' pastoral plea for
support and applied it to the university, saying, "A great
university is one of the necessities of the church." [38]

Before anything definite could be done in getting the
university project under way it was felt necessary to have
the Caldwell money in hand. With that in mind Archbishop Gibbons wrote Miss Caldwell early in January,
1885. However, the young woman was not inclined to turn
over the money until more definite plans had been made
for launching the enterprise. She wrote Gibbons in reply:

I have received your letter of Jan. 5th, and in reply
I beg to say that as soon as the money for the foundation
of the University is needed, it will be forthcoming. As long

---

[37] Peter Guilday (Ed.) *The National Pastorals of the American
Hierarchy (1792–1919)*, pp. 226–264.

[38] John Gilmary Shea, "The Pastoral Letter of the Third Plenary
Council of Baltimore," in *American Catholic Quarterly Review*, X
(Jan. 1885), 10.

as there is nothing definitely settled, I prefer to allow the investments to remain as they are.[39]

Gibbons sent this letter on to Archbishop Corrigan in New York, stating, "It is not as satisfactory as I would wish. You might show the letter to Bp. Spalding on the occasion of the dedication on the 25th, & perhaps another appeal might be made to her with more success. We can take no steps till we have her money. I suggested that she place it in your hands." [40] The dedication alluded to by Gibbons was that of the new Church of St. Paul the Apostle at 59th Street, New York City, which was to be dedicated on the feast of the conversion of St. Paul, January 25. Ten days previous to that event Spalding wrote Corrigan saying he was glad to hear that a meeting of the committee on the university was to be held. He added: "I have notified Bp. Ireland, but I beg you to have your secretary notify the others as it would look awkward for me to do it." [41] In the meantime word of the Baltimore council's work had reached Europe and on January 20, 1885, Herbert Vaughan, Bishop of Salford and later Cardinal Archbishop of Westminster, wrote Gibbons in congratulation on the council's accomplishments, "in having conducted everything to so satisfactory an end and in having excluded all Italian intervention in the shape of Italian delegation." Vaughan was curious about the university and he added:

I now write to beg your Grace to give me as full in-

[39] NYAA, C–7, M. G. Caldwell to James Gibbons, New York, January 9, 1885.

[40] NYAA, C–7, James Gibbons to M. A. Corrigan, Baltimore, January 11, 1885.

[41] NYAA, C–3, J. L. Spalding to M. A. Corrigan, Peoria, January 15, 1885.

formation as you can upon the prospect of an American
Catholic University. I hear that the 300,000 dollars have
been paid over to *you* & not to Peoria!

Any information, any views & wishes entertained I shd
be very glad of. Indeed if your Grace would write a full
account yourself which we might either print in [the]
Tablet or work up as our own, would be most acceptable.

I want to put the American Church forward as an
example to ourselves in this matter. There are a number
of [worldly?] Catholic laymen here who are sighing after
Oxford & Cambridge & the flesh pots of Egypt—and we
may make a strong case out by following your example.[42]

The dedication of the Church of St. Paul in New York
drew a large number of Catholic leaders from different
parts of the country who came to honor the mother church
of the Paulist Fathers. It afforded a good opportunity,
therefore, for the university committee to hold its initial
meeting which took place on January 26 at the residence
of Cardinal McCloskey. The members of the committee
present were Ryan, Corrigan, Ireland, Spalding, Farley,
and Eugene Kelly. At the suggestion of Archbishop Corrigan, the Archbishop of Philadelphia presided and Monsignor Farley acted as secretary. Archbishop Ryan explained the purpose of the meeting and suggested a formal
resolution be drawn up concerning the acceptance of the
Caldwell grant by the Third Plenary Council, "for the
purpose of founding a Grand Theological Seminary for
the higher education of the C. clergy of the United States,
said Seminary to form the basis of a future Catholic University . . ." The following conditions were embodied in

---

[42] BCA, 79–B–10, Herbert Vaughan to James Gibbons, London,
January 20, 1885.

the resolution, namely, that Miss Caldwell always be considered the founder of the university; that it not be under the direction of any religious order; that it form no part of any existing institution, and that the site be determined at the outset in such a way that it could not be changed during the life of the founder without her consent, nor after her death without grave reason.[43]

In this meeting in New York one of the first matters of business to arise was the site of the university. Mr. Kelly suggested that Seton Hall College at South Orange, New Jersey, be bought and made into a university, and a letter of Bishop Winand Wigger of Newark to Archbishop Corrigan was read in which Wigger proposed selling the college buildings and fifty acres of ground for $250,000. John Ireland proposed Washington, D. C., as the proper site for the new university. In the vote which followed, however, Kelly's proposal was carried for Seton Hall with an amendment to the motion that Miss Caldwell should first be consulted. Corrigan, Ireland, and Spalding were appointed the committee to interview Miss Caldwell concerning the South Orange offer.

The Committee discussed the endowment of professorships in the university and Spalding gave it as his view that since the salaries would range between $2,500 and $5,000, the endowments for each professorship should be between $50,000 and $100,000. Eugene Kelly pledged himself to endow one chair at $50,000, an offer which at the meeting the next day he said he would fulfill when the University

---

[43] Minutes of the meeting of the university committee, Monday-Tuesday, January 26–27, 1885, New York City. Archives of the Catholic University of America. Hereafter these archives will be designated as ACUA.

had five endowed chairs including his own. It was decided to name each chair or professorship for the donor of the endowment, and when one person was not found to have given the full amount necessary two or more might endow a single professorship jointly.

In regard to the name of the new institution, Bishop Ireland made a motion which was carried that it be called the Catholic University of America. After deciding that a lawyer be consulted immediately about the method to be pursued in incorporating the university and that Miss Caldwell be asked to transfer her money to the trustees, the meeting adjourned to the following day. On the second day there was further discussion on professorships and their endowment with an estimate made of how much principal each of the eight projected professorships would need to meet the salary. Of the eight chairs mentioned only two were thought to need more than $50,000 endowment, namely, science and elocution, in both of which cases salaries of $5,000 a year were assigned for the professors with a necessary endowment of $100,000 in each case. Certain prominent and wealthy Catholics were named as good prospects for these endowments and the "Catholic Irishmen of California" were to have a special appeal made to their generosity. The secretary of the meeting was instructed to write a letter to Archbishop Heiss of Milwaukee, explaining the reasons why this meeting was held and why he was not invited, that is, that a large number of the university committee found themselves accidentally together and felt it a good time to begin their work.

Bishop Spalding reported to the meeting on the result of his visit to Miss Caldwell concerning Seton Hall College. She consented, he said, to give $180,000 for the buildings and grounds attached. Mr. Kelly then submitted a letter from Bishop Wigger of Newark written that day, January 27, saying he had not proposed selling his college but that he had been approached by Bishop Spalding. Wigger said he felt it was worth $300,000, but he had agreed to $200,000 in conversation that morning with Corrigan, Ryan, Spalding, and Ireland. But the Bishop of Newark made it plain that he would not sell for less and he would require an immediate payment of $25,000. Spalding stated that Miss Caldwell had expressed a wish to examine some property in Washington, D. C., about which she had heard. It was supposedly about fifty acres, had a large building, and was located near the Soldiers' Home. Since, as Spalding said, she had been conceded the privilege of deciding the site and, too, since this proposed location was in the jurisdiction of Archbishop Gibbons, chairman of the committee, he thought it best to visit Washington and look at the property before any further action be taken. The members consented to this plan and Spalding promised to report to Archbishop Ryan on the Washington site within a week, Mr. Kelly suggesting an option of one year to be taken on the Washington property. The secretary, Monsignor Farley, entered into the minutes a copy of Spalding's letter to Ryan regarding the results of his trip to Washington.

Peoria, Feb. 8th, 1885.

Most Rev & dear Archbishop:

The place I went to Washington to inspect, seems to me a little too far from the city. My visit, however, makes me think that Washington is beyond doubt the proper site for the University, and Dr. Chappelle [sic] promised to look up suitable grounds which he thinks can be found without difficulty.

Washington is neither a Northern nor a Southern nor a Western city, but common ground upon which we can all meet to establish a National Institution. It has great advantages in the way of Museums, etc. The rate of mortality shows it to be exceptionally healthful. The Catholics there have social influence, and the more prominent men of the country are there more or less frequently. Unless it is absolutely necessary, it seems to me a mistake to buy a college like Seton Hall to start an absolutely new institution. When Dr. Chappelle [sic] reports, I will communicate his information to you. May I ask you to let Abp. Corrigan know the substance of this.

J. L. Spalding
Bp. of Peoria [44]

The rumors continued to be numerous in the press concerning the site of the university. The New York *Times* on February 3, 1885, mentioned Seton Hall College as the probable site and stated that the Caldwell grant had been greatly increased by donations from others, "showing the hearty interest felt in the establishment of the university."

Since the committee had deferred to Miss Caldwell in the matter of the location of the university, her word would, in the end, prove decisive. In that connection she wrote Archbishop Gibbons about ten days after the New York meeting:

I have been intending to write you for several days to tell you about a project in which I am deeply interested. It is, to locate the future University somewhere near Washington. You know, I have always been very much opposed to its being established in the North and there is no place in the South so advantageous as Washington. When several of the Committee met the other day here in New York, I

---

[44] *Ibid.*

was so anxious for them to at least look for some site near
Washington that Bishop Spalding was appointed to go
down and see what he could find. He wrote to me a few
days ago, telling me that he was convinced that a desirable
site could easily be procured, and at a moderate price.
Now, my dear Archbishop, I trust that you will give this
project your very kind consideration and warm approval.
Might I ask you to be so kind as to write me in which city
you prefer to have the University.[45]

The question of a site, however, was not settled finally
until there had been much discussion of the matter. The
Boston *Pilot* was correct, therefore, in reporting the New
York meeting in its issue of February 7, saying that so far
as the site was concerned, "no definite action was
taken . . ." Spalding became a strong supporter of Washington as he wrote Gibbons, "I am persuaded it ought to
be located there . . . Dr. Chapelle thinks he can raise as
much in Washington and you know [*sic*] doubt will find
more than one wealthy Catholic who will be willing to do
this." [46]

In February, 1885, Monsignor T. J. Capel who had
made so sad a failure as rector of Manning's University
College at Kensington in the Archdiocese of Westminster,
visited the United States. He was invited to speak by the
Xavier Union in New York at a dinner held at Delmonico's.
He chose as his subject, "The Catholic Scholar," and after
an introduction on the characteristics which should distinguish a Catholic scholar, he launched out into a com-

---

[45] BCA, 79–D–6, M. G. Caldwell to James Gibbons, New York
City, February 6, 1885.
[46] BCA, 80–E–14, J. L. Spalding to James Gibbons, Peoria,
February 9, 1885.

mentary on Catholic education in the United States. Capel gave it as his opinion that the need here was for Catholic elementary schools and he hoped his listeners would not be offended in his saying that the Catholics in America were far inferior to their Protestant fellow-countrymen in the matter of education. He said he had heard the ambitious talk about a university, and that while high ambitions were good, he would like to advise the American Catholics to strengthen their elementary schools before they began building universities.[47] Naturally, this untactful and impertinent speech from a foreigner, who was himself a failure as an administrator in higher education, aroused the ire of a number of American Catholics. James McMaster, editor of the *Freeman's Journal,* was quick to express his resentment at the comparison drawn between Catholic and Protestant education in the United States. To McMaster there was no such thing as Protestant education here. Moreover, he complained at the meekness of Americans in taking "lectures" from visiting Englishmen and those who were "English-Irish." McMaster, who himself was no ardent friend of the projected university, went on:

Instead of finding fault with the new Catholic university, Mgr. Capel, it was thought, would have been eager to give its projectors the benefit of his experience. American Catholics may not be worthy of a university yet; but alas! how unworthy must the English be, since they failed to appreciate Mgr. Capel's Kensington efforts in their behalf. Mgr. Capel's speech, published in pamphlet form, would be of great use to show what he really did say, and to give *"nous autres"* an opportunity of meditating how utterly weak and worthless we are.[48]

---

[47] New York *Times,* February 12, 1885.

[48] *Freeman's Journal,* February 21, 1885.

In the meantime the question of a site continued to occupy the minds of those interested in the university. In transmitting Spalding's report of his visit to Washington to Archbishop Corrigan, the Archbishop of Philadelphia said: "I perceived at our first meeting that Bishops Ireland & Spalding were inclined to select Washington, & therefore I expected such a note as this." Ryan added that since Mr. Drexel had been ill he had not approached him on the matter of a donation and he felt disinclined to do so until Miss Caldwell had paid over the money, "for until then, I fear the prospect may fall through at any time." [49] Bishop James O'Connor, Vicar Apostolic of Nebraska, wrote Archbishop Gibbons in February that he would stop in Baltimore on his way to Rome, "as I am most anxious to have a talk with you about 'the University.'" O'Connor was not favorable to the idea and he told Gibbons:

I was not at the session of the Council, at which it was decided to establish it, else I would have besought the fathers to postpone its organization till such time as our existing seminaries could be so improved, as to become feeders for an institution of the kind. As matters now stand, I cannot put aside the thought that the undertaking will be a lamentable failure. I pray God it may not be, but, short of a miracle, I do not see how any other result is possible.[50]

The *Catholic Mirror* of Baltimore, a promoter of the idea of a university for the past ten years, was naturally strong for Washington, and it reported Placide L. Chapelle, pastor

---

[49] NYAA, C–3, P. J. Ryan to M. A. Corrigan, Philadelphia, February 14, 1885.

[50] BCA, 79–E–12, James O'Connor to James Gibbons, Omaha, February 21, 1885.

of St. Matthew's Church in the capital, as saying that the chances were still good that Washington would win the university.[51] Chapelle had promised to look for sites and to inform Spalding, but the latter had heard nothing from him on the matter up to the last week in February.[52] At the two-day meeting in New York on January 26–27, 1885, Archbishop Gibbons and Archbishop Williams were not present. A month later, therefore, John Farley, acting in his capacity as secretary of the committee, wrote both arch-bishops a lengthy description of the business transacted.[53] Williams, ever cautious about committing himself to proj-ects until he had canvassed the ground, wrote Gibbons after receiving Farley's letter:

Before I give my opinion on their prompt and decisive action, I should like to know if you, as the natural chairman of the Committee, called the meeting in New York. I should certainly have been present, if any one had notified me in time to get there.[54]

Farley had apologized to the Archbishop of Boston for holding the meeting without informing him. "Your Grace was not advised previously, because the meeting was sug-gested only by the presence of so many of the Prelates at the dedication of the new Paulist Church on the above

---

[51] *Catholic Mirror*, February 21, 1885.

[52] BCA, 79–E–15, J. L. Spalding to James Gibbons, Peoria, Feb-ruary 23, 1885.

[53] BCA, 79–E–18, John M. Farley to James Gibbons, New York, February 27, 1885. The letter of Farley to Williams of the same date was copied for the writer by Robert H. Lord from the original in the Boston Diocesan Archives.

[54] BCA, 79–F–6, John J. Williams to James Gibbons, Boston, March 3, 1885.

date. This, the Prelates hope, will account to the absent members for any seeming discourtesy."

As in many of the important questions of these years in the Church in America, the Archbishop of Baltimore did not assume energetic leadership of the university business until time had been given for expression of opinion from all quarters. However, when he learned the results of the New York meeting he was pleased and from this point on Gibbons became more active in the matter. In reply to Farley's letter of February 27, he wrote:

I recd. your favor with the abstract of the Report of the meeting held in New York on the 26' of Jan.

I am glad that the University question is assuming a definite shape & with regard to the site, I will be heartily in accord with the majority regarding the place to be selected. I hope that Seton Hall is a healthy location, & not invaded by the terrible Jersey mosquitoes. Should Seton Hall be chosen, the work of the University could be begun with little delay, as the place would be ready to receive students.

Washington indeed has many [from this point two lines of the letter are almost completely illegible] we would have to create everything, which of course [would] involve delay unless Georgetown College would be offered for sale. The only ground I have for supposing that this might be offered for sale is a letter from Bishop Moore at New York, saying that his Eminence remarked they would be willing to sell. I would be surprised if they would consent to do so.

I did not see Bp. Spalding, but I learn he was in Washington, and consulted Dr. Chapelle on the subject. Any how a great step is gained by narrowing down the selection to Seton Hall or Washington, with the chances in favor of the former.[55]

---

[55] BCA, Letterbook of Archbishop Gibbons, p. 145, March 3, 1885.

At this time, too, there appeared the first private reactions from Rome on the university question. Denis J. O'Connell, soon to be rector of the American College, wrote Gibbons on March 8, 1885, a long letter in which he gave the archbishop Rome's impressions of the legislation of the council and of the pastoral letter of the American hierarchy. Regarding the university, O'Connell said:

Mgr. Jacobini is afraid the American University will conflict with the interests of the Amer. Coll. Bp. Spalding is not considered strongly attached to Rome nor to Roman training. Someone asked me if Spalding & Ireland were not severe on the Regulars in the Council! [56]

The friends of the university were not insensible of the fact that opposition was gathering to their plans. The Philadelphia firm, Hardy & Mahony, publishers of the *American Catholic Quarterly Review,* wrote Archbishop Gibbons to the effect that they had been approached by "several distinguished prelates and ecclesiastics" with the suggestion that Gibbons write an article for the *Review* to offset the "quiet opposition that is beginning to manifest itself in certain quarters." [57] They proposed he write it for the April number. For some reason Gibbons did not take on this assignment, but that particular issue of the journal did carry an enthusiastic article on the subject by John Gilmary Shea.

By late March, 1885, Archbishop Gibbons as chairman of the university committee was ready to act in calling a

---

[56] BCA, 79–F–9, D. J. O'Connell to James Gibbons, Rome, March 8, 1885.

[57] BCA, 79–F–11, Hardy & Mahony to James Gibbons, Philadelphia, March 10, 1885.

full meeting. He wrote Spalding first "as you are the
farthest removed," suggesting a date soon after Easter and
New York or Philadelphia as the place of meeting.[58] Gibbons concluded by saying that at the meeting "we can
then definitely determine the place & try to secure subscriptions." The reason for Gibbons' delay in acting is
made clear in a letter to Archbishop Corrigan:

I have been thinking for some days that some more steps
should be taken to expedite the opening of the university.
Otherwise the public may think that the subject has been
dropped. And I fear that I have the greatest share of the
fault of delay, if any fault there is. But I have not seen my
way, as the money of Miss Caldwell was not yet received.
I beg to have your advice about the expediency of calling
a meeting of the Board soon after Easter to meet in New
York as the most central place . . . I would also like to
know whom I should invite to the meeting. Your Grace
might be kind enough to invite the members living in New
York. Archbp. Williams, I presume, should be invited. If
Seton Hall is chosen, which seems most probable, all we
want, is money to make or announce some beginning of
the work. If you counsel the meeting, I will send the invitations on receipt of your letter.[59]

The rumors concerning Washington as a site caused great
distress to Archbishop Elder of Cincinnati who was convinced that it was not a proper city in which to train clerical students. Writing to Archbishop Corrigan on March 20,
1885, Elder said:

---

[58] BCA, Letterbook of Archbishop Gibbons, p. 150, March 20,
1885.
[59] NYAA, C–2, James Gibbons to M. A. Corrigan, Baltimore,
March 24, 1885.

Indirectly I hear there is a serious proposition to establish the University at Washington. It may be a good place —or may *promise* to *become* a good place—for pursuits of science;—chiefly however of Physics:—but I think it would be very unfavorable for studies, & for congregating of ecclesiastical students. The distractions of public affairs, —the intercourse with public men,—the gathering of unscrupulous men for their various interests from all parts of the country—the amusements—the social & convivial habits prevailing, appear to me very strong objections. The Jesuits can keep their young members out of these dangers: but secular Priests & Seminarians will be vastly more exposed. Even the Professors will have their serious dangers.[60]

Elder's suffragan, Bishop Gilmour of Cleveland, joined his metropolitan in opposing Washington. He told the Archbishop of Cincinnati:

I think Washington a very ill advised place for a catholic university, not only for the noise and bustle but far more for the unhealthy atmosphere of a capital. I am quite aware the Jesuits want to sell Georgetown to get them out of a heavy debt. But if they failed, why? Better keep clear of all these religious orders in this university affair. Or if they are to be in it, then let them care for it. But that would not be a university in the proper sense. I am favorably impressed with the Seton College proposition. For the west, I would say Cincinnati.[61]

While these Ohio bishops were ruminating about the site the committee was engaged in making its plans for the full meeting after Easter. In the light of later developments

---

[60] NYAA, C–2, William E. Elder to M. A. Corrigan, Cincinnati, March 20, 1885.

[61] AAC, Letters Jan. 1–Dec. 31, 1885, Richard Gilmour to William H. Elder, Cleveland, March 24, 1885.

a letter of the Coadjutor Archbishop of New York to Gibbons on March 25 is of interest. Corrigan wrote:

Concerning the University, I am convinced that it is of vital importance that the money offered by Miss Caldwell should be secured before any steps are taken by the Board.

The Cardinal declines assuming any responsibility in the premises as far as this Diocese is concerned. Under these circumstances, although he has allowed me to act for myself, according to my own discretion, I would suggest that a meeting of the Board, if deemed opportune, should take place either in Baltimore or Philadelphia. You may count on me always as ready to meet you and the other Bishops in either city, and as willing to cooperate as far as I can in whatever plan you think best.

I should say that all the Prelates named in the Council should be invited to attend, and also some prominent Priests and lay gentlemen, as e.g., Mr. M. Jenkins of your city,—Mr. B. N. Farren of Phila.; Mr. Eugene Kelly, if we can get him to come, etc., etc.

Bp. Wigger called on Monday to obtain the address of Miss Caldwell, when he informed me that he intended to write to her withdrawing his offer to dispose of Seton Hall. He had previously promised to allow the question to remain open until the 1st of May.

I think we should keep up interest in the University, and not abandon the project; but we cannot be the mere obedient servants of any Lady Bountiful. I had unexpectedly a cablegram from Dr. O'Connell, about which I hope to write or speak to you later.[62]

---

[62] BCA, unindexed in "Letters, Papers Various Administrations," M. A. Corrigan to James Gibbons, New York, March 25, 1885. On Easter Monday of that year Corrigan wrote Gibbons to the effect: "This afternoon I go to South Orange for a little visit, and expect to see Bp. Wigger, when I will mention what you say about Seton Hall. It will give me very great pleasure to attend the meeting in Baltimore May 7th, and I already begin to count it a holiday, so pleasant are the recollections of the last visit." BCA, 79–I–6.

Spalding meanwhile was glad to learn that Gibbons was ready to call a meeting of the committee, and he said he would do his best to come east for it, but, "in any event, I shall be quite ready to accept whatever the majority of the Board may decide upon." [63] To date John Ireland had not received word of any action and, impulsive as he was, he was beginning to get restive under the prolonged delay. He wrote Gibbons on March 26:

You will please bear with me if I ask, what is being done with our university project? I am afraid that with our delay the interest felt in it through the country will be lost. Already two of those whom we expected to be chief benefactors have died; others may pass away. I may not understand things in my remote quarter of the country; but it does seem to me that it were better if we were showing some signs of life.

It was very unfortunate that you were not able to attend the New York meeting. In your absence we would decide nothing. Is it not advisable, then, to have a meeting soon, at which there would be a full attendance? . . . I feel a deep interest in the University, both for the merits of the project itself and for the sake of the Council whose honor is staked upon the realization of all its measures.[64]

Gilmour of Cleveland was sceptical about the prospect of success, feeling Washington should not be the place, and that Miss Caldwell should not be "permitted to direct either location or management." The Bishop of Cleveland felt it would take the very best ability the Church could muster to carry through successfully on the university

---

[63] BCA, 79–H–7, J. L. Spalding to James Gibbons, Peoria, March 26, 1885.

[64] BCA, 79–H–5, John Ireland to James Gibbons, St. Paul, March 26, 1885.

project, and he seemed in favor of the western bishops holding back until the eastern prelates had come to more definite conclusions. "Let the West wait till the East is settled—God will direct those who are to deal with it." [65]

Archbishop Gibbons set Thursday, May 7, as the date for the first formal meeting of the university committee. He wrote John J. Williams inviting him for that date and saying, "I have been urged by some of the Prelates to call a meeting in the interest of the projected university." [66] The Archbishop of Boston replied several days later that he would be there.[67] Spalding wrote that since he was about to begin the building of his cathedral and would be busy with the contracts during April, a meeting early in May would suit his purposes.[68] Corrigan's letter of March 25, showing Cardinal McCloskey's unwillingness to have anything to do with the university, discouraged Gibbons, and he told the New York coadjutor, "I had almost given up the idea of calling a meeting in the interest of the University, after receiving yr. letter, as yr. views coincide with my own." However, meanwhile Spalding and Ireland's urging made him feel something should be done. He told Corrigan that the Bishop of St. Paul "almost reproaches me for seeming inaction." He gave Corrigan the date of May 7, therefore, and said if nothing else was accomplished at the meeting the committee might at least urge Spalding

[65] AAC, Letters Jan. 1–Dec. 31, 1885, Richard Gilmour to William H. Elder, Cleveland, March 26, 1885.

[66] BCA, Letterbook of Archbishop Gibbons, p. 153, James Gibbons to John J. Williams, Baltimore, March 30, 1885.

[67] BCA, 79–I–3, John J. Williams to James Gibbons, Boston, April 2, 1885.

[68] BCA, 79–H–14, J. L. Spalding to James Gibbons, Peoria, March 31, 1885.

"who has great influence with the young lady, to send her an ultimatum, saying that if she does not advance the money within a reasonable time without regard to the question of site, we will consider her promise revoked." Gibbons hoped Bishop Wigger would not withdraw his offer of selling Seton Hall College and he remarked that Miss Caldwell had called on him unexpectedly on the previous Monday evening.

I talked to her very plainly about her duty to fulfil [sic] her obligation without regard to site, that the selection of the place devolved on the Board, who were competent to make a judicious choice. It would be a great advantage if sufficient money could be obtained without her aid to purchase the site.[69]

Just at this time there appeared an article by John Gilmary Shea in the *American Catholic Quarterly Review* on the university question. Shea, who had progressive and clear ideas on the subject, argued strongly for prompt action and he instanced the examples of the Catholic universities at Dublin and Quebec as showing what could be done when there was a will to do it. Both Ireland and Canada had far less money and men to draw on than the Church of the United States. As for students, there could hardly be difficulty on that score with nearly 1,600 students then enrolled in the diocesan seminaries and colleges; surely some of these would be interested in higher studies. In regard to professors for a university, Shea believed that Woodstock, St. Mary's in Baltimore, Ilchester, Overbrook, Milwaukee, Troy and other seminaries could contribute

[69] NYAA, C–2, James Gibbons to M. A. Corrigan, Baltimore, April 1, 1885.

enough men to make up a good faculty. The writer pleaded for a school of jurisprudence which would be a real one, "and not a mere adoption nominally of some existing law school." Shea was against beginning the university in one of the existing colleges.

The attempt to elevate schools founded independently, with a life and spirit of their own, into component parts of the university, will be fraught with mischief. The university should be homogeneous in all its parts, actuated by one spirit and one consensus of ideas, not a mere collection of associations of independent schools.[70]

The historian spoke of the inadequacy of existing colleges in the United States for university education, and he concluded: "The Catholic university must come. The present generation seems ready to undertake it. Means are not wanting, professors and pupils will not be wanting." [71]

Due to the deep national feeling of many of the German Catholics in the United States it was considered important to have one of the prominent representatives of that nationality on the committee to help win support for the project from this numerous group of Catholics. Archbishop Heiss of Milwaukee had been chosen, although he had expressed himself even before the council as not feeling it was opportune to have a university. Heiss was, therefore, invited to Baltimore for the meeting on May 7 by Gibbons, but the Milwaukee metropolitan replied:

I have to ask to be excused on account of the great distance,

---

[70] J. G. Shea, "The Proposed American Catholic University," in *American Catholic Quarterly Review*, X (Apr. 1885), 320.
[71] *Ibid.*, p. 321.

and also on account of a good deal of work to be attended to at that time. If the proceedings of the meeting perhaps require the expression of my opinion by voting, I take the liberty in such a case to ask Your Grace to act as my proxy, being convinced, that my opinion in any question referring to it will coincide with that of Your Grace.[72]

Three weeks later the *Freeman's Journal* gave Gibbons' invitation to Heiss as a news item in its issue of April 25. Just why it should have special publicity is not clear as the Archbishop of Milwaukee was a regularly appointed member of the committee. In reply to Gibbons' letter about the meeting, John Ireland answered he would be there, and he added:

Miss Caldwell professes herself ready to pay over the money at any moment we need it to pay for ground, or for a building. She will not give it, she says, merely to have it lie in a bank. All this makes it the more necessary for us to go to work, as we are now allowing her too much time within which she may change her mind.

I have been myself very much in favor of Washington, as the proper place for the University. At the preliminary meeting in New York, those present were divided as between Washington & Seton Hall.[73]

Philadelphia's archbishop, too, let it be known he would be in Baltimore on May 7 and he remarked to Gibbons: "Until we have Miss Caldwell's money in our treasury, I look on nothing as certain about the University. Bishops Spalding & Ireland evidently favor Washington as the site

---

[72] BCA, 79–I–7, Michael Heiss to James Gibbons, Milwaukee, April 6, 1885.

[73] BCA, 79–I–8, John Ireland to James Gibbons, St. Paul, April 6, 1885.

—but I must not anticipate our discussion at the meeting." [74] The same day Ryan wrote to Corrigan, saying he
hoped the latter "will stop over in Phila. & we can go
together." [75]

Some three weeks before the meeting in Baltimore, Archbishop Williams of Boston wrote to his close friend, Bishop
McQuaid of Rochester, to get his views on the university.
In answer McQuaid outlined his ideas on the current trend
of the university question. Since the entire project would
not have in the ensuing years a more persistent foe than
McQuaid it may be of worth to give his reply in full.

In reply to your favor of the 6th, I have to say:
1.   There must in time be three great Catholic American
Universities; one for the East; another for the Mississippi
Valley and the third for the Pacific Coast.
2.   The University now in question is for the East, or the
Atlantic coast. The location of this University must be
determined by considerations of climate, population and
pecuniary resources in hand, or attainable. All these conditions are best answered in the neighborhood of New York
City. On no account should the University be located south
of Philadelphia; it must be placed somewhere between
Philadelphia and Boston. Within this district are congre-
gated the largest masses of people, and within thirty miles
around Wall Street, the money center of America, are to
be found two and a half millions of people.
3.   The placing of the proposed University at Baltimore or
Washington is the killing of the babe before it is born.
4.   A University at Baltimore or Washington would in
time be strangled by one in the vicinity of New York City.

---

[74] BCA, 79–I–9, P. J. Ryan to James Gibbons, Philadelphia, April
6, 1885.

[75] NYAA, C–3, P. J. Ryan to M. A. Corrigan, Philadelphia, April
6, 1885.

It is not probable that the blunder of monopoly committed at Quebec will be repeated.

5. The most suitable site will be a healthy one within easy reaching distance of New York City. There are such places in Westchester County and in New Jersey. There may be excellent places on Long Island, but I do not know them.

6. Seton Hall offers many advantages. It is easy of access from Newark, New York and Philadelphia. The healthfulness is all that could be desired. The property cost for ground and buildings about $300,000. The value of the land has greatly appreciated since I bought it in 1860. The buying price was at about $500 per acre, with the marble building thrown in. The land today, about 68 acres, should be worth from two to three thousand dollars per acre. The neighborhood is today one of New York suburban residences and in the future will have still more of them.

7. At $200,000, the price at which the bishop is willing to sell, so I am told, the University will have a great bargain.

8. The mystery to me is that the bishop of Newark is willing to part with such a property. When the proposition was made informally to me in 1866, I laughed at it. I had labored and made great sacrifices to build up a great diocesan institution, never dreaming that so many children of the household stood ready to tear it down.[76]

In the light of his later unrelenting opposition to the university this expression of qualified approval for the idea from Bishop McQuaid is of interest. Whether he would have supported a university in New Jersey there is no way of knowing, but its location in Washington sealed his opposition to it in the 1880's and his differences on other questions with the bishops who strongly supported the university

---

[76] RDA, McQuaid Copybook, pp. 187–188, Bernard J. McQuaid to John J. Williams, Rochester, April 13, 1885.

in the succeeding years helped to keep him in the camp of the opposition to the end of his long life.

Since no one of the members of the committee was a university-trained man with the exception of Spalding, whose experience in university life at Louvain, Freiburg, and Rome had been rather limited, it is understandable that they should have sought counsel where they thought it could be wisely given. In certain cases, as we shall see, advice was given even when it was not asked. Bernard O'Reilly, biographer of Pius IX and Leo XIII, was visiting in Ireland at this time and he wrote Archbishop Corrigan saying, "They are very anxious here, in high educational circles, about the way our Archbishops & Bishops propose to lay the foundations of the great Catholic University." O'Reilly gave Corrigan a lengthy explanation of the way in which Irish Catholic education was conducted and he said he felt that the American university must be "for the first decade at least of its existence, in a great measure if not exclusively an *examining body,* as the Royal University of Ireland is, and as is the Board of Intermediate Education." [77] Fortunately, this suggestion did not receive serious consideration by the American bishops.

The Archbishop of Cincinnati wrote to Gibbons two weeks in advance of the meeting stating that he hoped he was not too late to express his opposition to Washington and giving the same arguments against the capital as he had expressed to Corrigan some time before. Elder suggested Baltimore, Philadelphia, or New York, the advantages of which he conceded the eastern bishops would know

---

[77] NYAA, C–11, Bernard O'Reilly to M. A. Corrigan, Dublin, April 19, 1885.

better than himself. "It is only the disadvantages of Washington—or Georgetown—which I am impressed with." [78] Gibbons replied that he was not too late with his suggestion as the site had not yet been finally chosen, and he stated he would not like to see the university in Baltimore "as it might conflict with our Seminary & might embarrass the Sulpitian Fathers. Philadelphia is a very central place, & would be a desirable locality. I will mention your objection to Washington at the meeting." [79] The Bishop of St. Paul told Gibbons he believed one afternoon was not enough time to transact all the business and since they could not hope to gather the bishops for another meeting for a long time, "I hope the Prelates will come to Baltimore well provided with all the necessary patience to stay until something definite has been accomplished." [80] Spalding informed Archbishop Gibbons that Miss Caldwell was so opposed to Seton Hall that it was useless to try to change her mind. Her main objection was putting her money into "a broken down college." [81] In his last communication before leaving for Baltimore the Bishop of Peoria informed Gibbons that Miss Caldwell "would wish to have Dr. Chapelle appointed a member of the Committee." [82]

Up to May, 1885, therefore, little had been done to get

[78] BCA, 79–J–8, William H. Elder to James Gibbons, Cincinnati, April 20, 1885.

[79] AAC, Letters Jan. 1–Dec. 31, 1885, James Gibbons to William H. Elder, Baltimore, April 22, 1885.

[80] BCA, 79–J–9, John Ireland to James Gibbons, St. Paul, April 20, 1885.

[81] BCA, 79–J–12, J. L. Spalding to James Gibbons, Peoria, April 21, 1885.

[82] BCA, 79–J–19, J. L. Spalding to James Gibbons, Peoria, April 27, 1885.

the work of the university under way except to project it
in the council and to hold a preliminary meeting of the
committee in New York at which a few tentative decisions
were taken. No enterprise of the magnitude of a university,
of course, could reasonably be expected to progress very
fast. In fact, the American hierarchy had a number of
precedents from Europe which might well have tempered
their zeal and caused them to move with caution. As yet
Miss Caldwell's money was not in their possession and the
troublesome question of a site was likewise undecided. Dr.
O'Connell wrote just at this time to Gibbons: "The news
is spread everywhere in Rome that 'not one cent has been
paid in for the University.' " [83] As Bishop Ireland said they
would need plenty of time at Baltimore and "all the necessary patience to stay until something definite has been accomplished."

[83] BCA, 79–J–18, D. J. O'Connell to James Gibbons, Rome, April
27, 1885.

III

A Site and the Rectorship

THE FIRST formal meeting of the university committee took place at the residence of the Archbishop of Baltimore on May 7, 1885. Legally this group did not constitute the board of trustees since the institution had not yet been incorporated, nor had the Holy See given its approval to the plan for a Catholic university in the United States. Present on May 7 were the Archbishops of Baltimore and Philadelphia, the Coadjutor of New York, the Bishops of St. Paul and Peoria, and Monsignor John Farley of New York. Gibbons acted as chairman of the meeting and Farley as secretary. Following the opening prayer and an explanation of the object of the meeting, Archbishop Gibbons stated that the first subject for discussion would be the site of the university. Since Archbishop Williams of Boston had not arrived in the morning a decision on the site was postponed until afternoon. At that time Spalding read a communication from Miss Caldwell in which she promised to hand over the $300,000 to purchase whatever site might be selected by the committee, providing the original conditions of her grant be kept and that the interest accruing on this money should go to her as long as the capital was not called for by the committee. Miss Caldwell further stated that she would wish no more than $200,000 to be spent on buildings and grounds and the balance of $100,000 to be employed to endow professorships.

Following a discussion of the Caldwell communication, Spalding made a motion that Washington be chosen as the site for this university and the motion was carried. It was further decided that when the property was purchased it should be deeded to the Archbishop of Baltimore. A motion by Bishop Ireland that measures be taken to secure the refusal of property on the site near the Soldiers' Home in Washington for two weeks was passed and Dr. Chapelle, pastor of St. Matthew's Church, was to be instructed to engage the services of Mr. Thomas E. Waggaman of Washington to secure this refusal of property. Ireland and Chapelle were constituted a committee to secure an act of incorporation of the new institution in the District of Columbia with Richard Merrick to act as the lawyer in this instance. A copy of the act of incorporation was then to be sent each archbishop on the committee who would be requested to return the draft to Gibbons with whatever suggestions he cared to make, and the Archbishop of Baltimore would decide on the final form of the document.

Since the appointment of the original committee the previous November, two lay members had died, Reuben Springer of Cincinnati and William Drexel of Philadelphia. To fill their places the committee elected Michael Jenkins of Baltimore and Bernard N. Farren of Philadelphia, as well as Thomas E. Waggaman of Washington. The membership was likewise increased by the election of Bishop

John J. Keane of Richmond and by three additional priests, Placide L. Chapelle of Washington and John S. Foley and Thomas S. Lee of Baltimore. At a meeting on the following day, May 8, another bishop was added to the committee in the person of Martin Marty, O.S.B., Vicar Apostolic of Dakota Territory. An executive committee was formed within the general committee to consist of Gibbons, Corrigan, Spalding, Chapelle, Lee, Farren, and Jenkins. Spalding was asked to draw up an appeal to the public for financial assistance to the university which would be signed by all the members of the committee. Finally it was decided that the committee meet once a year on the last Wednesday of April, that the secretary notify members in advance, and that all general meetings be held in Baltimore. Following the adoption of a motion that the next meeting be held on November 11, the meeting adjourned.[1]

The most important business of this first formal meeting of the committee was, of course, the selection of Washington as a site. The choice was to cause a great deal of opposition during the next year or so. In fact, on the day of the decision Archbishop Gibbons wrote Elder, "I regret that after a long discussion, a place three miles from Washington was chosen for the University. I preferred Phila. for good reasons." [2] Gibbons, although chairman of the committee, was not, therefore, in favor of Washington, but he did not

---

[1] Minutes of the Meeting of the Board of Trustees, May 7, 1885, Baltimore. Archives of the Catholic University of America. Eugene Kelly, treasurer of the committee, was unable to be present at this meeting. He wrote Father Alfred A. Curtis, secretary to Archbishop Gibbons, on May 4 that "pressing matters of business deprive me of the ability to attend the meeting." BCA, 79–K–8.

[2] Archives of the Archdiocese of Cincinnati, Letters Jan. 1–Dec. 31, 1885, James Gibbons to William H. Elder, Baltimore, May 7, 1885.

urge his views when he saw the strong sentiment of Spalding and Ireland for the national capital and knew further that such was the choice of Miss Caldwell. The day of the meeting Gilmour wrote Elder at Cincinnati: "I send you [a] slip in which I was led to believe you were in Baltimore. Why not Emmittsburg for the University? It is well situated & cheap. Might you not urge this in Baltimore. It would flatter Baltimore & get Emmittsburg in line. Think of this & if you deem it wise act in the case." [3] However, Archbishop Elder was not a member of the committee and by the time Gilmour's letter reached Cincinnati the site had been chosen. The press through these months was filled with speculations concerning the amount of the endowment, and the *Catholic Mirror* of Baltimore believed that by the week of the meeting of the committee the amount, including Miss Caldwell's gift, was "over a million dollars." [4] This was entirely too optimistic an estimate; it would be still some time before the money given to the project would approach the million mark. If the New York *Times* had doubted the wisdom of the Catholics when it first learned the news of a Catholic university, selection of Washington as a site met with its approval. An editorial of May 11, 1885, read:

The selection of the city of Washington as the site of the new Catholic university is worthy of note as an evidence that the prelates of the Church of Rome in this country recognize the changed and rapidly changing character of the capital city and its promise for the future. Washington is no longer a mere seat of government—the

[3] AAC, Letters Jan. 1–Dec. 31, 1885. Richard Gilmour to William H. Elder, Cleveland, May 7, 1885.

[4] *Catholic Mirror*, May 9, 1885.

home of Congress and the President, sustaining an un-
settled population of office holders and office seekers. It has
already become a centre of social gayety, and social gayety
pretty certainly and promptly brings in its train the cultivation of letters and the arts, not only because that sort of
thing is looked on with favor by the world of society, but
because every social circle has a certain proportion of men
and women with the taste, the time, the money, and the
brains to engage in serious mental work. The Directors and
Curators of the National Museum have long foreseen that
Washington was to be an important centre of learning, and
it has been their ambition to stimulate its development in
that direction. The prelates have done a wise thing, no
doubt, in deciding to build the Catholic university at Washington. Now let them see to it that the teaching of the university is broad and liberal, not shunning any of the truths
of science or of history merely because it is the custom to
avoid them in most Catholic schools, and the institution will
be worthy of the city, even should Washington become the
Berlin of America.

This metropolitan daily had not overcome its misgiving of
the previous December concerning the kind of teaching
which a Catholic university would give in the sciences.

The *Catholic Mirror* gave a brief description of the Middleton property in Washington which had been chosen for
the university, stating that it was located at the eastern
gate of the Soldiers' Home and lying between the road to
the home and the old Bladensburg Road. They were quite
wrong, however, in adding that Archbishop Gibbons had
favored Washington after Baltimore. The writer in the
Mirror nonetheless did sense the importance of Washington for a university in mentioning "the great Congressional
Library, the National Museum and other national insti-

tutions, to which it is advantageous for scholars to have access." [5]

There continued a great deal of scepticism in some quarters about the success of the university venture. M. F. Morris of the Washington law firm of Merrick & Morris which had been approached by Ireland and Chapelle to make out a certificate of incorporation, wrote Archbishop Gibbons two weeks after the Baltimore meeting:

Several gentlemen, both Protestant and Catholic, have since spoken to me on the subject of the University; and if it would not be regarded as an impertinence on my part, I would be glad to submit to you for such consideration as they may deserve the views that have been elicited. I have had some experience myself as an educator; and I have an earnest and sincere interest as a Catholic that this enterprise should not prove a failure. Pardon me for venturing the opinion, that, as now formulated or proposed to be formulated, it will prove a most disastrous failure. No doubt the Council has considered the subject very fully; but it occurs to me, that, if the matter is not absolutely settled beyond re-consideration, the views of Catholic laymen, who have the interests of the Church at heart, might receive some consideration, even if ultimately they should be shown to be untenable and unfounded. [6]

Whether there was any response on Gibbons' part to this rather disquieting letter is not known. Precisely what fears Morris entertained it is impossible to say. However, his suggestion of getting the counsel of Catholic laymen had been acted upon in part by the bishops at their meeting in Baltimore since they there brought into the committee three

---

[5] *Ibid.*, May 16, 1885.
[6] Baltimore Cathedral Archives, 79–L–6, M. F. Morris to James Gibbons, Washington, May 23, 1885.

outstanding Catholic laymen in addition to Eugene Kelly, namely, Jenkins, Farren, and Waggaman. James A. Healy, Bishop of Portland, was likewise critical of the optimistic tone taken by some on the university. He wrote Archbishop Corrigan: "I observe with apprehension the 'Great Expectations' of the 'future contingent' the Catholic University. I do not share the enthusiastic hopes that have been uttered and printed." [7] But the choice of Washington met with the approval of Denis O'Connell who wrote Gibbons from Rome:

It is a source of pleasure to me to the [sic] Archdiocese of Balto. in possession of the new University and I congratulate the Catholics of Balto. I hope however that you can secure the resignation of Peoria to take control of it. It may be objected that he is to [sic] ardent for the office of presidency, but it will be some time yet before the place will be ready for the services of a calm presiding officers, [sic] and the ardor of Peoria is required to build it. I have reason to suspect that the choice of location made will do nothing to increase the assistance to be expected from other Sees, but if Peoria resigned he w'd be committed to it, and he would put forth all his energy to carry the plan through.[8]

[7] New York Archdiocesan Archives, C–2, James A. Healy to M. A. Corrigan, Portland, May 23, 1885.

[8] BCA, 79–L–15, D. J. O'Connell to James Gibbons, Rome, May 28, 1885. A letter of John Farley to Archbishop Corrigan on this subject and bearing no other date than "Tuesday, 188," was found in NYAA, I–33. Since it is impossible to fit this letter into its proper chronological place in the narrative, the pertinent passages are given here. "Should I say to the absent members of the Committee that Seton Hall was decided on, and that afterwards the very party who was anxious for it now proposes Washington? This is the fact. But it will look badly on paper. You know Bp. Spalding only went to look at Washington site out of courtesy to Abp. Gibbons, but had given his adhesion to Seton Hall. I am rather amazed at the change in his attitude. Will you kindly drop me a line at your convenience."

The news that the university site had been chosen
brought the inevitable offers of plans and designs from alert
architects and contractors. Archbishop Ryan of Philadelphia had such an offer from James McGrath of St. Louis
who, he assured Gibbons in transmitting McGrath's letter,
"has built what is probably the finest college in the country for the Christian Brothers of that city." Ryan was surprised to learn that matters had advanced to the state
where an architect in St. Louis might get the idea the
bishops were ready to begin building. He was still withholding whole-hearted co-operation in the venture until
the Caldwell money had been paid over.[9] Actually the
money for the ground had been paid by Miss Caldwell as
we learn from a letter of Archbishop Gibbons to Bishop
Joseph Dwenger of Fort Wayne. He told Dwenger about
the selection of Washington and continued, "The titles are
now being examined, & the purchase money is deposited in
[the] bank." [10] But Philadelphia's archbishop remained hesi-
tant about the whole matter. Early in June he expressed
his views to Corrigan:

Now what are we going to do when the circular proposed
at Baltimore to be signed by the Archbishops as an appeal
for the University shall be sent to us? Miss Caldwell has
given only $29,000, the price of the site for the university

---

[9] BCA, 79–L–18, P. J. Ryan to James Gibbons, Philadelphia, May
29, 1885, enclosing a letter of James McGrath to P. J. Ryan, St.
Louis, May 23, 1885, BCA, 79–L–5. It was not long, too, before
prospective professors began to apply for positions in the university.
Archbishop Gibbons received an application from a certain M. D.
Kavanagh of Ramsgate, Kent, England, for a professorship in law
written on June 22, 1885. BCA, 79–N–6.

[10] Archives of the University of Notre Dame, James Gibbons to
Joseph Dwenger, Baltimore, May 29, 1885.

& our promise to sign the appeal was conditioned on her placing the $300,000 in Mr. Kelly's hands for the University when the site should have been selected. Bp. Keane of Richmond lately informed me that she had only paid over the price of the site. *Perhaps* she has placed the rest in Mr. Kelly's hands as promised. As I foresaw, the next move is to have Bp. Spalding appointed Rector. This is a matter for grave consideration.[11]

The choice of a location occasioned some uneasiness in Rome since the American bishops had not as yet made any formal application for permission to begin a university. Dwenger wrote Gibbons from Rome, where he was engaged in advising the Propaganda officials on the decrees of the Third Plenary Council, to the effect that the question had been raised by some of the officials of Propaganda as to how the American hierarchy could proceed without the consent of the Pope. Dwenger stated that he had explained to Cardinal Simeoni that the American bishops were quite aware of the fact that they could not begin a university without the permission of the Holy See and that there were many steps between the selection of a location and the preparation for actual opening of the university. He added that he had told the cardinal the American bishops felt it more prudent not to ask the Holy Father while the matter was as yet somewhat uncertain. "This explanation was graciously recd and our course declared prudent and honorable to the Holy See." [12] The Bishop of Rochester was greatly provoked at the progress of the university matter and he wrote Corrigan:

---

[11] NYAA, C–3, P. J. Ryan to M. A. Corrigan, Philadelphia, June 4, 1885.

[12] BCA, 79–M–11, Joseph Dwenger to James Gibbons, Rome, June 12, 1885.

It will be time enough to go over the question of the *Grand American* Catholic University for the *Southern States* of the U. S. when we meet. We have all been badly sold. It did not enter my head that anything so preposterous could have been contemplated.[13]

Denis J. O'Connell, a young priest of thirty-six years of age of the Diocese of Richmond, had recently been named fourth rector of the American College in Rome. He had assisted Archbishop Gibbons in the preparations for the Third Plenary Council and when Louis E. Hostlot died in the office of the Roman rector in February, 1884, the post remained vacant until the appointment of O'Connell.[14] Denis O'Connell was destined in his ten years as the rector in Rome to have much of the business of the university pass through his hands since he acted in the capacity of an unofficial agent for the American bishops in the transaction of a great many questions with the Holy See. When the news of his appointment reached Richmond his bishop recorded in the episcopal diary:

Have received the news, for us a sad blow, of the appointment of Rev. D. J. O'Connell, D.D., to be Rector of the

---

[13] NYAA, C–16, Bernard J. McQuaid to M. A. Corrigan, Rochester, June 20, 1885.

[14] For the American College in Rome, cf. Henry A. Brann, *History of the American College, Rome* (New York, 1910). In the Bishops' Diary kept in the Archives of the Diocese of Richmond under date of November 9, 1884, the following entry was made by Bishop John J. Keane: "Rev. Dr. O'Connell has been in the service of the Abp. & the Council since Nov. 1883. It is a great embarrassment at the Cathedral here, leaving us shorthanded. But he was considered indispensable—and he will still be needed for several months to put the decrees in order, be one of the committee to take them to Rome, & then prepare for final publication," p. 132.

American College in Rome. It is a *great* loss to us, but as it is expected that he will have a quasi-representative character in Rome, his appointment will be a great blessing to the Church in this country.[15]

Fortunately, O'Connell was closely attached to Gibbons and Keane and he took a personal interest in the university. During the ensuing four years he did much to expedite the conduct of its affairs with the Roman officials.

The Boston *Pilot* for July 11 reported the purchase of the Middleton property in Washington at the figure of $29,500. The Boston paper, always friendly to the university project, stated that it was proposed to erect substantial buildings and "to make the University one which shall be second to none in the country." Bishop Spalding had meanwhile begun his travels over the country in an effort to raise money for the new institution. He wrote Gibbons on July 23 to the effect that:

Miss Caldwell's lawyer has sent me the document by which the transfer of the money she promised to found the University has been duly made in trust to Messrs. Kelly, Fry and myself. It is now in order I suppose to issue the appeal for endowment of chairs and bourses, as decided at our last

---

[15] Bishops' Diary, Archives of the Diocese of Richmond, July, 1885, p. 118. O'Connell had some misgivings about the university's fate in Rome. Just at this time he wrote Gibbons: "I hope that nothing will appear about the University in the public letter of the Prop. And launching off on that subject I am very much afraid the University at Washington will be a failure, considering the feeling in N. Y. and Phila., unless you can make sure of the undivided energy of Bp. Spalding. If he were to drop of [sic] the scene now, I do not know who there would be to take his place in carrying the plan through." BCA, 79–N–13, D. J. O'Connell to James Gibbons, Rome, June 28, 1885.

meeting. Please send me any suggestions you may have to make and I will at once draw up the Appeal and send copy for approval.[16]

By mid-September the appeal written by Spalding had been finished and approved by Gibbons and the executive committee for publication.[17] Spalding stated that the object of the appeal was to get Catholics of wealth "to provide the means to endow the eight professorships with which the University will enter upon its work, and also to found the burses of which mention has been made." The document called the university "the first work of general and national significance undertaken by the Church in this country." If it accomplished nothing more than to offer the occasion for a number of promising Catholic students to extend their education beyond the ages of eighteen or nineteen "it would be of inestimable value." The university would make a real contribution to the reconciliation of religion and science since:

. . . a true University, where all the sciences will be represented and where a chair will be assigned to each, will be not only a national and striking witness against the partial and erroneous views of those who have not a sufficient understanding of the Catholic system of truth, but it will also prove the most effective means of counteracting the tendency of the study of nature to make men indifferent or skeptical in matters of religion, which is due chiefly to the dissociation of the physical sciences from other sciences,

---

[16] BCA, 79–P–10, J. L. Spalding to James Gibbons, Peoria, July 23, 1885.

[17] *Freeman's Journal*, September 19, 1885, carried the text which bore the title, "An Appeal to the Catholics of the United States in Behalf of the University which the Late Council of Baltimore Resolved to Create."

whose office it is to explain their data and to assign their conclusions to the proper places in the sphere of human knowledge.

Further, a university would afford a meeting place for the best minds among the American Catholic clergy and laity and from this association much good would result. The various nationalities among Catholics of the United States would likewise find in the university a force which "must necessarily tend to harmonize and unify the many elements of which the Church in America is composed." The document quoted Cardinal Newman on a university:

In the nature of things greatness and unity go together; excellence implies a centre. Such is a university. It is the place to which a thousand schools make contributions, in which, the intellect may safely range and speculate, sure to find its equal in some antagonist activity, and its judge in the tribunal of truth . . .

In a final eloquent plea for all American Catholics to join hands in support of the undertaking, Spalding wrote: "Let this University be a standing monument to proclaim how meaningless are the words of those who say it is not possible to get Catholics to unite for any great purpose outside the domain of faith and morals."

The Catholic and secular press both published either extracts or the full text. The Boston *Pilot* warmly recommended the objective of the appeal in its issue of September 12. The *Catholic Mirror* of September 19 felt the plea of the bishops meant that "the Catholic University of America is now an assured fact." The same editorial stated that the Associated Press had carried the bishops' statement to all parts of the country and "the most able and representative American journals were receiving the news of this first authentic notification of the university's reality with great consideration, and treating it at length editorially." The *Mirror* quoted the reaction of one of the secular dailies, the New York *Sun,* which read:

On one ground, at all events, the creation of an American Catholic University at Washington will be viewed with satisfaction by all judicious friends of the higher education. The concentration of Catholic resources on a single great establishment will tend to convince every powerful Protestant denomination of the inexpediency of frittering its means among a multitude of petty local institutions. The funds thus dispersed and wasted will hereafter be more likely to feed and multiply the energies of the larger educational foundations; and the more universities of the highest type we have in the United States the better.

The published appeal of the bishops constituted the first official announcement to the American public of the projected university. As such it provoked comment from a number of quarters. Herman J. Heuser, editor of the *American Catholic Quarterly Review,* used it as the basis for a long article in his journal. Heuser appealed for the co-operation of all Catholics, particularly those engaged in education, for "the Catholic educators of our community, whether they think well or ill, or not at all, of the project, should have to bear a share in the loss, if it happened to be a failure, as they should be participants of its success." [18] Criticisms of the university which had appeared here and

---

[18] H(erman) J. H(euser), "American Catholics and the Proposed University," in *American Catholic Quarterly Review,* X (Oct. 1885), 636.

there, Heuser thought, only proved that "even in the circles of the better educated there is no clear understanding as to the precise aim and nature of such an institution." As an example of the generosity of American Catholics to higher education, the writer instanced the collections made thirty years before in the United States for the Catholic University of Ireland, the Dioceses of New York and Albany alone giving "above $25,000 within a very short time." As evidence of the need of a university among the Catholics of America he mentioned the lack of intellectual life, evident enough "when we take a glance at our literature and press." As for salaries, Heuser felt the professors should be paid as well as in other American universities and he added, "Johns Hopkins's regular professors receive, we understand, $5000. The majority of institutions rate, of course, much lower, but their influence is accordingly." The writer urged the establishment of a learned review or journal for the university, giving as an example the *Catholic University Gazette* begun in the spring of 1854 at Dublin by Newman's faculty. And as to numbers, they would not be important at first since Dublin's university began with only fifteen students.

The appeal was likewise sent abroad with the result that Cardinal Newman, who maintained a keen interest in university education after he left Dublin, wrote Archbishop Gibbons in October:

My Dear Lord Archbishop.
I have welcomed with the warmest interest the eloquent Appeal of your University Board to the Catholics of the United States, which has come to me from America through the kindness of an anonymous friend.
At a time when there is so much in this part of the world

to depress and trouble us as to our religious prospects, the
tidings which your Circular conveys of the actual com-
mencement of so great an undertaking on the other side
of the ocean on the part of the Church will rejoice the
hearts of all well-educated Catholics in these Islands.

With this thought before me I cannot help feeling it to
be out of place to notice what is merely personal to myself; still I may be allowed by your Grace and the other
members of the Board briefly to express my deep sense of
the singular honour they have done me by introducing into
their Appeal a quotation from what I wrote years ago
upon the subject of Universities.

It leads me in simple gratitude, were I not already bound
by faith and brotherly love, to pray for an abundant blessing from above on a design so necessary for the growth and
stability of the Church in the vast regions which Divine
Providence has opened upon her.

I am, my dear Lord Archbishop,
Your Grace's humble and affectionate servt.
John H. Card. Newman.[19]

Augustine F. Hewit contributed a brief commentary on the
appeal to the *Catholic World* for November in which he
said he was glad to see the bishops' statement "repudiates
the comment of those who have taken occasion to cast a
slur on the actual state of education among the Catholic

---

[19] BCA, 79–T–11, John H. Cardinal Newman to James Gibbons,
October 10, 1885, copy. The original of the letter is in the Mullen
Library of the Catholic University of America. Patrick Cardinal
Moran and the hierarchy of Australia sent a joint letter to the American hierarchy on November 29, 1885, in compliment of the work of
the Third Plenary Council in which, *inter alia,* they said: "The success
of your colleges now happily crowned by your National University, is
a matter of deep interest to us, and will, we trust, encourage our people
to second our efforts in imitating your noble example." BCA, 79–V–5,
Hierarchy of Australia to Hierarchy of the United States.

clergy." [20] To whom exactly Father Hewit was referring it is impossible to say, but he showed little patience with those who were raising objections to the university. "They are only the refrain of an old song we heard thirty years ago when the project of a university was first talked about . . ." In conclusion he asserted, "waiting for absolute unanimity, for the cessation of all objections, for the removal of all difficulties, would bring us to doomsday with nothing else."

Meanwhile the Archbishop of Milwaukee sent encouraging news to Gibbons to the effect that Mr. John Lawler of Prairie du Chien had stated he would "donate five thousand dollars absolutely and possibly more." Heiss asked that Ireland act as his proxy at the forthcoming meeting of the committee in Baltimore and remarked that Bishop Ireland could give Gibbons additional information on Lawler who "is a most pious Catholic and believes that all Catholics should show their piety by doing as much as they can for Catholic education." [21] During October, Ireland was in Washington and was interviewed on the university. The *Pilot* reported him as saying that there was $600,000 then in hand to begin the work. Questioned about what school would be opened first, the Bishop of St. Paul stated it would be the "philosophical and theological departments," and he added:

None will be admitted to the privileges of the University except those who have received diplomas from other institutions. There will be no collegiate course. Ours will be

---

[20] A. F. Hewit, "The American Catholic University," in *Catholic World*, XLII (Nov. 1885), 223.

[21] BCA, 79–T–21, Michael Heiss to James Gibbons, Milwaukee, October 24, 1885.

a University of a grade above anything that has yet been attempted in this country.[22]

The Bishop of St. Paul, if correctly reported, was apparently not aware of the character of Johns Hopkins University which had begun nine years before. While Ireland, Spalding, and Keane were traveling over the country in an effort to stir up enthusiasm and gather money other members of the committee were kept nearer home by the work in their dioceses. Archbishop Ryan wrote congratulating Archbishop Corrigan on his succession to the See of New York at the death of Cardinal McCloskey, and in anticipation of the forthcoming meeting of the university committee to be held in two weeks, he said:

I hope to meet you on the 10' of next month on your way to Baltimore. I will be very happy if you can pay me a little visit on your way to or from that city. I think of going by the "Congressional train" on the 10th. I should like to have a preliminary talk about the University so that we may if possible, act together. When do you propose to go? [23]

A week later Ryan thanked Corrigan for inviting him to preach the sermon on the occasion of his reception of the pallium and he added, "I will go to Baltimore by the train you mention, & will join you at Broad St. Depot when we shall talk over 'matters and things'!" [24] Bishop McQuaid heard of the meeting scheduled for November 11 and wrote

---

[22] Boston *Pilot*, October 24, 1885.

[23] NYAA, C–3, P. J. Ryan to M. A. Corrigan, Philadelphia, October 27, 1885.

[24] NYAA, C–3, P. J. Ryan to M. A. Corrigan, Philadelphia, November 2, 1885.

to warn his friend, Archbishop Williams of Boston, to be on the alert, to which Williams laconically replied, "Yours of the 2nd inst. is received, and I shall try to have my eyes well open to what may be going on at our meeting in Baltimore." [25]

Guidance to the American bishops in the matter of introducing the university subject in Rome was afforded by Denis O'Connell. Writing to James Gibbons on general business relating to the Third Plenary Council, he remarked:

The letter about the University will be written to you privately. The Cong. cancelled the decree that establishes the board of administration for the University. It says the Board must be formed after the approval of the charter or "statutes" for the University and those must be approved at Rome. This amounts to nothing, if kept quiet. The course of studies in Theology & Philosophy must be approved in Rome. All will be well in the end.[26]

The change mentioned by O'Connell was that referred to previously in connection with the Holy See safeguarding its right to establish pontifical institutions.[27] Three weeks later O'Connell wrote Gibbons again and this time he embodied the changes in phraseology which we have explained under the decree of the council on the university. The rector of the American College said he had heard through a letter received the previous day from Bishop Keane that the committee was meeting on November 11 and he wished

[25] Rochester Diocesan Archives, John J. Williams to Bernard J. McQuaid, Boston, November 6, 1885.

[26] BCA, 79–S–4, D. J. O'Connell to James Gibbons, Grottaferrata, September 21, 1885.

[27] Cf. p. 113 of this study.

"to render your minds perfectly free from any fear or anxiety," by sending the exact changes in the decree made by the Congregation of the Propaganda. After giving the verbatim changes, O'Connell told Gibbons:

This with what is found in the letter of the Prop. embraces everything. You know nothing of this officially yet, and you can communicate as much of it as you please. I shall explain to them here that the present Board is only created to have some reliable body of men before the public to inspire confidence and to carry out the plans and I do not imagine there will be the least difficulty. Besides Mgr. Jacobini said to me "to be frank with you, I have my doubts about the success" wherever he got the idea.[28]

A week following this letter Pope Leo XIII dispatched a private letter to Archbishop Gibbons in which he said that he was most gratified by the news that the American bishops were planning a Catholic university in America to be erected "quam primum fieri possit." The Pope stated he felt such a university would be a great benefit to religion and to the country. Leo XIII realized how much it would take to have the university begun properly and for that reason he was willing to forego for the time being the request which he had made of the American bishops when they were in Rome in 1883 to give generously to the mis-

---

[28] BCA, 79–T–13, D. J. O'Connell to James Gibbons, Grottaferrata, October 14, 1885. Cardinal Simeoni explained to Gibbons at the same time the changes made in article 187 of the decrees of the council pertaining to the university, viz., that it (the university) had to be approved by Rome before they could speak of the board or commission in charge of the project. BCA, 79–T–15, Joannes Simeoni to James Gibbons, Rome, October 17, 1885.

sions for the return of the peoples of the East to the Catholic Church.[29]

The second full meeting of the university committee was held on November 11, 1885, at Archbishop Gibbons' residence in Baltimore. Besides the old members, Bishops Keane of Richmond and Marty of Dakota along with Drs. Chapelle and Foley, Michael Jenkins, and Thomas E. Waggaman attended for the first time. Gibbons read the letter of Pope Leo XIII of October 22 giving his approval to the idea of a university, as well as Cardinal Newman's letter of the month previous. The committee then heard a report of some of the larger sums promised to the university fund, such as $10,000 from Jenkins, $10,000 from John Lawler of Prairie du Chien, Chapelle's estimate that the city of Washington would give $50,000, and Bishop Ireland's statement that he believed the family of the late William Drexel would give $50,000. But these were only promises. Therefore, it was thought wise to authorize Spalding, Ireland, Keane, and Marty to begin a systematic coverage of the dioceses of the United States for the purpose of collecting money and, to assist these bishops in their work, it was decided that Gibbons as chairman of the committee should write letters to the heads of the dioceses asking them to prepare their people for the campaign. The collectors were instructed to accept only cash or an equivalent, not promissory notes. Since a flaw had been found in the title to the Washington property due to the fact that one or more heirs to a 2/10 interest in the property had been missing for sixty years, Waggaman was requested to clear the title. The act of incorporation of the university

---

[29] *Acta et Decreta* (1886 edition), pp. lxiv–lxv.

was read and it was agreed the members of the committee should meet in Washington the following day to sign the petition for incorporation. Archbishop Williams was put in charge of preparing plans for the building which he would submit at the next meeting and Waggaman was given charge over the Washington property for payment of taxes thereon and for supervising the farm. The next meeting of the committee was set for April 28, 1886, and on the following day, November 12, all the committee members except Eugene Kelly went to Washington for the purpose of entering the petition for incorporation.[30]

Archbishop Gibbons had printed and sent to the bishops of the country a copy of Leo XIII's letter of October 22 in which the Pope had said:

Gratissimum Nobis accidit, quod accepimus, te, collata cum ceteris Episcopis sententia, egregium iniisse consilium Catholicam studiorum Universitatem in America, quam primum fieri possit, erigendi. Profecto Episcoporum auspiciis, patrocinio ac vigili cura, magno erit ipsa emolumento tum relligioni tum patriae vestrae; et Catholici nominis splendori, litterarum scientiarumque incremento quam maxime inserviet.[31]

But in this communication Gibbons contented himself with stating that the letter from the Pope had been written in

[30] ACUA, Minutes of the Meeting of the Board of Trustees, Baltimore, November 11, 1885. Gibbons made the following entry in his diary under November 11, 1885: "Recd. through Dr. O'Connell who arrived today, a letter from the H. Father in which he praises our efforts to establish a Cath. University, & refers to our promised collection in aid of the Eastern Missions—chiefly of Athens & Constantinople. BCA, Cardinal Gibbons' Diary, p. 188.

[31] AAC, Letters Jan. 1–Dec. 31, 1885. Printed circular of James Gibbons to William H. Elder, Baltimore, November 12, 1885.

reply to his own letter of December 18, 1884. He did not expand on the university question, perhaps feeling that the word of the Holy Father would carry its own weight. The lack of any definite statement as to the amount needed to begin the university led to some widely variant estimates in the press. The Boston *Pilot* on November 21 mentioned the forthcoming visit of the bishops to the dioceses and it stated the sum desired was $700,000 in addition to the Caldwell benefaction, "which . . . will give the work $1,000,000 to start on." But this was only a guess as no goal had been fixed by the committee itself. Bernard O'Reilly continued his interest in the project and told Gibbons in a letter from Rome that Archbishop Elder was leaving Rome that week and "I ventured to speak to him on your Catholic University." What he said to Elder he did not disclose but he assured Gibbons that he had "carefully abstained, in all my letters, . . . to touch this matter at all, except to Archbishop Corrigan." O'Reilly hoped the ideas in his articles on intermediate and university education in Ireland might be taken up by the American Catholics interested in higher education so that they might "raise the standards of studies, & gradually prepare for the great University you contemplate, a numerous body of young men *really fit to receive the full benefit of University courses, in every* professional department." [32]

Nearly three months after the meeting of November 11,

---

[32] BCA, 80–D–6, Bernard O'Reilly to James Gibbons, Rome, January 26, 1886. A few days later O'Reilly wrote Gibbons again suggesting that the bishops establish a monthly university magazine. "Through such a periodical you might convey to all Colleges & Intermediate Schools in the Union, the necessity of raising the standards of Teaching, & thereby preparing our youth for University education." BCA, 80–E–8, Rome, February 7, 1886.

Gibbons had not yet written the letter to the American bishops preparing them for the collectors. John Farley, at the instance of John J. Keane, reminded him, therefore, on January 29, 1886, of this obligation. "I would have reminded your Grace of this long ago, but I was told by Bps. Ireland & Spalding soon after the last Board meeting, that you had made up your mind not to send this note, deeming it unnecessary." [33] But the collectors were in some instances meeting with a rather cool reception and consequently Bishop Keane suggested to Farley that he have Gibbons write the bishops. Keane had gone to New York that winter for the purpose of collecting only to learn to his amazement that Archbishop Corrigan was not in sympathy with the university project "in its present shape and could therefore not cooperate in my efforts at collecting." [34] Corrigan told Keane he felt it a mistake to have located the university "in the South." The Archbishop of New York did suggest that Keane address the Xavier Union, a Catholic club, on the subject of the university with the understanding that he, Corrigan, should issue the invitations. Keane agreed, but the occasion proved anything but successful and he stated that several men told him that the failure "could easily be found in the wording of the invitation, which put the money feature so prominently and baldly as to repel all not already interested." [35] From New York Keane went with Spalding to Brooklyn. "But there

---

[33] BCA, 80–D–11, John M. Farley to James Gibbons, New York, January 29, 1886.

[34] ACUA, Manuscript Memorial of John J. Keane on the Early Years of the University, p. 2. Hereafter this document will be referred to as Keane Memorial.

[35] *Ibid.*, p. 4.

was an evident want of interest and but little response, and although I spent several days calling on individuals, the total was not at all worthy of the place."

The efforts of the bishops were not all so discouraging as Keane's first experiences. In a meeting in Chicago on January 28 it was reported that "enthusiastic speeches were made by prominent clergymen, who expressed the opinion that $100,000 could be secured in Chicago alone." [36] One would gather from the tone of Keane's letters that no such enthusiasm had yet been shown in the East. He wrote Gibbons that he had returned to New York from Albany and expected to go back to Brooklyn and then on to Boston and Philadelphia in company with Spalding, but he added, "I do not find that University stock stands high." [37] He spoke at a dinner at Delmonico's on February 18 with Corrigan, Ryan, Spalding, McQuaid, and Eugene Kelly among those present. Keane told the gathering that "two-thirds of the money necessary to start had already been raised, and he hoped those present would follow the example of one of their number, Eugene Kelly, who had contributed $50,000, and help raise the other third." [38] Bishop Keane was more optimistic in his public utterances on the subject than in his private correspondence with Archbishop Gibbons.

Just at this time there reached America the news that Gibbons had been made a cardinal. He was first informed of it through a telegram from Archbishop Corrigan and by February 11, 1886, he wrote in his diary: "Telegrams

---

[36] *Freeman's Journal,* February 6, 1886.

[37] BCA, 80–G–2, John J. Keane to James Gibbons, New York, February 11, 1886.

[38] New York *Sun,* February 19, 1886.

and messages of congratulation are pouring in from all parts of the country." [39] Among the letters of congratulation was one from Bishop Charles J. Seghers of Vancouver Island, soon to meet a tragic death in Alaska, who told the new cardinal, "I seize this opportunity to transmit the application of a trustworthy gentleman of Belgium for the position of Librarian of the future Catholic University." [40] The chairman of the university committee continued to receive proposals of this kind from interested parties, as well as gratuitous advice on the mistakes which the committee was making. Thomas P. Kernan of Utica, New York, wrote complaining of Washington as the location and he drew up a petition which he hoped might change the views of the committee. He was disappointed, he said, that the site of the university "should not have been selected somewhere on the coast, where it would attract students and visitors during all season [sic] of the year, and where it would always enjoy cool weather which predisposes and greatly aids all intellectual work." [41]

Rumors multiplied in the press and by late March, 1886, the Washington *Sunday Herald* was quoting a despatch from Washington to a New York paper that serious dissension had arisen among the committee members, and that the personnel of the committee as well as a reconsideration of the site would come up at the next meeting. A question of sectional difference was mentioned since the committee "contains twelve men from the Atlantic coast to five from

---

[39] BCA, Cardinal Gibbons' Diary, p. 197.

[40] BCA, 80–R–10, Charles J. Seghers to James Gibbons, Victoria, B. C., April 5, 1886.

[41] BCA, 80–O–12, Thomas P. Kernan to James Gibbons, Utica, March 9, 1886.

all the rest of the country." Chapelle was apparently interviewed in Washington by a reporter but he did not give any
definite answers to questions. The matter of beginning the
building would depend, said Chapelle, on reports from
Keane and Spalding who were out collecting.[42] In the
meantime the collectors were continuing their efforts and
John Ireland wrote Gibbons to say that he felt the date of
the meeting, the Wednesday after Easter, should be postponed for several weeks to enable Bishop Marty to be
present. Marty would have difficulty in getting away Easter
week and, "as he represents the Germans, it will be rather
unfortunate if we have the meeting without him." Ireland
felt, too, that a postponement would give Spalding and
himself a few more days after Easter for collecting which,
he believed, "would have good results." In closing he returned to his earlier point, "the absence of Bp. Marty from
our meeting, if held, Easter week, would, I repeat, be a
serious drawback . . ."[43] Spalding agreed with Ireland
and the result was the meeting was postponed until May
12. John J. Keane wrote suggesting a meeting of the principal Catholics of Baltimore be held on the evening of the
gathering of the committee for the purpose of asking for
contributions. "It is rather galling that New York should
be claiming to have done nearly all that has thus far been

---

[42] *Catholic Mirror,* March 27, 1886, quoting Washington *Sunday
Herald.* An effort to secure this paper at the Library of Congress
was unsuccessful. The library's file of the *Sunday Herald* begins only
with the issue of March 22, 1886, and the item was not in that issue.

[43] BCA, 80–Q–9, John Ireland to James Gibbons, St. Paul, March
30, 1886. Heiss was still a member of the committee, although he
was soon to resign. Perhaps Ireland knew this when he referred to
Marty in a manner which would lead one to believe the South
Dakota bishop the only representative of the Germans.

done in the cause. Does it not seem time for Baltimore to speak out & act?" [44] Archbishop Heiss took the opportunity of the invitation to the meeting on May 12 to resign from the committee, pleading his preoccupation with the forthcoming provincial council in Milwaukee, the great distance to Baltimore, and the little that he could contribute. "Hence Your Grace will allow me to tender to the Board my resignation through you as the President of the Board, requesting most respectfully hereby Your Grace to explain to all in the meeting my reasons for doing so." [45] Heiss reiterated his decision in a letter about two weeks later, saying, "Your Grace will allow me to repeat what I said in my forgoing letter; it is for me a great difficulty to attend the meetings of the Board, and to be a member of the Board without complying with my duties punctually, I am really ashamed." [46] The loss of Heiss deprived the university work of the most influential of the leaders of the German Catholics. As we have seen, he was not enthusiastic about a university from the outset, although there is no evidence for believing that his action in the spring of 1886 was for any other reasons than those he assigned.

Among the speculations regarding the university it was only natural that the choice of a rector should play a lead-

---

[44] BCA, 80–S–8, John J. Keane to James Gibbons, Richmond, April 13, 1886.

[45] BCA, 80–S–17/1, Michael Heiss to James Gibbons, Milwaukee, April 17, 1886.

[46] BCA, 80–U–9, Michael Heiss to James Gibbons, Milwaukee, May 5, 1886. Regarding this resignation O'Connell added a postscript to a letter to Gibbons three months later in which he said: "It has been pretty well circulated that Abp. Heiss withdrew from the University and it was made to look ominous." BCA, 81–R–10, D. J. O'Connell to James Gibbons, Rome, August 14, 1886.

ing role. As early as February 27, 1886, the *Catholic Mirror* quoted a New York *Sun* despatch from Washington to the effect that, "it is practically settled that Bishop Spalding, of Peoria, Ill., will be the rector, and it was long ago decided that Dr. Chapelle, pastor of St. Matthew's Church, in this city, should be professor of history." There was little or no information on the subject of Chapelle as a professor of history but there was more reason for the belief that Spalding would be the first rector. Aside from Bishop Becker, who ten years before had written on the need for a Catholic university in the United States and thereby attracted attention to himself as a possible rector, no American bishop seemed so qualified for the post as Spalding. In view of Becker's withdrawal from plans being made and in view, too, of Spalding's early espousal of the cause and his influence in getting the Caldwell gift, his name suggested itself for the leadership of the institution.

The subject of the rectorship arose first at the meeting of the committee in Baltimore on May 12, 1886. The initial business transacted at that meeting was the question of a clear title to the Washington property. A lawyer of the capital, Irving Williamson, had made a trip to Kentucky to interview heirs of the Henry Duley family which had owned the property. Williamson reported that as soon as he had full information about the Duley family in his possession "there will then be nothing in the way of instituting the necessary proceedings to get the outstanding interests, and making the title perfect." [47] Following this detail, a motion was made and carried that the four Arch-

---

[47] ACUA, Minutes of the Meeting of the Board of Trustees, Baltimore, May 12, 1886.

bishops of Baltimore, New York, Philadelphia, and Boston be constituted a committee to choose a rector. Later that day the archbishops reported to the general committee that they had agreed on a rector but that the name would be withheld until the next meeting set for November 17.

The choice of the four archbishops was originally John Lancaster Spalding. However, Spalding refused to accept the post and they then chose John J. Keane, Bishop of Richmond. Keane was at first quite unwilling to assume the responsibility for a task for which he did not feel qualified. Speaking of this meeting at which he was present, the Bishop of Richmond wrote:

The Archbishops of the Board were asked to be a committee to select a Rector. They conferred on the subject during the midday recess. Then the Most Rev. Chairman came to tell me that their choice had fallen on me. I was utterly astonished, for I had always considered it a matter of course that, as the establishment of the University was mainly owing to the eloquent appeal of Bishop Spalding and to the generousity [sic] of his protegee Miss Caldwell, it would naturally be he that would have charge of it. All this I said very emphatically, adding my profound conviction that I was utterly unfit, by education and by inclination to be at the head of a house of study and, still more, to organize a University.

Archbishop Gibbons answered that the committee of Archbishops had first offered the post to Bishop Spalding, and that he had refused it most positively, and that he was as earnest as they in urging that I should accept. This Bishop Spalding himself repeated to me, adding that, for years to come, the post would practically be that of the President of a Seminary, a post which he could in no way be induced to fill. Finally Archbishop Gibbons said that it simply came to this, that I must accept the position or that the whole project must fall through. I answered that the failure of the project was a responsibility which I durst not assume, adding that to me it was a matter of complete indifference where or at what I was to be engaged, if only I were in the line of God's will. My consent, subject of course to the approval of the Holy See, was communicated privately to all the Bishops on the Board, but not announced as a matter of public prudence.[48]

The committee was, of course, not free to divulge the name of the new rector until his appointment had been approved by the Holy See. Since Keane was a resident bishop proper disposition would have to be made as well for his diocese. For this reason it was still many months before the public was informed as to the name of the rector chosen to head the university. At the meeting in May, 1886, the chairman was asked to communicate with the superior general of the Sulpician Fathers with a view to asking that community to assume charge of the discipline of the priest-students of the university.[49] The bishops who had been out over the country collecting money gave an account to the committee of the results of their work. Keane reported a total of $24,780 either paid in or to be paid on demand, the largest item of which was $20,000 from Patrick Quinn of Philadelphia. Spalding reported a total of $91,000 from his efforts, of which $50,000 from Miss Lina Caldwell for a chapel was the largest item. Bishop Marty said he had been unable to collect personally but that from the responses of a circular he had sent out he thought $100,000 could be realized. John Ireland was not at this meeting and, therefore, the fourth member of

[48] ACUA, Keane Memorial, pp. 4–5.
[49] ACUA, Minutes of Meeting, May 12, 1886.

the episcopal committee appointed to collect could not be heard from. Archbishop Williams laid before the committee ten plans for buildings drawn up by various architectural firms and he was authorized to award prizes for these plans of $400 to the first, $300 to the second, and $100 to the third in order of merit. Williams offered to make these prizes his own gift and the committee gratefully accepted his offer. In place of Archbishop Heiss who had resigned, Caspar H. Borgess, Bishop of Detroit, was named a member of the committee.

One of the final items of business at this meeting of May, 1886, was a motion passed unanimously that Archbishop Gibbons submit to the Pope a report of what had thus far been done by the committee in regard to founding the university. On the occasion of Keane's visit to New York the previous winter in the interest of collecting money, Archbishop Corrigan had told him that he felt that there should be a university in New York with the Jesuits in charge.[50] For that reason when the motion about a report to the Holy See was before the Baltimore meeting, Keane insisted that Rome be requested not to give any approbation to another Catholic university in the United States for a period of twenty-five years. Gibbons was puzzled at this request and stated he did not feel such a demand of the Holy See was necessary. However, Keane insisted with the result that the motion as finally framed stated that the Holy See be requested not to give approbation to another university until the next plenary council. The change from twenty-five years to the next plenary council had been suggested by Corrigan himself, a change which Keane ac-

---

[50] ACUA, Keane Memorial, p. 3.

cepted. Regarding the incident, Keane later wrote, "of course, I afterwards explained to Abp. Gibbons in private the reason of my action, at which he was not a little astonished." [51] During the course of the discussion Gibbons had pressed Keane to know why he feared another university but since the Archbishop of New York was present and maintained silence, Keane did not feel free to state that the rival institution had been mentioned for New York by Corrigan himself.

The Boston *Pilot* of May 22, 1886, reported the Baltimore meeting of May 7 and stated that, "it is understood Bishop Spalding, of Peoria, Ill., is to be rector of the university . . ." Details, too, of the building were beginning to be discussed in the press with the *Freeman's Journal* of May 22 carrying a brief story taken from the Baltimore *Sun* to the effect that the buildings would be of the Romanesque Renaissance style, "which is admitted by competent art critics of historic style as affording the best opportunity for harmonizing modern demands with classic forms of brick and cut-stone architecture." These repeated stories in the press did not contribute much to a clarity of view on the part of the reading public, for in a good many cases the editors and news writers were anticipating decisions which the university committee itself had not reached.

The time was nearing when the whole university plan would have to be laid before the Holy See for formal approval. Not much more progress could be made without Rome's approbation of the arrangements. On July 24, 1886, the *Freeman's Journal* reprinted a story of Bernard

---

[51] *Ibid.,* p. 6.

O'Reilly's from Rome which had been published in the New York *Sun* and in which O'Reilly reported that Leo XIII had shown a lively interest in the work of the Third Plenary Council. "This was in a very particular manner the case with the creation of the new Catholic University at Washington, whose progress he watches with a keen interest, which extends itself to every detail." Bishops Ireland and Keane had been chosen as the two representatives of the university committee to lay the plans before the Holy Father, and Keane wrote Gibbons asking him to set the next meeting of the committee for October 20, "and we will sail the Saturday following." [52] In the meanwhile Keane continued his travels in an attempt to secure more money for the enterprise and to inspect university and seminary buildings. He was in Boston in late July [53] and then went on to visit Montreal and Quebec. He informed Gibbons from Lake George in early August after his return from Canada:

I will now, in compliance with your Eminence's wish, make all preparations for starting to Rome with Bishop Ireland on the following Saturday (following the committee meeting). A very important matter will be the preparation of the statement of our business & our requests, to be presented by us to the Holy See, & to be signed at our next meeting by your Eminence and the other Prelates of the Board of Trustees. If you desire it, I would try to prepare the document & have it ready for the meeting.[54]

---

[52] BCA, 81–P–1, John J. Keane to James Gibbons, Fortress Monroe, July 25, 1886.

[53] Boston Diocesan Archives, Archbishop Williams' Episcopal Register, July 29, 1886.

[54] BCA, 81–Q–14, John J. Keane to James Gibbons, Lake George, August 6, 1886.

Some confusion took place concerning the exact date of the next meeting since Keane and Ireland were trying to arrange a date which would best fit into their plans for sailing for Europe. Keane asked the Cardinal of Baltimore at Ireland's request to make the meeting as late in October as possible, and he continued:

My recent trip to Harvard and Laval Universities, & Boston & Montreal Seminaries, & my conferences with all the long-headed clerics & laics whom I could find, capable of giving advice on the University question, have considerably modified my views as to the best plan of organization.[55]

If Bishop Keane knew little or nothing about a university at the time of his appointment as rector, and we have his own word that this was the case, he must be given credit for approaching the difficult assignment in an intelligent manner and for showing himself so open-minded about suggestions from those who had been trained in the university tradition. A good part of the next two years would find him inspecting universities in America and Europe and taking counsel with university administrators whenever the opportunity presented itself.

At the request of Keane and Ireland, therefore, Cardinal Gibbons changed the date of the meeting from October 20 to October 27 and notified John Farley to send out the notices to the members for the latter date.[56] While the plans for the Washington university were progressing the Bishop of Rochester was in no way won over to what

---

[55] BCA, 81–R–9, John J. Keane to James Gibbons, Fortress Monroe, August 12, 1886.

[56] NYAA, 14, James Gibbons to John M. Farley, The Stockton, Cape May, August 17, 1886.

seemed to him its grandiose ambitions. He was at this time
making preparations for his diocesan seminary and he had
already sent several priests abroad to be trained for its
faculty. In reporting to the diocese on the year 1885 he
wrote his customary pastoral letter in which he made reference to the university.

The Baltimore Council takes another step in advance,
and proposes to establish a principal, or higher seminary
for theological studies. This proposed seminary is sometimes
spoken of as a University. As the funds for its founding and
maintenance are to come from the wealthy Catholics of the
country, our interest is comparatively small. We wish it
and its work all success. The formation of such a higher
seminary is in harmony with the church's action in the
educating of candidates for the Sanctuary.[57]

McQuaid's interest was not, however, so slight as to cause
him to refrain from setting down his ideas on the Washington university in the form of a memorial which, he informed Archbishop Corrigan, he was having translated and
would then send to him for his perusal.[58] Although the
letter does not specifically say so, it is safe to presume that
the memorial was intended for the officials of the Holy See.
Some ten days before McQuaid wrote the Archbishop of
New York, the Cardinal Prefect of Propaganda, Simeoni,
had addressed the latter saying a responsible person had
told him that regarding the university there was not among
the hierarchy "uniformità di vedute," and that the committee itself "opinano diversamente." Simeoni would, there-

---

[57] RDA, Pastoral Letter of Bernard J. McQuaid, August 20, 1886.
[58] NYAA, C–16, Bernard J. McQuaid to M. A. Corrigan, Rochester, September 23, 1886.

fore, appreciate Corrigan's candid opinion in the matter.[59] That Rome was curious to know the views of the American hierarchy on the question was, indeed, true, for the same week in which Simeoni wrote Corrigan the rector of the American College addressed Gibbons saying:

I dropped Bp. Keane a note today about the University. He had better come well fortified with letters showing the "opinions of the Bishops." Everything moves on very pleasantly and the future promises well. The rumor is now filling us that Spalding is to be Bishop of Washington.[60]

And the last week in September the Archbishop of New York told McQuaid, "I have received this afternoon a letter from Propaganda, a letter asking in the most *confidential manner* my opinion on the University." [61] Doubtless this was the letter Simeoni had written Corrigan two weeks before.

In these months of 1886 during which those interested in the university were exerting considerable effort to gather a substantial endowment for the undertaking, they had to contend with discouragement from certain quarters. If one may trust the *Catholic Mirror*—although its reporting on the university was frequently inaccurate—the East was supporting the project better than the West at this time. In its issue of September 4, 1886, it stated that the Caldwell gift had been about doubled since the previous November. The *Mirror* went on to say:

---

[59] NYAA, I–41, Giovanni Simeoni to M. A. Corrigan, Rome, September 11, 1886.

[60] BCA, 81–V–3, D. J. O'Connell to James Gibbons, Rome, September 17, 1886.

[61] RDA, M. A. Corrigan to Bernard J. McQuaid, New York, September 25, 1886.

It appears that the East has been quite generous, while the West is yet somewhat apathetic toward the project. The prelates deny the reports to the effect that Western bishops are dissatisfied with the proposed location of the university, and that they do not like so many Eastern men in the board of trustees, still it is evident that there is not so much enthusiasm as there might be west of the Mississippi river. Of all the States, Ohio has contributed the least. The reason assigned is that Catholics out there, with the remembrance of Archbishop Purcell's failure fresh in their minds, cannot muster up a great deal of confidence in any costly project directed by ecclesiastics. The collectors have found the Ohio people thoroughly apathetic to their appeals, and have not collected enough money there to pay traveling and other personal expenses. Illinois has not done much better, although the one Diocese of Peoria has contributed freely, owing to the prominent place taken by its bishop (Spalding) in the movement. Indiana has done little better, and the far Western States have done nothing to speak of. New York leads in contributions.

And yet there were encouraging aspects to the dreary task of collecting money. For example, Mr. John Sweetman of Currie, Minnesota, wrote to Cardinal Gibbons to offer $500 toward the endowment of a Brownson chair of philosophy in the university. In thanking him for his generous offer the cardinal said, "I regard the proposition to establish and endow a Brownson Chair in the new University as a most admirable one, and know of no way in which the memory of the illustrious Dr. Brownson could be more fittingly honored." [62] Responses of many small donors of this kind gave the bishops courage to go on with the work.

The correspondence between Rome and America on the

[62] BCA, Letterbook of Archbishop Gibbons, p. 181, James Gibbons to John Sweetman, Baltimore, October 13, 1886.

university question was increasing as time went on. John J. Keane reported to Gibbons that he had a letter from Denis O'Connell which "agrees entirely with your view of the University business." He continued, "I will prepare a second paper for Card. Simeoni & the Propaganda, as he advises, & will send it to Dr. Magnien, to submit to you & have copied like the other." [63] The Archbishop of New York had about the same time completed his report on the university for Simeoni in the preparation of which he used McQuaid's memorial mentioned previously. Corrigan wrote the Bishop of Rochester from St. Dominic's Monastery in Newark:

I stole over here last week to make a short Retreat of a day and also to be away, for a purpose, from New York when a certain Italian Monsignor should arrive.

Yesterday morning my letter regarding the University was mailed to Card. Simeoni. Your memorial was very opportune and very valuable. The line of thought in the letter was this. While the University was very desirable in the abstract, the method employed to effect it was open to grave objection.

I. from the *place* (Washington)
　1) not a large center of population
　2) a corrupt political centre
　3) a Southern city
　4) Title deed imperfect
　5) Another University there already.
　6) Washington a poor site for either medical or legal studies, in any case.

---

[63] BCA, 82–B–9, John J. Keane to James Gibbons, Richmond, October 12, 1886. Alphonse Magnien, S.S., (1837–1902), superior of St. Mary's Seminary, Baltimore, mentioned by Keane, assisted Gibbons in the preparation of documents for the Holy See.

II. from the *personnel*
   a) Professors too expensive, etc.
   b) students not to be had.

III. from the *system* proposed
No regular training, or uniform training in advance; no unity of studies or ideas; impossible in 3 or 4 years to go over the immense field mapped out by the Council or the programme of Committee. These points were all more or less developed, e.g., the first argument was illustrated by a schedule showing a score of cities with larger population, and more Catholic churches than Washington. Then the centres of population, of thrift and of wealth were shown to lie on the Atlantic seaboard, and in the North, etc.

In conclusion two other methods were indicated as less expensive, more feasible, more satisfactory, viz.

1. A Religious Order

2. A Board of Examiners for the whole country, like the London University. This would excite a healthy competition, and lead to the survival of the fittest . . .[64]

We have in this letter of Archbishop Corrigan to Bishop McQuaid a summary of the objections which the two prelates would continue to urge against the university both in Rome and in the United States. Their criticisms of Washington as the location were shared by others, but, in view of the special advantages offered to scholars and research students in the Library of Congress, the Smithsonian Institution, and other centers of scientific effort, Washington was even at that early date a highly desirable place for a university. Others besides the Catholic bishops

[64] RDA, M. A. Corrigan to Bernard J. McQuaid, Newark, October 9, 1886.

realized the advantages of Washington for a university. A year and a half before the opening of the Catholic University of America the former president of Cornell University, Andrew D. White, wrote an article in which he strongly urged the establishment of a national university in the capital city. Speaking of the possibility of finding some millionaire to endow such a university he wrote concerning the city of Washington:

He will find the eight or ten millions it will require, a small price to pay for the glory which it will bring to the nation and to him; he will see that the number of men distinguished in science and literature who live there or go there; the scientific collections streaming into that center from all points in our vast domain; the great national library and the precious special and private libraries accumulating there; the attractiveness, accessibility, beautiful climate, and increasing salubrity of the place; the facilities of every sort for bringing the best thought of the world to bear upon the political center of the nation; that all these constitute an argument than which none can be more cogent for the establishment of a teaching university, in the highest sense of the word, at Washington.[65]

True, Washington was not a large city in comparison to New York or Philadelphia, but there was every prospect that its 200,000 inhabitants would be increased greatly as the years passed. As for its being a southern city, while a large number of southerners made Washington their home and the town did have a good deal of a southern tone, by the days of the first administration of Grover Cleveland and that of Benjamin Harrison southerners could hardly

---

[65] Andrew D. White, "The Next American University," in *The Forum*, V (June, 1888), 373–374.

be said to dominate the city. Geographically it might seem the South to a New Yorker but as the national capital, as Spalding once said, it was neither southern nor northern. The flaw in the title to the property was a minor matter and was settled without great difficulty, and as for there being another university in Washington, the Jesuit Fathers at Georgetown were concentrating on their undergraduate college and the professional schools and they gave at this time no evidence of widening the scope of their university to include graduate work. Archbishop Corrigan's objection to the personnel on the score of the salaries for the professors being too high could hardly be regarded seriously, for as yet only a rough estimate of salary scales had been made within the committee. Likewise it was too soon to say that students were "not to be had," for no effort had as yet been made to enlist a student body. As for Corrigan's criticisms of the system proposed for the university, it is true no plan of studies had been worked out. In this the Archbishop of New York had a real point. The absence of any concrete, even if tentative, plan of studies was a weakness. Of course, this could not be done in a definitive way until the Holy See had given its approval to the university itself and until the program of studies for the school of theology had been drawn up in consultation with Rome, and that was the only school intended by the committee at first. But the total absence of any plan of studies did give a certain cogency to this part of Corrigan's memorial. In the suggestion of an alternative by the Archbishop of New York one is reminded of his statement to Bishop Keane the previous winter that he hoped for a university in New York under the Jesuits. But the bishops of the committee were of the mind from the outset that it would be preferable to have the university under the administration of the hierarchy and when the first formal approach was made to the Holy See this point was specified. In reading the second alternative offered by Corrigan, namely, of constituting an examining university rather than a teaching institution one wonders if the suggestion of such made to him by Bernard O'Reilly some months previously had not made an impression on the archbishop's mind.

By October, 1886, plans were being made for the meeting of the university committee at which the letters to the Pope and to the Propaganda would be finally approved. It was decided to combine the business of the university with that of the problem of the secret societies in a two-day meeting at Baltimore, although Cardinal Gibbons wrote Archbishop Corrigan, "I am afraid we will hardly be able to get through our work on the University & the Societies in two days." [66] A week before the meeting Denis O'Connell wrote Gibbons from Rome, telling him that in an audience granted Bernard O'Reilly a short time before, Pope Leo XIII "suggested that he give the proceeds of one of his works towards the Cath. University of America." [67] Keane was winding up his affairs in Richmond and on October 25 he confided to the episcopal diary:

After finishing the visitation of the Diocese, I start for Rome, with Bp. Ireland of St. Paul, to lay the business of the proposed Catholic University before the Holy Father. I leave the finances of the Diocese in a very satisfactory condition as the "Balance Sheet" for 1886 shows. Very

[66] NYAA, C–15, James Gibbons to M. A. Corrigan, Baltimore, October 18, 1886.

[67] BCA, 82–C–10, D. J. O'Connell to James Gibbons, Grottaferrata, October 22, 1886.

Rev. A. Van De Vyver, V.G. is administrator & attorney during my absence.[68]

Bishop Borgess of Detroit, newly elected to the university committee, sent word to Gibbons on October 26 that through a misunderstanding he had been told by Bishop Marty the meeting would be on November 17, "but at 9:45 this morning a telegram is handed me, stating, that the meeting takes place tomorrow at eleven o'clock A.M. I am sorry, that this mistake makes it impossible to attend the meeting." [69]

The fourth meeting of the committee convened on October 27 at the cardinal's residence in Baltimore. A few corrections were made in the minutes of the former meeting as read, among them that the $50,000 promised by Miss Lina Caldwell was not an absolute promise but a sum that might reasonably be hoped for. There then followed the reading of the two letters which had been composed by Bishop Keane, one addressed to the Pope and the other to Cardinal Simeoni. Some slight objection was raised by Archbishop Corrigan as to the form of the letters whereupon he was requested to revise them and put them in a better style which he agreed to do.[70] Following the modifications suggested by Corrigan, all the members of the committee present signed the documents. Since the Archbishops of St. Louis, Chicago, Cincinnati, New Orleans, and Santa Fe were in Baltimore for the meeting on the secret societies they were asked to add their signatures to

[68] Archives of the Diocese of Richmond, Bishops' Diary, October 25, 1886, p. 147.

[69] BCA, 82–D–1, Caspar H. Borgess to James Gibbons, Detroit, October 26, 1886.

[70] Keane Memorial, p. 6.

the Roman letters, although they were not members of the university committee, and this the metropolitans did in order to give the petition more weight.

Bishop Keane, along with the Bishop of St. Paul, was commissioned to carry the letters to Rome. Cardinal Gibbons asked what Keane proposed to do on his visit to Europe to which the Bishop of Richmond replied that he hoped first to obtain the Holy Father's consent to their undertaking and then to visit some of the universities of Europe to acquaint himself with problems of administration and programs of study. Likewise he hoped to make inquiries concerning suitable professors to fill the chairs in the new university. Keane stated to the committee that there was not enough enthusiasm among the clergy of the United States for the university and he hoped upon his return to remedy this by arranging to speak in its behalf before clerical conferences and retreats; for a similar reason he hoped to visit the seminaries of the country in an effort to arouse interest among the students and to enkindle in their minds a desire to be among the first students of the university. The committee agreed that nothing should be said publicly concerning Keane's rectorship until the Holy See had formally approved his selection.[71]

The letters to Pope Leo XIII and to Cardinal Simeoni, both bearing the date of October 27, 1886, are important documents in the evolution of the university. The American

---

[71] ACUA, Minutes of the Meeting of the Board of Trustees, Baltimore, October 27, 1886. Under October 27, 1886, Gibbons wrote in his diary: "The University Board met. Bps. Keane & Ireland were commissioned to go to Rome—present letters to the H. Father & the Propaganda praying for a sanction & blessing in the work." BCA, Cardinal Gibbons' Diary, p. 211.

bishops complimented the Pope for the emphasis of his pontificate on the richness of supernatural truth and, they remarked, "to this is added the encouragement through which Your Holiness has aroused the minds of all to a deeper and more thorough research into sacred studies and those subjects connected with them." With that consideration in mind the bishops in the Third Plenary Council gave major attention to Catholic education "in all its degrees." While they were solicitous in the council about primary and intermediate education, the bishops told the Pope they felt they would not be conforming themselves to the desires of His Holiness had they not made provision for higher education as well. In the United States conditions were such that the protection of souls against error could be afforded best by a more thorough research into truth "both revealed and natural." The instruction given in the schools, colleges, and even in the ordinary seminaries was not sufficient. Prompted by this need as well as encouraged by a private benefaction for the beginning of such an institution, the fathers of the council, therefore, decreed the beginning of a principal seminary, "ad Universitatis instar," to which would later be added the other faculties. And this decree, along with the others of the council, the Pope had already acknowledged. To establish this institution the council had appointed a committee of bishops with whom had been associated priests and laymen. Its hopes were not in vain, for the prelates had learned that a sum of money could be collected which would endow the theological faculty *in perpetuum.* But the bishops would wish His Holiness to know that they did not contemplate proceeding further with the project until they had the full approval of the Holy See. To clarify the issue they, therefore, would list certain explanations of their plan and ask the Pope to approve them.

Among these major points of the bishops' letter were the following: the university should always remain under the complete direction of the hierarchy and never be entrusted to a religious order. Nonetheless, they would wish to have it understood that distinguished professors from among the religious orders, as well as the diocesan clergy, would be invited to do the teaching in the sacred sciences. In order to maintain a proper ecclesiastical spirit among the students of the university, the bishops of the committee were unanimous in desiring to entrust the discipline of the students to the priests of St. Sulpice. Further, after due consideration they had determined that this first Catholic university of the United States should be located in Washington which as the national capital was the center of the political and intellectual forces of the entire nation; Washington had as well growing facilities and resources for education, and its healthful climate attracted many people already distinguished in culture. Although in the future other universities would be founded elsewhere, there was little doubt that the university erected in the very center of the nation would always hold the primacy. Moreover, the bishops begged the Pope that no one be allowed to begin another pontifical university until the next plenary council should be called so that the minds and resources of the faithful might not be distracted from this initial undertaking by the foundation of several universities. Since experience warned that their efforts might be vague and uncertain without a rector for the university who would have in hand the tasks of arousing enthusiasm among the faithful, collecting money, securing professors, and performing other work under the general direction of the committee, the prelates, therefore, had selected John J. Keane, Bishop of Richmond, as first rector. Bishop Keane was happy in his present position but he was willing to do this work if the Holy See would deign to approve the choice. The bishops for that reason requested the Holy Father to free Keane from his diocese so that he could devote his entire time to the university. They mentioned that since "it seems to be highly desirable and in the opinion of the people wholly necessary that the Rector be distinguished by the dignity of the Episcopacy," they had selected a bishop for the position. The committee wished to make it very clear to the Pope that in the founding of a university they intended to detract in no way from the honor or usefulness of the American College in Rome. They would endeavor at all times to maintain there a chosen number of students who would draw from the apostolic source itself their sacred studies and their spirit. The resources of the United States would undoubtedly suffice for the future prosperity of both institutions. Finally, in order that the points related in the present letter might be made clearer to His Holiness the committee was sending two of its members to Rome.[72]

The letter of the bishops of the university committee to Cardinal Simeoni followed in the main the outline of that to Pope Leo XIII. After stating the need for a Catholic university in the United States, as they had done for the Pope, the writers added to Simeoni that such a university would obviate the difficulty of Catholics sending their children to non-Catholic universities where there was great danger to their faith. In explaining that money was

---

[72] BCA, 82–D–3, Letter of the bishops of the university committee to Pope Leo XIII, Baltimore, October 27, 1886.

already at hand or could easily be secured for permanently endowing the faculty of theology, the bishops told the cardinal that "only the wealthier of the faithful need be invited to found the University," while the resources of others could be left for the building and support of parochial schools. Regarding the site and its purchase, the bishops left the matter open for change since, they remarked, the question of location of the university was secondary, "and so could be solved in another way if the need and the advantages otherwise demanded, without endangering the principal question of the foundation of the University itself." The question of a rector was stated much as it had been in the letter to the Pope, but to Simeoni the bishops expressed themselves in a slightly different way. "Since indeed, according to the common opinion concerning the magnitude of the work, hardly any priest would meet the requirements, even if otherwise suitable, the Committee thought that, at least for the present, the Rector should be a Bishop." The request that no other university be approved until the next plenary council was repeated to Simeoni. The bishops closed their letter to the Cardinal Prefect of Propaganda by asking for the necessary faculties for the *seminarium principale* with the ordinary privileges of universities, and they stated that if these requests were granted they would see to it that the special rules for the university would be made at the proper time and submitted to the supreme judgment of the Holy See.[73]

The *Church News,* a Catholic weekly paper of Washington, carried in one of its first issues an account of the meet-

---

[73] BCA, 82–D–5, Letter of the bishops of the university committee to Cardinal Simeoni, Baltimore, October 27, 1886.

ing of the university committee in Baltimore, remarking
that nearly a million dollars had been collected and that
Archbishop Williams and Bishop Keane had been authorized to make contracts for the erection of the building
which would begin next spring.[74] The Boston *Pilot* had a
similar story in its issue of November 6. The *Freeman's
Journal* of the same date carried an editorial on "The
Proposed Catholic University," which contained little or
no editorial comment but simply summarized the news
previously printed on the meeting of October 27, and
added that Bishop Ireland and Keane had sailed from
New York on the *Aurania* on October 30 to lay the university question before the Holy See. The *Catholic Mirror*
of November 6 published a long editorial on the results of
the meeting ten days before. They were more cautious
about the amount of money in hand, saying "it is impossible to state the exact amount of money that can be
depended upon, but it ranges close upon a million." The
Mirror felt this sum had justified the hopes of the bishops
in the generosity of wealthy Catholics and that the five
million dollars necessary for the undertaking in its full
character could be raised. To the critics who were urging
that the elementary Catholic schools should be given first
consideration, the editorial writer of the *Mirror* replied:

In view of the fact that some hostility to the project has
been exhibited, on the ground that elementary education
should first be provided for, a short consideration of the
university's functions may not be out of place. Of course,
elementary education—the parish school—is the first thing
to be considered; but, as we shall presently show, the university will not interfere in any manner with the growth of

[74] *Church News,* October 31, 1886.

the parochial school, but will certainly contribute greatly to its extension.

The writer then proceeded to develop the argument that one of the most certain guarantees for sound instruction in the elementary and secondary schools was the presence out over the nation of a group of university-trained Catholic educators. "Such a class of Catholics we do not at present possess, howsoever great may be individual learning."

When Bishops Ireland and Keane sailed on the *Aurania* on October 30, 1886, for Rome to lay the entire university question before the Holy See and to secure its approval, the scene of the activities shifted and during the ensuing weeks the committee in the United States awaited the outcome of the Roman conversations.

IV

The Roman Negotiations

THE INCEPTION of the university project was contemporary with the emergence of the American Church upon one of its most critical periods. A number of problems, some arising from without the fold and others springing from the very composition of the American Catholic body, were coming to engage in a serious and often an acrimonious manner the attention of thoughtful Catholics. Few of these questions were connected in any vital way with the university problem, but through circumstances or design a number of them were ultimately resolved into an alignment of issues and personalities that rendered unpleasant the final stage of the institution's establishment, and some endured to plague the harmony of its nascent years.

At the very time of the arrival of John J. Keane and John Ireland in Rome in early November, 1886, a number of these problems had reached an acute stage in their development. The mounting immigration from southern and eastern Europe in the 1880's rose steadily during the decade, bringing hundreds of thousands of new Catholics to American shores. The Catholic population, estimated at about six and a quarter millions in 1880, reached close to nine millions by 1890.[1] This large increase among the foreign-born Catholics aroused the latent suspicion and dislike of many native-born American Protestants. Since the Civil War the United States had been happily free from any organized nativist movements against the Catholic Church. But as one historian of immigration expressed it, "Nativism is a hardy perennial, and the storms of the Civil War and Reconstruction did no more than sear its leaves." [2] The result was that in 1887 there was founded in Clinton, Iowa, by Henry F. Bowers, the American Protective Association, familiarly known as the A.P.A. Confined at first to the Middle West, its growth was slow, but with the economic havoc wrought by the panic of 1893 the membership and the propaganda against the Catholics increased in volume.[3] The new nativists thought they had found in the foreign-born Catholics a scapegoat for the economic ills from which the nation was suffering in the early 1890's.

Closely related to the startling growth of foreign-born Catholics in the United States and the unfriendly reactions

---

[1] Gerald Shaughnessy, *Has the Immigrant Kept the Faith?* pp. 161, 166.

[2] Carl Wittke, *We Who Built America. The Saga of the Immigrant* (New York, 1939), p. 498.

[3] There is no satisfactory history of the A.P.A. A popular work by a Catholic journalist is Humphrey J. Desmond, *The A.P.A. Movement* (Washington, 1921). An unpublished doctoral dissertation done at Harvard covers this movement, Alvin Packer Stauffer, "Anti-Catholicism in American Politics, 1865–1900," Widener Library, Harvard University, 1933. Cf. also Gustavus Myers, *History of Bigotry in the United States* (New York, 1943), pp. 219–247.

against them, was the increase in these years of the secret
societies. The Church had repeatedly stated in forceful
terms its opposition to societies which embodied in their
rules a religious rite and a pledge of secrecy of their members, and which denied to legitimate authority the right
to question them as to their purposes. From the time of
Pope Clement XII and his condemnation of the Free
Masons in 1738 the Church had often reiterated her position on these societies. Among the most recent pronouncements of the Holy See were the encyclicals of Pope Leo
XIII, the *Etsi nos* of February, 1882, and the *Humanum
genus* of April, 1884. When the American hierarchy met
in Baltimore for the Third Plenary Council they devoted
a lengthy decree to these secret societies,[4] and the pastoral
letter at the close of the council carried a full explanation
of the Church's reasons for opposing them. "One of the
most striking characteristics of our times is the universal
tendency to band together in societies for the promotion of
all sorts of purposes." [5] The bishops were careful to distinguish between legitimate social organizations which were
but "the natural outgrowth of an age of popular rights and
representative institutions," and those whose purposes were
kept secret. The crux of the Church's stand was expressed
in these words:

. . . if any society's obligation be such as to bind its members to secrecy, even when rightly questioned by competent
authority, then such a society puts itself outside the limits
of approval; and no one can be a member of it and at the

---

[4] *Acta et Decreta* (1886 edition), pp. 137–144.
[5] Peter Guilday, *National Pastorals of the American Hierarchy
(1792–1919)*, p. 256.

same time be admitted to the sacraments of the Catholic Church.[6]

These were years, too, when giant strides were being made in the industrialization of America. There naturally followed upon the advent of "big business" a widening rift between the forces of capital and labor. The laboring classes found themselves victimized by the powerful monopolistic interests and, in an effort to protect themselves, they sought a remedy through organization. It was that motive which led to the founding of the Knights of Labor in 1869. The Knights at first grew but slowly. However, the 1880's witnessed a phenomenal increase and by 1886 their numbers were estimated at between 600,000 and 700,000 members. To avoid persecution by employers, the Knights of Labor at first maintained complete secrecy regarding their affairs. This, of course, heightened suspicion of them in many quarters and a number of the bishops were highly critical of Catholic workingmen holding membership in the organization. However, in September, 1879, Terence V. Powderly was chosen Grand Master Workman and with their growing strength the Knights threw off the cloak of complete secrecy. Thousands of Catholic workingmen held membership in the society and as the debate concerning the organization's true character grew more intense Powderly, a Catholic, was asked by Cardinal Gibbons to give an explanation of the Knights' aims and purposes. The subject of the secret societies, and the Knights of Labor in particular, was on the agenda for the meeting of the archbishops who had been constituted a special committee to study the question preparatory to the assembly scheduled in Baltimore for late

---

[6] *Ibid.,* p. 259.

October, 1886. The final decision in this matter, as in others, was not made until it had been referred to the Holy See.[7]

Stirred by the evils of the industrialism which were becoming more and more apparent, an American reformer by the name of Henry George (1839–1897) published a book in 1879 entitled *Progress and Poverty*. It was a severe indictment of working conditions in the factories of the capitalist system as a whole, although George did not advocate the overthrow of the system, as did some of his more extreme contemporaries. He maintained that every man had a right to land as he had to air and water, and therefore, a system which denied him this right was undemocratic. George urged a tax on land so adjusted as to take away the "unearned increment" as he called it. From this nucleus there grew the so-called single tax movement. One of George's most articulate followers was Father Edward McGlynn, pastor of St. Stephen's Church in New York City. McGlynn's advocacy of the George reforms attracted the attention of the Congregation of the Propaganda and in 1882 Cardinal Simeoni questioned McGlynn's superior, Cardinal McCloskey, concerning the priest's views on land. A number of these movements found a focal point in the

---

[7] The question of the Church and the secret societies still awaits definitive treatment. Allen Sinclair Will, *Life of Cardinal Gibbons* (New York, 1922), I, 268–276, 320–360, discusses the subject as does Frederick J. Zwierlein, *The Life and Letters of Bishop McQuaid* (Rochester, 1926), II, 378–474. A master's dissertation is in progress at the Catholic University of America on "The Catholic Church and the Secret Societies in the United States," by Fergus Macdonald, C.P.; likewise a master's dissertation has recently been completed at the University by Henry J. Browne on the subject of "Terence V. Powderly. His Relations to the Catholic Church, 1879–1888."

mayoralty election in New York City in the fall of 1886 when Henry George was a candidate. The campaign was one of the most spectacular in years. Powderly addressed a mass meeting in behalf of George's candidacy and Father McGlynn, against the better judgment of Archbishop Corrigan, also participated actively in behalf of George. Although George lost the election to Abram S. Hewitt, candidate of Tammany Hall and the reform Democrats, the incident served to intensify class feeling and there followed, insofar as it concerned the Church, a suspension of McGlynn from his priestly functions and a summons for him to come to Rome.[8]

In addition to these questions which pressed for solution on the part of the American churchmen, there was the growing agitation of the German Catholics in the United States for a stronger guarantee against the loss of their national language and customs. At the very time that Ireland and Keane arrived in Rome the question of the German Catholics of America had been brought sharply into view at the Holy See by the report submitted to the Congregation of the Propaganda by the Reverend P. M. Abbelen, vicar general of the Archdiocese of Milwaukee. Father Abbelen was at the time the leader of the movement which later came to be called Cahenslyism. It was sufficiently serious to warrant a meeting of the Archbishops of Baltimore, New York, Philadelphia, and Boston in Philadelphia in December, 1886, when the four eastern metropolitans drew up plans to counteract this divisive

---

[8] *Dictionary of American Biography*, XII, 53–54. The story of Father McGlynn likewise remains to be told from documentary sources. Stephen Bell's *Rebel Priest and Prophet. A Biography of Edward McGlynn* (New York, 1937) is not a definitive work.

force within the Catholic Church of the United States. The archbishops transmitted an account of their meeting to Ireland and Keane and asked them to act as their representatives before the Holy See.[9]

These acute problems, which seemed to converge in the late 1880's, brought at times a severe strain within the ranks of the American hierarchy itself. On the matter of the secret societies there was general agreement among the bishops that organizations which persisted in maintaining strict secrecy as to their aims should be condemned. But the difficulty was to determine just which organizations were secret and what were the purposes of the various societies. Some of the bishops were inclined to forthright condemnation while others felt the whole subject should be approached with great caution. On the Knights of Labor particularly, men like Gibbons feared for the cause of the Church among the working class if a hasty condemnation were issued, while Kenrick of St. Louis regarded the Knights as worthy of rebuke. All the bishops sympathized with Archbishop Corrigan in the difficulty which he had to meet in the case of McGlynn, but differences arose among them as to whether or not the book of Henry George, *Progress and Poverty*, should be denounced to the Congregation of the Index for condemnation. In the German question virtually all the non-German members of the hierarchy were opposed to the movement sponsored by Abbelen, but, as was natural, the German bishops gave

---

[9] Will, *op. cit.*, I, 517–521. On the German question cf. John J. Meng, "Cahenslyism: The First Phase, 1883–1891," in *Catholic Historical Review*, XXXI (Jan. 1946), 389–413. A sequel to this article which will carry the movement into the twentieth century will appear in the *Catholic Historical Review* later in the year 1946.

sympathy and support to its claims. The over-all result was a series of deep differences between the American bishops on the method of handling these questions, differences which carried over into the 1890's and appeared in the Americanism quarrel and the school controversy of those years.[10] In all this the fate of the university was involved and it is not surprising to find that its enthusiastic friends were more than once countered in Rome and in America by bishops who disagreed with men like Keane, Ireland, and Spalding on these other disputed questions before the Church. The mission of Keane and Ireland to Rome, therefore, in the autumn of 1886 had a broader significance than the interest of the university, although that was the ostensible and principal reason for their journey. During the long and tedious negotiations which ensued the university question was more than once interrupted by the pressure of other business.

While Keane and Ireland were still on the high seas bound for Rome the Archbishop of New York, in a communication which has not been found, had apparently called Cardinal Gibbons' attention to the fact that the plan for a university had not been recommended in Rome at the time the archbishops were there in 1883 to make arrangements for the council. Gibbons was under the impression that it had been in the original schema and when informed of his mistake he wrote to Corrigan:

I must hasten to confess my error when I stated that the

---

[10] For a recent brief treatment of these problems and the attitudes of the various bishops, cf. Thomas T. McAvoy, "Americanism, Fact and Fiction," in *Catholic Historical Review,* XXXI (July, 1945), 133–153.

Principale Seminarium was recommended in Rome, & that reference was made to it in the original Roman schema. Whilst I feel bound to labor for this work as emanating from the Council, I must confess that my zeal for the undertaking was stimulated by the strong impression resting on my mind that it had originated with the Holy See & that it recommended [it] to us in Rome.

My stomach is not in working order, & disturbs my hand.[11]

There is little doubt but that in the development of the university question up to this time the Archbishop of Baltimore had shown hardly more than passive interest. This hesitancy on Gibbons' part was not extraordinary since he displayed the same attitude toward other questions until such time as sentiment had crystallized and begun to take a definite course. His reluctance to take a more decided stand on the university became the source of embarrassment to Keane in Rome, and it was only after the official approval of the Holy See in the spring of 1887 that the cardinal gave the undertaking his wholehearted backing. From that time on his support of the university was unquestioned.

The Bishops of Richmond and St. Paul were not long in Rome before they began to be confronted with arguments in opposition to the university. These views, as we shall see, came from the United States and it was only prudent that the Roman officials should present them to Keane and Ireland so that the entire question might be thoroughly investigated before the Holy See gave its judgment. In order to systematize their case, the two bishops prepared a document for the information of the Propaganda which they

---

[11] New York Archdiocesan Archives, C–15, James Gibbons to M. A. Corrigan, Baltimore, November 4, 1886.

entitled, "Animadversiones Quaedam de Universitate in America Fundanda." Therein they took up point by point the principal objections raised. To the question of whether there was sufficient money available for the foundation, Ireland and Keane answered that while it was not all in hand it was certain from inquiries which had been made that the necessary funds would be provided. Since, as they said, a rumor had reached the bishops that the Holy See had a certain hesitation about approving the plan, they had not wished to accept any money until Rome's approval of the undertaking was granted. Once they had the approbation of the Holy See there was little doubt that within two years the total sum necessary would be collected. To the question how a sum large enough for the beginning of a university could be raised so quickly, the bishops replied that if a complete university were intended now that would, indeed, be impossible. But, following the mind of the Third Plenary Council, the theology faculty alone was contemplated at the outset and for that, they estimated, $650,000 would be needed. The university committee had already $500,000 in hand or in "scriptis authenticis." Therefore, only $150,000 remained to be collected which could undoubtedly be done within a year after papal approval of the university.

To the objection that the project presupposed a sufficient number of provincial seminaries already existing, the bishops answered that such was the case, for all the nine provinces of the United States east of the Mississippi River had at least one seminary, and in some cases two or three, apart from the novitiates of religious orders. True, the area west of the Mississippi had shown less progress in regard to erecting seminaries, but Keane and Ireland stated that they did not feel the project for a university, which was so necessary, should be delayed until every section of the immense territory of the United States was provided with ordinary seminaries. To the question of whether or not the American College in Rome might not serve the purposes intended by the university, the bishops reiterated their intention to support that institution, but just as other parts of the Christian world maintained colleges in Rome and at the same time had universities in their own countries, so there seemed no reason why the Church of the United States should not do the same. In regard to any question raised about the unanimity of the American bishops in this matter of the university, it was considered impressive by Ireland and Keane that the entire membership of the committee, along with all the other archbishops gathered for other business, should have assented so unanimously. As for the lack of unanimity on the location of the university, there were, it was true, varying opinions, but all finally agreed with the opinion expressed by the Archbishop of Boston that in the future there would be other universities in so vast a country, but that the first and at present the only university, should be located in the capital of the nation. As it appeared in the petition, all the members of the committee subscribed to this view.

Since this matter of a site was the chief difficulty which had so far arisen, Bishops Keane and Ireland took the pains to outline in detail the reasons for locating it in Washington. In any other city the university would be a local institution while in Washington it would be national. While other cities had larger populations and greater commercial activity, Washington was the center of the "moral and spiritual forces" of the whole nation. Moreover, Washington offered fewer inducements to vice than other cities, and it was the mind of the bishops that those students who would come from a distance should be kept under a salutary discipline. No student would be permitted to live outside the university unless at the special request of his bishop, and when the time came for lay students they, too, would have to live at the university unless they were able to live at home with their parents or relatives. When the gift of $300,000 was given it was stipulated that no change of location should be made without the donor's consent and if a change were made now the entire gift would undoubtedly be lost. Furthermore, almost the entire country saw in the choice of Washington a proof of the harmony which Catholics profess as existing between Church and State, and now to withdraw from the decision would be to give the enemies of the Church an argument against the American Catholics.

In answer to the question why the bishops requested no other university to be founded until the next plenary council, Keane and Ireland answered that they had heard from many French clergymen that the condition of the French Catholic universities was weak and uncertain, due not only to the hostility of the government, but as well to the fact that they tried to found several universities at the same time. In America there was evidence of this happening in the case of institutions of lesser rank than universities and for that reason, too, they requested that there be only one university for the time being. The more immediate reason for the request of the bishops was, of course, the threat of another Catholic university in New York. In the meeting of the university committee of May, 1886, it was first thought wise to ask the Holy See to withhold approbation from any other university for twenty-five years, but at the suggestion of the Archbishop of New York the time limit was changed to the next plenary council, a decision in which all of the committee agreed. The privilege of being the only Catholic university in the United States was, therefore, requested only for a short time and not forever. In answer to the objection that the university would be detrimental to other institutions of learning already existing, Keane and Ireland said this could hardly be the case since the course of studies to be offered in the university would be for those who had already completed their training in other seminaries. In the course of time other faculties besides that of theology would be added, but in that case care would be taken that such faculties might not prove a detriment to any other school but rather a help to them all.

In regard to the report which they heard in Rome to the effect that some of the bishops signed the petition without wishing to favor the undertaking which it proposed, Keane and Ireland stated they wished to reprove and reject with fitting indignation such a shameful charge concerning the honesty and truthfulness of the bishops. They felt they had a right to regard the signatures as given in good faith until such time as anyone wished to accuse himself clearly of having acted in bad faith. In conclusion the two American bishops assured the Roman officials that there had been mature deliberation on all these points before action was taken in America, and they consequently requested the Holy See to give the undertaking its approval. Should any further information be desired they were ready to give it. To offset the danger of a postponement of the entire plan, the bishops stated that they wished

to say with the greatest reverence but with all sincerity
that for the American people, the clergy, and the hierarchy
such a decision might imply that the project had been entirely abandoned and it might result, therefore, in no little
embarrassment to the bishops and scandal to the people.[12]

This lengthy document of the Bishops of St. Paul and
Richmond summarized their defense of the university proposal. They had presented to Cardinal Simeoni soon after
their arrival in Rome the petition of the university committee and Ireland, in his capacity as Bishop of St. Paul,
took the occasion of an audience granted by Leo XIII to
present the committee's letter to the Pope. At the same time
he asked for a joint audience for Keane and himself on
the university question and Leo XIII promised to grant it
soon. The two bishops visited Camillus Cardinal Mazzella
who for over ten years had resided and taught in various
Jesuit houses in the United States. They asked him to tell
them if he thought Georgetown College should be considered an objection against establishing the university in
Washington. The Jesuit cardinal saw no objection on this
score since the two institutions would have an entirely different character.[13] The report concerning the good faith of
the signatories to the petition naturally disturbed Keane and
Ireland very much. They made careful inquiries concerning
the source of this report and were informed "unofficially"
that the Propaganda officials had received the word from
the Archbishop of New York.[14] This information, of course,
had a tendency to confirm the suspicions of the two bishops

---

[12] Baltimore Cathedral Archives, 82–G–6, Animadversiones Quaedam de Universitate in America Fundanda, Rome, December 6, 1886.

[13] Keane Memorial, pp. 6–7.

[14] Ibid., p. 7.

as to the attitude of Archbishop Corrigan in the whole university matter.

After a wait of about six weeks for an audience with the Pope, Ireland and Keane were told by Archbishop Domenico Jacobini, Secretary of the Propaganda from 1882 to 1891, that the university question was to be quietly laid aside until the arrival of Cardinal Gibbons who was coming to Rome for the red hat and that then the matter would be tabled indefinitely. This report aroused the indignation of Ireland and Keane and they went to the Vatican immediately, saw one of the secretaries, and demanded an audience. The following day they saw Pope Leo XIII who received them very kindly, but expressed concern about the Jesuit university already in Washington. The bishops told the Pope of their conversation with Cardinal Mazzella and they suggested that the Holy Father consult him. The Pope made careful inquiries concerning the course of studies, and the age of the students admitted to Georgetown. When Ireland and Keane explained that an alternative to the university in Washington had been offered in the form of a university in New York directed by the Jesuits, the Pope replied with considerable feeling that although he loved and honored the Society of Jesus, the kind of university envisaged must be organized, like the Church, hierarchically.[15] Leo XIII concluded the audience by saying that his mind was not fully made up but he wished the two bishops to remain in Rome until the arrival of Cardinal Gibbons.

Despite the urgency felt by the two Americans in the objective of their mission, Rome was not to be hurried.

---

[15] *Ibid.*, p. 8.

Denis O'Connell writing Bishop McQuaid on December 9 on various matters, said, "The University goes over to January." [16] The day following he wrote Gibbons on the Knights of Labor case and he alluded to the trouble which had arisen regarding the university. "The University meets with the difficulties anticipated and great faith is not given here to the signatures. Ireland had his audience today. He spoke at length on the actual question and he is much pleased with the Holy Father's words." [17] In writing Archbishop Corrigan the same day O'Connell said he presumed he knew all about the university question. He mentioned that the German problem was to the forefront of Ireland's and Keane's attention at the moment and "the Henry George question is pushed back especially as McGlynn is coming." [18] By mid-December the two American bishops in Rome were thoroughly aroused at the opposition the university was meeting; particularly did they feel chagrin at the doubts cast on the sincerity of the signatures to the petition. Apparently they believed that no amount of talking on their part would clear the matter and that only individual letters from the signers could lift the cloud that hung over the university's future. For that reason Ireland and Keane wrote the members of the committee and asked that they reply to them personally.

Since our arrival in Rome, we have done all that we could in furtherance of the petition concerning our pro-

---

[16] Rochester Diocesan Archives, D. J. O'Connell to Bernard J. McQuaid, Rome, December 9, 1886.

[17] BCA, 82–G–9, D. J. O'Connell to James Gibbons, Rome, December 10, 1886.

[18] NYAA, C–13, D. J. O'Connell to M. A. Corrigan, Rome, December 10, 1886.

posed Catholic University, which the representatives of the American Hierarchy signed and commissioned us to lay before the Holy See. But we find that our efforts are paralyzed by an unexpected obstacle of a most painful character. Somebody has whispered that some of the Prelates' signatures do not mean what they say,—in other words, were not given in good faith but deceptively. This is said in the Propaganda, and by the Holy Father himself; it is even asserted among the laity!

The consequences are obvious. Suspicion is cast upon all the signatures; our mission is turned into a farce; and, worst of all, the most shocking discredit is thrown upon the character of our Prelates for truth and honesty.

We have, as in duty bound, repelled the imputation with the indignation it deserves. But we are powerless to remove the wretched impression produced. This can be done only by the declaration of the Prelates individually. We therefore appeal to each of the Prelates who have signed the petition, to send us, and that immediately, such a declaration on the subject as will enable us to silence this calumny.[19]

At the end of the month Keane wrote Gibbons a letter which must have been received with something of a shock by the Archbishop of Baltimore. He repeated the story of the doubtful signatures and asserted that Ireland and himself had denounced it as strongly as they could. Then Keane continued:

. . . but I cannot help recognizing with what crushing force they can say to us: "Why look, even your Cardinal puts his name to statements & recommendations which he will afterwards take back or modify;—if even he can send

---

[19] Boston Diocesan Archives, printed letter of John Ireland and John J. Keane to John J. Williams, Rome, December 14, 1886. Hereafter these archives will be referred to as BDA.

us important documents, not because he believes them best for the interests of the Church, but in order to please this one or that one, what confidence can we repose in any of these signatures? " They do not always say this in full honest words; but they say it quite as gallingly in meaning shrugs, and smiles, and insinuations. Even the Holy Father himself has thus intimated his apprehension that Your Eminence was uncertain & vacillating in your views as to the University's location etc.[20]

Painful as this letter may have been to Gibbons he could not but recognize that it was prompted by the generous impulse of a sincere friend and admirer and that his own hesitancy to commit himself squarely on the issue of the university had helped to make the lot of Keane and Ireland a difficult one in Rome. Since Gibbons himself was soon leaving for Rome he would have an opportunity to rectify his policy.

When the Ireland-Keane circular to the bishops of the university committee reached America it caused something of a stir. The Archbishop of Cincinnati called it "a sensational document," but it would seem he had forgotten that he had affixed his signature to the petition on the previous October 27 in Baltimore, for three months later he told Gibbons that he did not remember distinctly signing a letter on the subject, apart from the signature which he gave to the acts of the council. "Your Eminence no doubt is acquainted with the matter; & if you remember my signing a special letter on the subject, will you be good enough

[20] BCA, 82–J–4, John J. Keane to James Gibbons, Rome, December 29, 1886. Gibbons said no more in his diary about this letter other than to write under date of January 14, 1887: "Wrote to Bp. Keane in reply to his letter from Rome of the 29." BCA, Cardinal Gibbons' Diary, p. 213.

to recall to me the circumstances—& also the substance contained in the letter." [21] Archbishop Ryan of Philadelphia
mentioned hearing of the matter through a letter from
Denis O'Connell, and he told Gibbons, "a Delegate he
thinks will be appointed & they are waiting on [it?] to
consult with your Em." [22] A week later Ryan again referred to the matter in a letter to Gibbons and this time he
was more explicit in stating where he believed the trouble
lay.

This is one of the many annoying effects of referring everything to Rome. When the Holy Father gave a general
sanction to the University, this was, I think, all sufficient
"pro tem." I foresaw & foretold that more than this would
lead to embarrassing postponements. It is the history repeated of the Irish Catholic University. Hence I think a
Delegate might be of advantage if his powers were sufficiently extensive & he be a man who would have at once
the confidence of Rome & of the American Church. [23]

It is difficult to see how the Archbishop of Philadelphia
could believe the university would be able to make progress

---

[21] BCA, 82–J–6, William H. Elder to James Gibbons, Cincinnati,
December 30, 1886. About a week later Elder had refreshed his
memory of the incident and he wrote Gibbons: "I remember now
signing the letter about the University in Your Eminence's room in
October. I have written Bp. Keane that although I did not read it,
& I do not know its details, yet I signed it understandingly as an
expression of my interest in the University, & my confidence in those
who are directing it, & that I adhered to the signature." BCA,
82–L–3, William Henry Elder to James Gibbons, Cincinnati, January
8, 1887.

[22] BCA, 82–K–1, P. J. Ryan to James Gibbons, Philadelphia,
January 2, 1887.

[23] BCA, 82–L–8, P. J. Ryan to James Gibbons, Philadelphia,
January 10, 1887.

on the altogether general approbation given to the idea by Pope Leo XIII in his letter of October 22, 1885, to Gibbons. Something far more explicit by way of papal approval was necessary if plans were to be advanced beyond the stage of mere discussion.

It soon became evident that the opposition to the university in this country was centered in Archbishop Corrigan and Bishop McQuaid. Early in the new year McQuaid wrote Corrigan saying that he (McQuaid) could, of course, "say things in a stronger and less dignified way than it would become one in your position to say the same." He stated that he had written Miss Ella Edes about the German question with the intention that she should show his letter to Canon Sbarretti. Miss Edes had been his private agent in Rome and Corrigan's as well. He mentioned that he had sent his memorial "*in re University*" to Sbarretti through Miss Edes, and he expected, therefore, that the canon would know all about it. But apparently he did not, for Sbarretti had asked for a translation of the document so that he might place it before the cardinals of Propaganda. McQuaid went on to say, "The idea I threw out was that the American Hierarchy ought to be consulted before any definite action should be taken by Rome. Ireland and Keane have sent me nothing. Please to let me have the paper. Perhaps they do not intend that it shall reach my eyes." [26] Two days later the Bishop of Rochester told Corrigan he would write Rome once more about the university and advise them to send a circular to the American bishops on the question of the choice of Washington as a site and of their willingness to call on their poor people for con-

[26] NYAA, C–16, Bernard J. McQuaid to M. A. Corrigan, Rochester, January 14, 1887.

tributions. "Ireland and Keane will get answers only from those who favor the bantling they are coddling into puny existence. Bp. DeGoesbriand [of Burlington] was very indignant at the idea of a general collection. The Germans as a body have lost all heart in the work." [25] In these weeks McQuaid kept up a lively correspondence with New York on the problems under discussion in Rome and concerning the university on January 14 he declared, "the more I think it over the more opposed I grow." [26] He wondered if Keane and Ireland knew of his opposition.

They may, or they may not know that my letters to Rome on the University question are blocking their game in that direction. It is likely they know how I stand, as I have made no secret of my views since Washington was pitched on as the site of the University.[27]

Fearing that the letters which Keane and Ireland had requested from America would all be friendly to the university, McQuaid said that in his last communications with Rome he had urged the Propaganda to send a letter to all the American bishops, presumably hoping that the replies from others in agreement with him would cancel out the opinions of the prelates on the university committee.

McQuaid at the same time was endeavoring to persuade Bishop Gilmour of Cleveland to join hands with Corrigan and himself against the university. He wrote Gilmour in late January, asking him if he understood when the council

[25] NYAA, C–16, Bernard J. McQuaid to M. A. Corrigan, Rochester, January 13, 1887.

[26] NYAA, C–16, Bernard J. McQuaid to M. A. Corrigan, Rochester, January 14, 1887.

[27] NYAA, C–16, Bernard J. McQuaid, to M. A. Corrigan, Rochester, January 22, 1887.

gave permission to begin a university, that the bishops in general had assumed any responsibility for its support, and that as in Belgium for Louvain there would be diocesan collections for its support. "There has been so much scheming in this whole affair that no rascally trap sprang [*sic*] on us will surprise me . . . I for one do not propose to build a University in the South, to be governed by a Board of Southern bishops, priests and laymen in a large majority." [28] The Bishop of Rochester's dislike of the whole project made him prone to see failure where there was no failure. For example, in writing Corrigan he mentioned receiving a letter from Dr. Hanna,[29] one of his priests studying in Rome, in which Hanna told him Ireland and Keane had had their audience with Leo XIII in regard to the university and remarked, "I did not ask them the details, but they seemed pleased on the whole." [30] Hanna's statement prompted McQuaid to add to Corrigan, "this would indicate that they did not get just what they wanted." The rest of the letter was filled with the Bishop of Rochester's familiar objections to the university, namely, that the poor would have to support "this abortion," that it was a pure assumption that the hierarchy had taken any responsibility for either the university itself or for the site chosen, and that he did not believe the bishops "for a

[28] RDA, Bernard J. McQuaid to Richard Gilmour, Rochester, January 26, 1887. Copy from Archives of the Diocese of Cleveland.

[29] Edward J. Hanna (1860–1944) was a professor of theology in St. Bernard's Seminary, Rochester, from its opening in 1893 up to 1912 when he was named Auxiliary Bishop of San Francisco. He was Archbishop of San Francisco from 1915 to 1935.

[30] NYAA, C–16, Bernard J. McQuaid to M. A. Corrigan, January 26, 1887.

moment thought that success was possible at Washington. I shall regret to see Rome mixed up in this failure."

At the risk of becoming tedious it may be worth while to see a little more of the correspondence of Bishop McQuaid on this issue, for although his friend, the Archbishop of New York, was clearly in the camp of the opposition, it was McQuaid who formulated the main arguments of that party. On January 31, 1887, he wrote the Bishop of Cleveland again, recounting the failure of the university committee to gather in the money they had anticipated from a few rich people and reiterating his position that his attitude from the beginning had been that if the committee could get enough money for a university from some of the wealthy Catholics, then McQuaid thought "they might build a university when and where they pleased." But now that the necessary funds could not be raised in this way he foresaw the threat of diocesan collections in all the churches of America. "This will be the next move. The instance of Belgium will be cited where there is an annual collection in every church and chapel of the country for the support of Louvain University. Mind my words." Apparently suspecting that his friend in Cleveland might not have received the appeal of the university committee, McQuaid sent along a copy.

If you will read the passages marked in the "Appeal" I send you, you will perceive the plan on which these gentlemen propose to run this scheme. First they will implicate the Holy See. Then they will cry out, Do we who *assumed* the *founding* of the University, propose to dishonor the Holy See by letting it fail after having pledged ourselves to give it success? [31]

[31] RDA, Bernard J. McQuaid to Richard Gilmour, Rochester,

Although Bishop Gilmour had favored a university even before the Third Plenary Council, he agreed with McQuaid that Washington was an unfortunate choice for its location. He wrote to the Bishop of Rochester on the question:

I fully agree that the site for the University & some of the [sic] have hurt very much its prospects. I will be slow indeed to consent to have it saddled on us for support. We are carrying enough as it is.

Troy, Seton Hall, Phila. would have all been better than Washington. In God's name what has infatuated them at Rome about Fort Wayne? He has not one single quality for the position.[32]

But the definite decisions in the whole matter were not to be made in America through the private correspondence of the bishops. Such action was reserved to the Holy See whose sole privilege it is to erect a pontifical university. Fortunately for the university, the Archbishop of Baltimore was soon to sail for Rome and upon his arrival there the negotiations would be definitely speeded up. Pope Leo XIII had, as we have seen, postponed final action until the arrival of Gibbons. This news got about Rome and Miss Edes communicated it to Bishop McQuaid which made the latter not a little uneasy, for as he told Corrigan, " Of course, if the Pope settles the affairs with Baltimore, the latter will have all his own way." [33]

January 31, 1887. Copy from the Archives of the Diocese of Cleveland.

[32] RDA, Richard Gilmour to Bernard J. McQuaid, Cleveland, February 2, 1887. The reference at the end is to Bishop Dwenger who had been sent to Rome to see the decrees of the Third Plenary Council through to final approval.

[33] NYAA, C–16, Bernard J. McQuaid to M. A. Corrigan, Rochester, February 1, 1887.

Early in the new year 1887 Cardinal Gibbons sailed for Rome where on March 17 in a public consistory Pope Leo XIII bestowed the red hat on the newly-created cardinals.[34] Such was the formal occasion which called the Archbishop of Baltimore to the Vatican. But once in Rome he had to discuss many important affairs affecting the welfare of the Church in America, for it was just at this time that the secret societies, the Knights of Labor, the Henry George theories, the German problem, and the university were all pressing for settlement. We are concerned here only with the negotiations pertaining to the university. When Gibbons arrived in Rome, Keane and Ireland who had been there nearly three months, without getting definite action, naturally informed him of the current of Roman opinion on the university. Gibbons was irked at what he regarded as the hidden character of the opposition from the United States. He wrote to Archbishop Elder of Cincinnati:

There is an undercurrent of opposition to the University coming from our own country. I have no objection whatever to an honest opposition. Nay more, I regard opposition as a duty when dictated by conscience. But it is regrettable when done in a covert way. The Propaganda tells me that some of the Bishops are opposed to it, & signed out of complacency. Hence I intend to advise that the H. See consult the Bishops individually & ascertain their true sentiments. Till then I will have nothing to do with the

---

[34] As a special courtesy to Cardinal Gibbons the Pope sent Monsignore Straniero to Baltimore with the red zucchetto and biretta which were conferred in the Baltimore cathedral on June 30, 1886, the twenty-fifth anniversary of the cardinal's ordination. Archbishop Kenrick of St. Louis bestowed the biretta in the presence of a large number of the American hierarchy and the sermon was preached by the Archbishop of Philadelphia, Patrick J. Ryan. Will, *op. cit.,* I, 280–290.

enterprise. Liberavi animam meam. We can afford to wait as the matter is not pressing.[35]

It would be difficult to quarrel with the judgment expressed in this letter, namely, that opposition was a duty in conscience when sincerely held but that it should be stated openly. Gibbons likewise showed prudence in soliciting the opinions of the American bishops before taking final steps with the Holy See, for on their support in the final analysis would rest the success of the university. Although Keane and Ireland might feel they had already waited long enough, the course pursued by Gibbons at this time proved to be worth the delay.

In a conference which Cardinal Gibbons held with Cardinal Simeoni, the Prefect of Propaganda, the latter told him of having received a lengthy protest against the university from a leading American bishop. Unofficially it was made known that it emanated from Archbishop Corrigan of New York. We have already seen the substance of this protest in Corrigan's summary of it to Bishop McQuaid.[36] The knowledge of this report discouraged the Cardinal of Baltimore very badly and he told Bishop Keane that he believed they should abandon the whole idea and let the responsibility for the university's failure rest where it belonged. "To this," wrote Keane, "I agreed very willingly, only too glad to escape from such contention." But John Ireland, who had been out of Rome for a few days, returned in time to be informed of the state of mind of Gibbons and Keane before they had taken any action.

[35] Archives of the Archdiocese of Cincinnati, Letters, 1887, A–K, James Gibbons to William H. Elder, Rome, February 19, 1887.

[36] Cf. p. 185 of this study.

The Bishop of St. Paul protested indignantly against what he termed, "so cowardly a surrender to so unworthy an opposition." Ireland insisted that they pursue their original plan of getting the official papal approval and then if the university committee felt it necessary the whole matter might be dropped. "His advice prevailed. Cardinal Gibbons answered the various objections to the entire satisfaction of the Holy Father, and the final decision was taken." [37]

Gibbons' manner of answering the objections for the Pope took the form of a lengthy letter written in French which bore the date of March 9, 1887.[38] In this document the cardinal told Leo XIII that the project of founding a university had found favor among the bishops of the Third Plenary Council. True, some had expressed their fear concerning the lack of money, but when the gift of Miss Caldwell was made known, "leur approbation de l'Université fut la plus cordiale." The laity in the United States had received the proposal well and there was not much doubt that they would respond with money to secure the financial support of the theological faculty which was all that was intended for the time being. Gibbons explained to the Pope the personnel and work of the university committee. He likewise alluded to the Pope's knowledge of opposition among the American bishops on the choice of Washington. For that reason he suggested that for the moment this matter of site be considered as secondary until he could secure from the American hierarchy their votes on

---

[37] Keane Memorial, p. 11.
[38] BDA, Printed copy of letter of James Gibbons to Leo XIII, Rome, March 9, 1887, sent to John J. Williams.

the question. The cardinal then asked the Holy Father, in order to eliminate further difficulty, if he would give his approval without delay to the university. "Cette approbation sera pour nous le prix du succès le plus complet." The university committee had already had proof of Pope Leo's favorable disposition towards the project, but the cardinal felt that the time had now come when it was necessary to obtain a formal and explicit letter of approval. Gibbons assured Leo XIII that the Catholics of the United States wished him to know that they were convinced the project of a Catholic university in their country was entirely in harmony with the instructions which His Holiness had given to the world more than once during his pontificate. "Les Catholiques des Etats-Unis se feront un devoir de vous prouver leur reconnaissance pour cette nouvelle marque de votre amour à leur égard. Le peuple Américain prend un intérêt profond à notre projet, et sera heureux de le voir béni par Votre Sainteté."

The news of Gibbons' success was not long in reaching America. The *Church News* for March 27 reprinted a story bearing a Roman dateline of March 21, to the effect that the Pope had that day approved the plan of the university after the Secretary of the Propaganda had presented the Holy Father with a letter of approbation. The story continued, "The brief will be signed by the Pontiff next week. Bishops Ireland and Keane are delighted at this manifestation of cordial approval, and will leave for America as soon as the brief is received." Gibbons informed Archbishop Corrigan on March 28 that the Pope had consented to issue the brief of authorization for the university and the cardinal added, "my request is granted that the question of site be reconsidered." [39] Three days later he wrote Archbishop Elder a letter the concluding sentence of which read, "The H. Father's heart is set on a university. We must not disappoint him." [40] It was on Easter Sunday, April 10, that the Pope issued his brief giving his approbation to the university in the style requested of him by the American bishops. Leo XIII alluded to the dangers which beset youth both in Europe and America from false doctrine and he looked to the university as a source for disseminating the truth to offset the errors of the age. "We therefore most gladly welcome and heartily approve your project for the erection of a University, moved as you are by a desire to promote the welfare of all and the interests of your illustrious Republic." Knowing of the opposition which the university had met, the Pope spoke a strong closing exhortation to Gibbons and the other members of the committee when he said:

Go on therefore, Beloved Son, together with all Our other Venerable Brethren the Bishops of the United States, to carry to perfection with one mind what you have begun; and let not any one of you be deterred by any difficulty or labor, but let all take courage from the assured hope that they will receive an abundant return for their cares and sollicitudes, having laid the foundations of an institute destined to provide the Church with worthy ministers for the salvation of souls and the propagation of Religion, and to give to the Republic her best citizens.

Deferring to the difference of opinion about the site, that

[39] NYAA, C–15, James Gibbons, to M. A. Corrigan, Rome, March 28, 1887.

[40] AAC, Letters, 1887, A–K, James Gibbons to William H. Elder, Rome, March 31, 1887.

matter was left open in the papal brief until a vote could be taken among the bishops. In the document as drawn up by Archbishop Jacobini, Secretary of the Propaganda, no mention was made of the request of the committee not to have another university approved until the next plenary council. This item was taken up later with the officials of the Propaganda and satisfactorily settled.[41]

With the official brief of papal approval the immediate business of the American bishops in Rome insofar as the university was concerned was at an end. Bishop Keane set out soon thereafter on a tour of European universities to gather ideas on courses of study, professors, and administrative techniques. In the meanwhile on March 25 Cardinal Gibbons had taken possession of his titular church, Santa Maria in Trastevere, where he made his remarkable speech on the relations of the Church and State in the United States. The cardinal, whose health had been impaired during his Roman visit, left for home with stops in Paris, Louvain, and London. While in London during May he was the guest of Cardinal Manning with whom he found much in common. He reached Baltimore on June 7, where an enthusiastic reception awaited the city's first cardinal.

Varying reactions were shown in the United States to the papal approval of the university. The *Freeman's Journal* of New York, never enthusiastic about the project, conceded in its issue of April 30, "this brief will no doubt give a strong impetus to the movement in favor of a Catholic

---

[41] Keane Memorial, pp. 11–12. For the text of the papal brief cf. BCA, 82–P–10/1, Pope Leo XIII to James Gibbons, Rome, April 10, 1887. John J. Keane made the brief the subject of an article in the *Catholic World*, XLVI (Nov. 1887), 145–153, entitled, "Leo XIII and the Catholic University of America."

university in this country." However, the editorial writer expressed a certain misgiving that the bishops would find the
prospective students so eager to earn money that "it will be
a long time before the money-making spirit of our time will
so lose its grasp on the young men of the country as to
permit them to 'lose time' in higher education." But he
concluded it was nonetheless well that the Church should
begin the great work which would have a tendency "to
reduce the chance of materialism choking up all that is best
in this country." The *Church News* of Washington was
more enthusiastic in its editorial of May 1 and spoke of the
Pope's brief as urging "fearless resolution in the prosecution
of the plan . . ." About this time the United States Bureau
of Education sent an inquiry to Eugene Kelly, treasurer of
the university committee, concerning the institution. Kelly
told Archbishop Corrigan he had had a similar request
"last Fall" but had neglected to answer it. Since the federal
bureau wanted to include accurate information on the
institution in a report which it was getting out, Kelly
stated he felt Corrigan should give him a few lines on the
university.[42]

Shortly before leaving Rome, Bishop Keane wrote Cardinal Gibbons saying that Archbishop Williams of Boston
had arrived the previous Thursday. "This sets me free, and
I start next Monday." The Bishop of Richmond continued:

I have fully explained to him the status of every question
that we had in hand, and find him thoroughly in sympathy
with the views of your Eminence on every point. I have
shown him the necessity of some clear strong words to clinch

---

[42] NYAA, C–9, Eugene Kelly to M. A. Corrigan, New York,
May 6, 1887.

the nails, and I am sure that he will say them;—in fact he has begun already.[43]

Keane went on to suggest to Gibbons that he have Monsignor Farley call a meeting of the university committee for the Tuesday or Wednesday after the diocesan retreat. He enclosed copies of Leo XIII's brief in Latin and in French and also a copy of the circular to all the bishops which he had sent as Gibbons had directed. Regarding the sentence in the papal brief which stated that "all things" [de his omnibus] done by the university committee be referred to Rome, Keane felt it was too wide and might lead to trouble so, "I asked & obtained an authentic interpretation limiting it within the bounds of constitution, laws, & organization of studies."

During the spring and summer the replies from the American bishops on the university site trickled slowly into the cardinal's office in Baltimore. Of those which have been preserved few were more pronounced and enthusiastic for Washington than that of Bishop Camillus P. Maes of Covington. He advanced six points in favor of the national capital, one of them being the acquaintance which future bishops, priests, lawyers, and doctors would make in Washington as students with the officials of the government which, he felt, would be all to the good. "There will not be a mark or dark corner left in the Country where lying bigotry can hide its head without being mercilessly exposed by the light of knowledge acquired by the better classes of our non-Catholic people and communicated, thanks to

---

[43] BCA, 82–Q–1, John J. Keane to James Gibbons, Rome, May 14, 1887.

their innate sense of justice and bold assertion of fair play, to the masses." Maes concluded his letter by saying:

I have heard no arguments that could induce me, so far, to change my opinion on the subject. In answer, therefore, to the letter of your Eminence, I name Washington, D. C., as my first and only choice for the establishment of our Catholic University.[44]

Two weeks later there came the answer of the Bishop of Rochester. McQuaid's very lengthy communication to Gibbons rehearsed all his objections to the university which we have already seen in detail. He proposed a set of five questions which he wished answered before deciding definitely on the matter of a site: was the university to include all departments normally associated with a university; were the American bishops to be held financially responsible; were the poor people to be called on for money, and if not, then how were the funds to be provided; and finally, was it only a theological faculty that was intended and for which the American hierarchy was to be held responsible. These were questions which it was fair for any American bishop to propose, but there was evidence in his letter that Bishop McQuaid was too impressed by stories he had read of the plans in the public press. Conflicting stories there had been, indeed, concerning the amount of money it would take and how much had been thus far contributed. In this McQuaid was quite justified in asking for "an accurate financial statement, not of moneys promised, but of moneys paid in to the University treasury and disbursed therefrom." The Bishop of Rochester was correct in sensing that an appeal to the

---

[44] Archives of the Diocese of Covington, Camillus P. Maes to James Gibbons, Covington, May 27, 1887, copy.

Catholics of the United States would be made through their bishops and for that reason the bishops would have a right to know the financial standing of the project. But he was expecting too much haste on the part of the committee since they had not yet held a meeting following the papal approval and up to that time the entire matter was on only a tentative basis. In regard to the question of a site, McQuaid suggested the university course in theology be attached to St. Mary's Seminary in Baltimore, a suggestion which he thought all the more appropriate since it seemed to be settled that the Sulpicians were to be in charge of the discipline of the university students. "For many reasons I consider Washington City the least desirable of any for the site of a university." Bishop McQuaid closed his letter by saying, "Your Eminence will please to bear with my frankness, but it is better to be warned in time before plunging into an abyss from which it may be difficult to extricate ourselves." [45]

Since we have seen Bishop McQuaid's views on the university in more than one connection it is not necessary to give his long letter to Cardinal Gibbons in more than summary. However, the cardinal had not committed himself so openly and in detail on the subject and for that reason it may be worth while to cite Gibbons' reply to the Bishop of Rochester in full text. In one of the few letters extant of the Cardinal of Baltimore to Bishop McQuaid the former replied:

I thank you cordially for your kind message of welcome to me on my return home.

---

[45] BCA, 82–T–4, Bernard J. McQuaid to James Gibbons, Rochester, June 11, 1887.

In reply to the series of questions you propose I would say that in my judgment it is proposed to adhere as closely as possible to the letter and spirit of decree no. 182 of the Third Plenary Council. The aim of the Board will be to confine their efforts to the Theological & Philosophical Department for a good while to come. It is only after this work is well grounded that any attempt will be made to institute any other branches. The theological Department will be the "nucleus vel germen quoddam, unde favente Dei gratia perfecta suo tempore efflorescet studiorum universitas."

It is not the intention to make any appeal to the poor. If I remember well, this fact is expressly stated in the letters which were addressed to the Holy Father & to the Propaganda. The Right Rev. Rector even informs me that he does not intend to make an appeal to the Bishops, except to ask their permission & influence in approaching the wealthier Catholics in their dioceses. He says the Committee will charge themselves with raising the necessary funds, & I presume they will mainly rely on the voluntary contributions of the wealthier classes.

I am not desirous of having the University established in Baltimore City, or even in the diocese, & I will be glad if the majority of the Prelates recommend some other place. I am already burdened with as many duties as I can well attend to, & I am sure that my responsibilities will be increased if the University is placed in the diocese. My sole wish is to aid as far as I can in carrying out the wishes of the Fathers of the Council.

The next meeting of the Board is called for September 7th. I think it is the judgment of all that in this great undertaking we should proceed slowly & cautiously, & take no steps without careful deliberation.[46]

Gibbons' letter to McQuaid was about as complete a

---

[46] RDA, James Gibbons to Bernard J. McQuaid, Baltimore, June 15, 1887.

summary of the cardinal's position as he had given in a
private letter up to this time. It was consistent with the
caution he had displayed towards the whole question from
the beginning and it was consistent, too, in showing that
he did not care to have the university either in Baltimore
or in Washington. It is interesting to find this opinion
against Washington so strong in Gibbons, for in the years
that were to follow he came to be so closely identified with
the university and its history through thirty years that it
may come as something of a surprise to know that he
originally was opposed to having it in his diocese.

Before leaving Rome the Pope had given his approval to
the selection of Bishop Keane as first rector of the university,
but it had not yet been publicly announced. Furthermore,
at the personal suggestion of Leo XIII the bishop had a
long conversation with Monsignor Désiré Mercier of the
University of Louvain who happened to be in Rome, as
well as with Francesco Satolli, professor of dogmatic theology in the College of the Propaganda.[47] He arrived in
New York on the *Servia* on June 13 and at the end of the
week the *Freeman's Journal* reported him as the rector of
the university and quoted the bishop as having said that the
new institution would in no sense "be a rival of any existing
Catholic college." [48] Keane reached his diocese in mid-June
and was given a cordial reception in Richmond in which

---

[47] Richmond Diocesan Archives, Bishops' Diary, June 17, 1887,
p. 148.

[48] Keane Memorial, p. 12. The *Catholic Mirror* of November 19,
1887, quoted the London *Weekly Register* to the effect that Keane
and Ireland held a conference with "a former professor of the Sorbonne at Paris, and adopted, at his suggestion, a proposal for giving
periodical lectures before the public, practiced as so important a
part of the work of the Sorbonne."

Governor Fitzhugh Lee joined.[49] The bishop confided to his diary on June 17 the information of his approval by Leo XIII to which he added, "but he advises my retaining my Diocese till the University project is more solidly and practically under way." [50] Looking back on these troubled early years of the university's development, Keane stated in 1897 that he returned to Richmond in the summer of 1887 "with a rather heavy heart." He acknowledged that his diocese was not one among the first in America, but he was very happy in Richmond and he believed his work, especially among the Protestants and the Negroes, had been beneficial and "very congenial to my wishes." He remarked that Leo XIII had said that although he should return to the diocese it would be only a question of time until he would have to resign that position since it was obvious that he could not fill both offices. This news naturally got around among the priests and people of the Diocese of Richmond and "the situation was painful to all." [51]

Meanwhile the final decision concerning the university site was held over until the next meeting of the committee which was scheduled for Baltimore in early September. Archbishop Corrigan informed Elder of Cincinnati that it would come up at that time,[52] and McQuaid requested

---

[49] *Freeman's Journal*, June 18, 1887.

[50] Richmond Diocesan Archives, Bishops' Diary, p. 148.

[51] Keane Memorial, p. 13.

[52] AAC, Letters, 1887, A–K, M. A. Corrigan to William H. Elder, New York, June 5, 1887. John Farley, secretary of the committee, was apparently puzzled about the status of Bishop Borgess. He wrote Gibbons in regard to the forthcoming meeting on September 7 and he asked: "What shall I do about Bp. Borgess? Does he still represent Abp. Heiss? I wrote Mr. Farren that your Eminence begged him to reconsider his intention to resign. He thanks your Em. very much

the Archbishop of New York to ask for a reading of the
bishops' letters in reply to Gibbons on the site when the
committee should meet.[53] In answering, Corrigan stated
that he expected to write Gibbons and to suggest Philadelphia as more advantageous than Washington and as
being more closely in line with the council's resolution that
it be located near a large city. The Archbishop of New
York reminded McQuaid that it could not be attached to
St. Mary's in Baltimore since Miss Caldwell's gift stipulated
that the university not be an appendage of an existing
institution. At the close of his letter Corrigan said, "I am
very much disposed to resign my seat on the University
Board,—having lost confidence in the good faith of some
of the members. What would you advise me to do?" [54]
The response from Rochester was immediate. "I would
advise you by all means to sever all connection with the
University. You have been shabbily treated, and the worst
is to come. Have nothing to do with it, and especially do
not permit it to be placed in your diocese." McQuaid went
on to say that the committee would come to proposing
New York in order to avoid failure. In time, he continued,
Corrigan would wish to establish a "higher course of
theology" in his new seminary and "we do not want to
have anything to do with a Southern Seminary." At the
close of this letter the Bishop of Rochester said he thought

& gratefully for your good opinion, but insists on having his letter of
resignation submitted to the Board. He leaves for Europe shortly and
cannot be at the next meeting." BCA, 82–U–3, John M. Farley to
James Gibbons, New York, June 16, 1887.

[53] NYAA, C–16, Bernard J. McQuaid to M. A. Corrigan, Rochester, June 17, 1887.

[54] RDA, M. A. Corrigan to Bernard J. McQuaid, New York, June
22, 1887.

it was strange Gibbons had not told him that the Caldwell gift barred the possibility of locating the university at St. Mary's. "He only wrote of his inability to assume new responsibilities in addition to his already great burdens. He did not answer my main questions. He dodged them adroitly, or ignored them." [55]

As far as extant documents go it is difficult to see how McQuaid could reason that the bishops of the university committee had treated Archbishop Corrigan "shabbily." He had been a party to the undertaking from the outset and no major steps were taken in the matter without Corrigan's knowledge. Moreover, the archbishop had been given any number of opportunities to state his views in the meetings of the committee; and whenever he did choose to express an opinion it was given consideration as, for example, his suggestion to change the language of the petition to Rome not to approve another university for twenty-five years to the time of the next plenary council. Again, when he had stated that he thought the wording of the petition needed to be revised before being finally submitted to the Holy See, the committee agreed that he should make the revisions himself. It is true that the committee went counter to his wishes about locating the university in Washington, but they could hardly be charged with shabby treatment of the Archbishop of New York when he was present at the meeting and voted for Washington himself. Nor could the committee be expected to guess the fact that Corrigan had an idea of a university in New York to be staffed by the Jesuits. Of this matter he said nothing in the committee

[55] NYAA, C–16, Bernard J. McQuaid to M. A. Corrigan, Rochester, June 23, 1887.

meetings; it was only in private conversation after the first full meeting that he revealed this intention to Bishop Keane. It is difficult to escape the conclusion that had Archbishop Corrigan spoken his mind more frankly in meetings of the committee a number of the unfortunate episodes which arose might have been avoided. It is certainly true that Cardinal Gibbons wavered in his support of the university project up to the time of the papal approbation. As we have seen, his hesitancy and seeming effort to please both sides led to a sharp letter from Rome from his friend, John Keane.[56] But a careful reading of his reply to McQuaid will reveal a candid tone and as full an explanation as one could reasonably ask to the questions which the bishop had put to him. For McQuaid to have written Corrigan that the cardinal "dodged them adroitly, or ignored them," was hardly a fair judgment under the circumstances.

The reply of Archbishop Corrigan to Cardinal Gibbons' request for his mind on the site for the university was sent on June 27, 1887. He was strongly opposed to Washington because of the demoralizing political atmosphere of the capital, because it was not a large city, and in the South at that, and also because there was already there a Catholic university. For all these reasons Corrigan gave his vote for Philadelphia as being healthier and cheaper than New York and more centrally located than Boston.[57] He entirely excluded any western city, "as their Bishops in the Plenary Council expressly waived their rights to the *first* University, in favor of the East and hence we look to some Eastern city." McQuaid kept his friend the Bishop of Cleveland

---

[56] Cf. p. 214 of this study.

[57] NYAA, C–39, M. A. Corrigan to James Gibbons, New York, June 27, 1887, copy.

informed of his various moves in regard to the university. He wrote Gilmour a summary of his letter to Cardinal Gibbons and quoted the questions he had asked. He stated that he had never believed in the practicability of a university in the real sense and now he was growing sceptical about "the practicability of even a higher seminary." He concluded his letter to Bishop Gilmour by an admonition to observe the background of the bishops who were in favor of a university. "Keep in mind in thinking over this subject that those who are most prominent in the movement, and who do the most hifaluting never accomplished any work in this line. If the disgrace of the failure is to fall on them alone we might stand by and laugh." [58] McQuaid was, perhaps, thinking of his successful venture in founding Seton Hall College when he was a priest of the Diocese of Newark and he was correct, of course, in saying that none of the bishops on the committee had yet done anything along this line.

Cardinal Gibbons received a strong recommendation for Washington from John J. Conroy who had resigned the Diocese of Albany in 1877. Conroy wrote the cardinal that he had " become more and more confirmed in my opinion in favor of its location in the City of Washington. No change that could be now made would improve its prospects of success, nor enlist more widely the sympathies of the public." [59]

Bishop Keane reported to the cardinal on July 12 that the editor of the *Moniteur de Rome* had written him, telling

---

[58] RDA, Bernard J. McQuaid to Richard Gilmour, Hemlock Lake, June 28, 1887, copy.

[59] Archives of the University of Notre Dame, John J. Conroy to James Gibbons, New York, June 30, 1887.

how satisfactorily that journal had treated the various American questions before the Holy See. In a postscript Keane said, "I hope all the Bishops have sent your Eminence their vote on the University question." [60] About the same time McQuaid reported that Bishop Marty had just arrived in Rochester from Baltimore and Washington and that Marty reported a majority of the bishops in favor of Chicago. "He speaks as though there could [be] no doubt about the matter." The thought of the university going to Chicago struck Bishop McQuaid as surprising. "But they cannot expect us to send on money to Chicago. It will all be needed for the East." Just how Marty got the impression that the majority of the bishops were in favor of Chicago is, indeed, difficult to say, for when the votes were all in at the meeting in September it was found that only one vote had been cast for Chicago. McQuaid consoled Corrigan that when the time came the archbishop would be ready to have his own university in New York and he apparently felt that the votes for Chicago of which he had been informed, indicated a deliberate by-passing of the metropolis of the nation since he concluded by saying, "it is wonderful the jealousy there is with regard to New York." [61] Later that month Denis O'Connell wrote Gibbons of the departure from Rome of two students of the American Church, Hanna and Deasy. O'Connell had presented the two men in a farewell audience of the Holy Father during which the Pope, "of his own prompting, told Hanna to prepare himself

---

[60] BCA, 83–B–9, John J. Keane to James Gibbons, Richmond, July 12, 1887.

[61] NYAA, C–16, Bernard J. McQuaid to M. A. Corrigan, Rochester, July 14, 1887.

for 'the University at Washington.' " [62] How pleased McQuaid was to have Father Hanna designated by the Pope himself for a professorship in the future American university we have, unfortunately, no means of knowing.

In the printed circular which Cardinal Gibbons had sent to the American bishops in the late spring of 1887 he had asked that they reply to the question about the site of the university by July 1. The cardinal enclosed a copy of Pope Leo's brief of April 10 and called attention to the fact that the brief gave strong approval to the university idea but that it directed that a vote be taken among the bishops on the site. As Gibbons said, while the Pope appreciated the reasons prompting the university committee to select Washington, yet " he is desirous that the decision and the action of the Bishops should be as unanimous as possible, since it is evident that on their unity of sentiment and action the success of this undertaking which he has abundantly shown to be very dear to his heart, must mainly depend." [63]

Three days before the committee met, Miss Caldwell wrote Gibbons to remind him of the letter she had sent him before the meeting in the fall of 1886. She asked that the cardinal have her letter read at the coming meeting. She said:

The Bishop of Richmond told me last spring that it was the intention of the board to commence the University buildings very soon after this meeting. I hope and expect, however, that the money which I have given, will not be used until a

---

[62] BCA, 83–D–12, D. J. O'Connell to James Gibbons, Grotta-ferrata, July 31, 1887.

[63] NYAA, C–15, James Gibbons to M. A. Corrigan, printed letter bearing no place or date.

sufficient sum to secure the full endowment of the University has been raised.

A rumor also has reached me that there is question of changing the site. Of course, however, according to the original conditions of my gift, this cannot be done without my consent.[64]

The university committee assembled on September 7, 1887, in the cardinal's residence in Baltimore with fourteen members present. One of the first matters of business was to accept the resignation of Bernard N. Farren of Philadelphia and Bishop Borgess of Detroit as members of the committee. In their places there were elected Bishops Kilian C. Flasch of La Crosse and Camillus P. Maes of Covington. Bishop Keane read a full report covering his own and John Ireland's activities in Rome for which they received a vote of thanks from the committee. Keane then presented the members with a set of questions which he asked them to consider: (a) would Washington be retained as the site of the university; (b) would a course of popular lectures to be given in connection with the university be acceptable to the committee and, if so, would it be expedient to erect a lecture hall in the city; (c) should not a committee of bishops be appointed to draft statutes for the government of the university and to outline a course of studies; (d) should the building committee be authorized to begin construction at once; (e) was there not need to institute more active measures to raise funds; (f) finally, should not a committee be appointed to take charge of investing the funds of the university.

Before considering the questions posed by Keane, Car-

---

[64] BCA, 86–L–2, Mary Gwendoline Caldwell to James Gibbons, Newport, September 4, 1887.

dinal Gibbons, as chairman of the committee, stated that he had received a letter from Rome listing certain difficulties in the way of the success of the university and that he had sent a full reply to the Holy See covering all these matters. He remarked that Pope Leo XIII was not only anxious for the establishment of the university but really enthusiastic on the subject. The Pope had taken a number of opportunities to speak of it with approval and his words had been quoted all over Europe. Following these remarks of the cardinal, the question of the site was taken up for final settlement. Gibbons stated that he had received replies from fifty-three bishops in response to his circular on the subject. Of these thirty-three voted for Washington, seven for New York, three for New York or Philadelphia, three for Philadelphia, one for Philadelphia or Baltimore, one for Chicago, and five declined to give an opinion, preferring to leave it to the judgment of the committee. On the basis of these returns Archbishop Williams moved that Washington be adopted as the permanent site and the motion was carried.

With this long controverted point out of the way the committee turned to Keane's questions. The suggestion of a series of popular lectures was discussed and that gave rise to another question, namely, whether it might not be wise to locate the university nearer to the city than the property already chosen. Keane moved to locate the institution nearer to Washington than the Middleton estate, but his motion lost by a vote of seven to six. The lectures, so the committee felt, could be given effectively in a hall which might be leased in the city. In regard to the title flaw, Waggaman stated that a perfect title could be secured by payment of $5,000, which the committee authorized.

The appointment of a building committee followed, with Williams as chairman and Keane and Waggaman as committee members, this committee being empowered to make contracts as well as to settle disputes of title. Keane submitted the estimate of E. F. Baldwin of the firm of Baldwin and Pennington of Baltimore for the building. Baldwin estimated the building proper would cost $170,000, steam fitting $20,000, and drawings and improvements to the grounds an additional $10,000. These expenditures would cover all necessary accommodation for forty-five students and the faculty. The Baldwin estimate was regarded as moderate by the members and it was moved to refer it to the building committee for action. The question of the university statutes then came before the meeting, along with the need for a course of studies. It was decided that a special committee be appointed for the purpose which would also have power to make contracts with professors, these contracts to have the signature of Cardinal Gibbons to make them valid. Gibbons named as the committee for these tasks, Archbishop Ryan, Bishops Ireland, Keane, Marty, and Spalding and Father Chapelle.

Bishop Keane was directed to draw up a letter to be sent to all the bishops of the United States urging them to assist the collectors, and the original committee of collectors was continued with Flasch and Maes added as members. Archbishops Ryan and Williams along with Eugene Kelly were constituted a separate committee to invest the funds of the university. Kelly as treasurer of the original group reported $18,000 on hand. Keane told the members that he was the bearer of a gold medal for Miss Caldwell from Leo XIII and it was decided that he should communicate with her and learn whether she preferred to receive the honor

in private or in public on the day of the laying of the
cornerstone of the university. Monsignor Farley, as secretary, was instructed to send Miss Caldwell a copy of the
minutes of this meeting. The committee then heard a
motion that John J. Keane should be formally appointed
first rector of the university, a motion which was carried by
a unanimous standing vote. Following this action the members asked Bishop Keane to write a letter of thanks in their
name to a certain Mr. Huffer of Paris for his gift of $8,000
to the university, and Keane and Marty were likewise
instructed to prepare diplomas which would be presented to
donors of $1,000 or more to the university fund. The next
meeting of the university committee was set for May, 1888,
on the occasion of the laying of the cornerstone of the new
building.[65]

On the day of the meeting, September 7, Gibbons wrote
to Elder of Cincinnati and told him, "Washington has been
selected as the site for the University by about two-
thirds of the Bishops who have voted." [66] There were
probably few bishops, except McQuaid, who would be
more greatly disappointed at the selection of Washington
than the Archbishop of Cincinnati, for he had opposed
Washington from the beginning. The usual rumors in the
public press began to circulate after the meeting. The New
York *Tribune* of September 8 reported the election of
Keane as rector and then added: "It is said that $8,000,-
000 will be required to build and place the University on
a solid basis. Of that amount about $700,000 has been

---

[65] Archives of the Catholic University of America, Minutes of the
meeting of the Board of Trustees, Baltimore, September 7, 1887.

[66] AAC, Letters, 1887, A–K, James Gibbons to William H. Elder,
Baltimore, September 7, 1887.

secured, including the $300,000 given by Miss Caldwell." [67]
These irresponsible stories in the press led to considerable
confusion and embarrassment in the university committee,
since some people placed credence in the reports. An even
more fantastic story than that of the eight millions appeared
on September 9 in the Brooklyn *Standard-Union* to the
effect that Miss Caldwell had withdrawn the money she
had given to the university. The article carried, too, a story
on McGlynn and his troubles with the Holy See which,
the writer said, had been shown to McGlynn and found to
be accurate, although the priest "could not or would not
say anything about the alleged withdrawal of Miss Caldwell's gift." The story in the *Tribune* about the eight
million dolllars needed for an endowment prompted Archbishop Corrigan to assure the Archbishop of Cincinnati that
they "had a very pleasant meeting in Baltimore, although
not a breath indicated the possibility of spending 'eight
millions' on the University." [68] The *Tribune* repeated the
story of the eight millions in a lengthy editorial on the
university in its issue of September 10. The same editorial
contained the following interesting opinions on the university's foundation:

In view of the doctrines of the Church regarding secular
education, the wonder is no steps should have been taken
before toward the creation of such an institution. The
Church has a number of excellent colleges, but none that
rank in importance with the leading colleges of the country,
which, though they are, most of them, nominally under the
control of some religious denomination, are practically to

[67] New York *Tribune,* September 8, 1887.
[68] AAC, Letters, 1887, A–K, M. A. Corrigan to William H. Elder,
New York, September 10, 1887.

all intents and purposes secular schools. With the rapid growth of the country, and the consequent great increase of the Church in numbers and wealth, its far-seeing prelates have no doubt believed that the day was fast approaching, if it had not already arrived, when the need of such a university would be felt. The primary aim will doubtless be, as shown in the Pope's letter to Cardinal Gibbons, the education of young men for the priesthood, but such a project would fall short of much of its utility if it did not secure to Catholic youth most of the advantages to be gained in other colleges. The sagacity that is characteristic of the Church is not wanting in this case. Its traditions have been followed in establishing the university at the seat of power. Planted at the National Capital, it will be the centre of a strong influence for Catholic ideas.

In fact, Washington seems almost an ideal site for a university. It has long been a cherished dream of some of our public men that a great National University should grow up there, in the very shadow of the Government. The city is not one of commerce and trade, but a quiet aggregation of homes. It has a characteristic intellectual atmosphere, because a large proportion of its inhabitants are more or less connected with the work of carrying on a great Government. The Government libraries and scientific bureaus and the presence of numbers of scientific men contribute to this. The climate is mild, and living can be comparatively cheap. Perhaps the example of the Catholic Church will result, some day, in the establishment of a great secular university in Washington.

Aside from the item concerning the amount of the endowment needed for the university, the editorial in the New York *Tribune* was intended to do only good to the cause. But the circulation of false rumors concerning not only the university but the McGlynn case and Gibbons' role in the latter, caused trouble. The *Catholic Mirror* of

September 17, 1887, ran an editorial entitled, "Sensational Newspaper Stories," in which it took the daily press severely to task. Gibbons, so the *Mirror* said, had regarded the story about his intervening in the McGlynn case of sufficient import to issue a formal denial, and as for the university story, the editorial writer remarked: "While the cardinal, in common with the prelates of the country, was anxious in the interest of education and religion, to see a university established in this country, he has abstained from giving his vote in favor of any particular locality. The cardinal has no knowledge of any change contemplated or effected in the original endowment." The Boston *Pilot* of September 17 carried an enthusiastic news story on the Baltimore meeting of September 7 and the decisions taken and here, too, appeared the item that "the completed University will cost about $8,000,000." It is just possible this story originated in the expansive mind of Bishop John Ireland. The *Church News* for September 18 published what would appear to have been an interview with the Bishop of St. Paul since it employed direct quotations. Ireland was quoted as having said it would cost a million dollars to put the theological school in operation and, "I have no doubt that we will require fully $8,000,000 to carry out our idea of what the university ought to be, but we do not expect to collect so large a sum in a few years." Ireland went on to say that subscriptions would be taken up in every diocese and that he and Keane would travel Maryland and Pennsylvania "next January" on this mission. The Bishop of St. Paul said that the university "will be a sort of post-graduate course." He further remarked that three of Europe's most distinguished professors had been engaged, among them Ludwig von Pastor as professor of history, Henri Hyvernat as professor of Assyriology and Egyptology and "the third I am not at liberty to mention." Hyvernat was in time engaged for the university but this reference to Pastor is the sole bit of evidence we have that the university officials had approached the great historian of the popes. Enthusiastic interviews with the press such as Bishop Ireland had given were, of course, intended to give the movement spirit and doubtless they did, but it was unfortunate that more care had not been used as to the accuracy of details. It would have saved the *Church News* of September 18 from characterizing the rumors of the previous week as "rather unique specimens of what it would be uncourteous, perhaps, to call lying, but I don't just now recall the euphemism for it."

Five days after the meeting of the committee in Baltimore, Denis O'Connell cabled Gibbons, "Ajtum [*sic*] approbatum potes incipere aedificare postea programme submittere sileas responsum dubiorum germanorum." [69] He followed the cable a week later with a letter in which he said the question of site had first to go to the Pope for approval, "hence the delay in my cable." O'Connell told Gibbons that the committee was now at liberty to proceed with the building "whenever you please," but the course of studies was to be submitted to Rome for approval. O'Connell remarked to the cardinal:

The Holy Father questions me most closely about the number of Bps. votes for each place. I began by saying "Your Holiness remembers it was question about a site for the University." "Yes, he said "between Balto. & New York." When I gave him the vote, such as I had it, he

---

[69] BCA, 83–M–9, cable, D. J. O'Connell to James Gibbons, Rome, September 12, 1887.

replied "it is clear." He also enquired if Bp. Keane would not remain the Rector.[70]

The false press reports had reached Europe by late September and the indefatigable Bernard O'Reilly wrote Gibbons from Glengariff to say he had seen the misrepresentations, "but with two men like your Eminence & the Bishop of Richmond to watch over its beginnings, its friends need not be apprehensive."[71] Returning to the subject in an editorial entitled, "False Newspaper Statements," on October 1, the *Catholic Mirror* said the tale about the withdrawal of Miss Caldwell's gift had been repeated "through the entire press of the country, and even found its way over the borders. The original announcement emanated from a certain source in Brooklyn. It was given with enough of the appearance of authenticity to deceive secular journalists who knew little and cared less about the truth or falsehood of it . . . The whole thing was, in fact, a pure fabrication from beginning to end." The point of these stories should not, of course, be unduly emphasized and yet they did play an important part in spreading confusion and scepticism about the university in circles far removed from the responsible members of the committee. At a time when public confidence in the undertaking was of vital importance they furnished unfriendly critics with an opportunity to cast doubt on the practicability of the enterprise.

The *Freeman's Journal* stated that it had been given the courtesy by the editor of the *Catholic World* to read the

---

[70] BCA, 83–N–4, D. J. O'Connell to James Gibbons, Grottaferrata, September 18, 1887.

[71] BCA, 83–N–11, Bernard O'Reilly to James Gibbons, Glengariff, September 22, 1887.

advance sheets of a series of articles being written on the
university by Bishop Keane. The writer acknowledged the
need for higher education for priests, but to him, "well-
educated laymen are badly needed—more badly needed,
in fact, than well-educated priests." [72] The Bishop of
Rochester meanwhile pressed his friend, the Archbishop of
New York, to follow up on his thought of resigning from
the university committee. "Now that you have started to
build your own Seminary, you can resign from the University on the plea that you have this work to attend to;
that it needs all your attention and resources, etc." [73]
McQuaid was irked at the recent press stories on Cardinal
Gibbons' trip to Portland, Oregon, to confer the pallium
on Archbishop Gross. "This everlasting talk about *head* of
the *American church* annoys me. The good little man can't
see that he is making himself ridiculous. He will go so far
that somebody will have to call him to order." The *Catholic
Mirror* of the previous week was one paper guilty of the
offense when it described the cardinal's progress across the
continent in the following words: "Reports from points
en route indicate that the beloved head of the Church in
America has been everywhere received with the strongest
tokens of affectionate respect and esteem by all classes of
citizens without regard to creed." [74]

In the November, 1887, issue of the *Catholic World* the
newly-elected rector of the university began a series of
articles in which he endeavored to acquaint the American
public with the Catholic universities of Europe and with

---

[72] *Freeman's Journal,* October 8, 1887.

[73] NYAA, C–16, Bernard J. McQuaid to M. A. Corrigan, Rochester, October 9, 1887.

[74] *Catholic Mirror,* October 1, 1887.

what had been done to date concerning the Catholic university for the United States. His series appropriately was inaugurated by an article on the relations of Leo XIII to the university. Keane traced in a few broad strokes the progress of the Roman negotiations from the papal brief of April 10, 1887, through the frequent references which the Pope had made to the undertaking in his audiences. On the ninth anniversary of his elevation to the papal throne and again in an assembly of the cardinals on Easter Tuesday, the Pope had referred in enthusiastic terms to the American university. Keane stated that Leo XIII wished the university to be American as well as Catholic and the bishop quoted him as having said,

I wish that it should be founded by American means, and that it should be conducted by American brains; and if at first you have to call in the help of foreign talent in your faculties, it must be with the view of developing home intellect, of training professors who will gradually form indigenous faculties worthy of the name the university bears.[75]

Pope Leo XIII had favored Washington as the site since he wished the beneficial effects of the university to be felt by the entire Church and people of America, "and he is convinced that from no other centre could it so well do this as from the national capital, the heart of the republic." [76] Keane told his readers how Leo XIII had personally directed him together with Bishop Ireland to Professor Mercier of the University of Louvain who was then in

---

[75] John J. Keane, "Leo XIII. and the Catholic University of America," in *Catholic World*, XLVI (Nov. 1887), 150.
[76] *Ibid.*

Rome at the Pope's behest, in order that they might learn
Mercier's ideas. "And certainly he was right. Our conferences with Professor, now Monsignor, Mercier will be an
invaluable assistance in determining the course of studies of
the university . . ." [77] A final point which Keane emphasized was that Pope Leo wished the university to remain
always under the bishops of America for various reasons
but, principally, "that thus the university will always be
most sure to remain thoroughly American, thoroughly in
sympathy with the spirit of the church in the whole
country." [78]

This article was commented on widely in the Catholic
press, as was natural, and the New York *Tribune* used it
as the basis for another long editorial on the university in
which they cited Leo XIII's ideas on the new foundation
with warm approval. The editorial writer concluded:

Whatever may be the feeling of Americans toward the
Church of Rome, they cannot object to such a fair and
generous rivalry as is implied in the equipment of a great
university of learning. If they did object they would certainly cease to do so when they read the words of the Pope
in regard to it: "I wish that it should be founded by American means, and that it should be conducted by American
brains, and if at first you have to call in the help of foreign
talent in your faculties, it must be with the view of developing home intellect, of training professors who will
gradually form indigenous faculties worthy of the name the
university bears."

An institution of learning which is thus to remain forever
"under the authority and protection of the bishops of the

---

[77] *Ibid.,* p. 152.
[78] *Ibid.,* p. 151.

country," and which in its government and curriculum is to reflect the spirit and needs of the people for whose benefit it is to be established, deserves all the success which will undoubtedly come to it.[79]

[79] New York *Tribune,* October 10, 1887, editorial, "The American Catholic University."

V

Bishop Keane Takes Control

THE FORMAL appointment of John Joseph Keane as first rector of the Catholic University of America took place at the meeting of the university committee in Baltimore on September 7, 1887. Keane had been present in the Third Plenary Council of 1884 and had voted for a university, but it was not until May, 1885, that he was elected to membership on the university committee. A year later at the meeting of May 12, 1886, the four archbishops of the committee had selected Bishop Keane to be the first rector after John Lancaster Spalding had declined the position. In the intervening year between his appointment to the committee and his selection as rector Keane had shown himself a tireless worker in collecting funds for the undertaking. His industry, his outstanding ability as a public speaker, his zeal for the university cause, and finally his generally high quality of intelligence recommended him to the archbishops as the proper man to lead in the difficult work of laying the foundations for a successful university enterprise.

254

John J. Keane was born in Killbarn, Ballyshannon, County Donegal, Ireland, on September 12, 1839. He was one of five children, the other four of whom died at an early age. The family emigrated from Ireland during the famine year of 1848 and went first to New Brunswick. Two years later they moved to Baltimore where young John attended St. Vincent de Paul School and then entered Calvert Hall, the Christian Brothers' school, where he graduated at the age of seventeen. He worked for several months at the bookseller's establishment of John Murphy Company and then for a year or more was employed in the wholesale dry goods store of John S. Barry & Company. While working he studied Latin, Greek, and history on the side. When he was nearly twenty John Keane entered St. Charles College at Ellicott City, Maryland, a preparatory seminary conducted by the Sulpician Fathers which had opened eleven years before. Young Keane made the six-year course in half the time and was ready by 1862 to begin his theology at St. Mary's Seminary in Baltimore which then had between forty and fifty students under the presidency of Joseph P. Dubreul, S.S. He defended his thesis for the baccalaureate and with four others, among them John J. Kain, the future Archbishop of St. Louis, was awarded the degree on June 24, 1863. Keane was ordained to the priesthood on July 2, 1866, by Archbishop Martin J. Spalding and immediately appointed as an assistant at St. Patrick's Church in Washington where he spent his entire period as a priest of the Archdiocese of Baltimore. In March, 1878, six months after the transfer of James Gibbons to the Archbishopric of Baltimore, he was appointed fifth Bishop of Richmond. Keane was consecrated in St. Peter's Cathedral in Richmond by Archbishop Gibbons on August 25 of that year.[1]

While John Keane had made a good record as a preacher and a zealous parish priest during his twelve years at St. Patrick's in Washington and had followed that service by eight years of able administration of the Diocese of Richmond, he was not, as he said himself, in any way qualified by training for the position of a university executive. He was the first to recognize this handicap and he put his limitations honestly before the archbishops. But since the only bishop who had any university experience, namely Spalding, had refused to accept the responsibility, Keane was persuaded to make the attempt. It can be said for John J. Keane that although he knew little or nothing about universities at the time of his original selection in May, 1886, he intelligently set about learning what was expected of him. During the three and a half years which intervened between his choice by the university committee and the formal opening of the university, he traveled widely through America and Europe visiting university foundations and discussing problems of administration and curriculum with leading university minds. The result was that by the time he was ready to begin his active administration in Novem-

---

[1] There is no biography of Bishop Keane. Besides the sketches in the dictionaries of the hierarchy there is the one written by William J. Kerby in the *Dictionary of American Biography*, X, 267–268. Cf. also John T. Reily, *Collections and Recollections in the Life and Times of Cardinal Gibbons* (Martinsburg, West Virginia, 1892–3), II, 648–649. The day that Keane received his A.B. degree, St. Mary's Seminary conferred the doctorate of divinity on five priests, among them Henry B. Coskery, Joseph Paul Dubruel, S.S., and Thomas Foley. Baltimore Cathedral Archives, 32B–Z–1, Acta Episcopalia of Archbishop Kenrick, p. 222.

ber, 1889, an appointment which, incidentally, carried no specified term of years, Keane was better informed than any American bishop on how to conduct a university. He was destined to give the infant institution a vigorous leadership and direction during its first seven years of life when the going was often very rough indeed, and his administration, while not without flaws, when seen through the perspective of over fifty years more than justified the choice of Keane by the archbishops.

From the autumn of 1887 the direction of the university business quite naturally was in Keane's hands. But the formal announcement of his appointment and its approval by Pope Leo XIII did not silence the critics. The first of his series of articles on Catholic universities in the *Catholic World* for November, 1887, drew from Bishop McQuaid the comment, "If Dr. Keane cannot do something better than his first article on the University the latter will have a sickly birth." [2] The Bishop of Rochester continued his opposition to the enterprise and when his obstructive tactics failed to prevent Roman approval of the university he consoled himself by telling Archbishop Corrigan, "having done my duty in warning Rome against too much implication in the University business I can wait patiently further developments. When the enthusiasts go out to get the money the hollowness of the scheme will appear." [3]

While the dark foreboding of the Bishop of Rochester was not to be borne out entirely, it is true that the bishops who had been appointed to collect for the university during

[2] New York Archdiocesan Archives, C–16, Bernard J. McQuaid to M. A. Corrigan, Rochester, November 6, 1887.

[3] NYAA, C–16, Bernard J. McQuaid to M. A. Corrigan, Rochester, November 11, 1887.

the winter of 1887-1888 experienced the inevitable disappointments, but there were heartening responses, too. In order to assist them in their difficult work Cardinal Gibbons, as chairman of the university committee, had printed a circular which he sent to all the bishops of the country. In this communication Gibbons summarized the result of the American bishops' votes on the question of location and he informed them that the decision had been ratified by the Holy See with the results that the Holy Father had "cordially encouraged us to begin at once the erection of the building." [4] The cardinal went on to say that, "from all this it is evident that the Providence of God has committed us in the most absolute manner to the realization of this great project." Therefore, he made a plea that the various ordinaries assist the collectors in raising funds in their respective dioceses. He assured the bishops that it was not the plan of the university committee to lay further burdens upon the poor in general whose contributions were needed for local works of religion and charity. Rather it was the hope of the committee that the bishops would help by their co-operation and encouragement with the wealthier Catholics of their dioceses. Gibbons concluded:

Permit me then, Monseigneur, taking for granted your kind and zealous interest in the noble work to which the voice of the Holy Father and the Providence of God summon us, to ask you that you will inform me at your earliest convenience, whether the Bishops engaged in collecting may not hope to find something in your Diocese, and also at

---

[4] Archives of the Archdiocese of Cincinnati, Letters, 1887, A–K, printed circular of James Gibbons to William H. Elder, Baltimore, November 11, 1887.

what time during the next eight months it will best suit you to invite them and to give them your kind assistance.[5]

The response of the cardinal's circular was, of course, influenced by the opinions of the individual prelates on the university itself. Bishop Stephen V. Ryan of Buffalo wrote to say that he was "perfectly willing to have any of the Most Rev. Committee do what they can in Buffalo at any time that may be convenient for them, but I do not expect that they will do much here, as we have very few of that class on which they rely for help." [6] From the Southwest, John C. Neraz, Bishop of San Antonio, wrote two weeks later, stating, "any bishop who will come to the Diocese of San Antonio has my full approbation, good will & best wishes, and although poor, I hope our people will do their best & I am sure that his Lordship will be well received everywhere. I think the best time to visit the Diocese would be after Easter, as the rains are less frequent and traveling easier." [7] These were encouraging returns, but the last week of November brought a letter which more than offset the generous replies from Buffalo and San Antonio. The promising possibilities of the Archdiocese of New York were closed by Michael Corrigan's reply to Gibbons:

In reply to the printed Circular, just received, asking when the Bishops who propose to collect funds for the University may come to this Diocese *"within the next eight months,"* I beg to say that I cannot invite them to come

---

[5] *Ibid.*

[6] BCA, 83–T–8, S. V. Ryan to James Gibbons, Buffalo, November 29, 1887.

[7] BCA, 83–V–2, John C. Neraz to James Gibbons, San Antonio, December 13, 1887.

here at any time within that period; and with your kind permission, I will state some of the reasons on which this reply is based. 1. The mortgage of $400,000 which was placed on the Cathedral some years ago, is now reaching maturity, and it becomes an urgent duty to provide ways and means to meet the impending obligation. With an annual interest to pay on the large sum of four hundred thousand dollars, I cannot see that attending to this debt should be postponed in favor of any good work, which does not so intimately affect the welfare of this Diocese. 2. The late Mgr. Quinn made a contract for finishing the spires of the Cathedral at a cost of $192,000 promising at the same time to raise the necessary funds. Sickness and death prevented him from fulfilling his promise, and I find this debt pressing on me, while not one dollar has been collected to meet it.

Thirdly, in the Synod of 1886, the Clergy requested me to build a new Seminary, and ground has already been secured for the purpose. The work of building ought soon to be begun. The present Seminary is one hundred and sixty miles distant from the Cathedral, and since the division of this Province, in 1875, is no longer in a *Central* position. Space forbids any further enlarging on these reasons; but even in this crude form, they suffice to explain my position.[8]

A debt of nearly $600,000 was, to be sure, a heavy obligation but the refusal of Archbishop Corrigan to allow the collectors into New York came as a severe setback to prospects for an ample endowment for the new university.

But if this discouraging news brought a disappointment to the university committee another letter of Corrigan's, written the same day to the cardinal, was destined to have

---

[8] BCA, 83–T–6, M. A. Corrigan to James Gibbons, New York, November 28, 1887.

even a more shocking effect. We have seen that Corrigan
had for some months contemplated withdrawing entirely
from the university committee and that he had asked his
friend, Bishop McQuaid, for his advice in the matter.
McQuaid had been quick to urge his resignation. After
deliberating over the matter for some time Corrigan wrote
to Gibbons:

As the care of my Diocese requires all my time and attention, and as I find that I am unable to keep up with
the work to my own satisfaction, I find it necessary to
relieve myself, as much as possible, of all other anxieties
and responsibilities; and I therefore most respectfully tender
Your Eminence my resignation as a member of the Board
of the Catholic University.[9]

Gibbons was deeply affected by this news. He waited for
four or five days and he then wrote Corrigan:

Your letter of the 28th ult. is received in which you
express your determination to resign as a member of the
university Board. I am very much grieved in reading the
letter, for, if Your Grace insists on withdrawing, your action I fear, will have a very depressing effect on the whole
undertaking.

After thinking over the matter for a few days, I have
concluded to ask Your Grace to kindly reconsider your action. I wish I had the persuasive influence of St. Fr. De
Sales to induce you to reconsider. The meetings will be
rare. What is needed is the influence of your name. I hope
you will forgive my importunity, & give me joy by yielding
to my request. Your resignation at a later period after the

[9] BCA, 83–T–6/1, M. A. Corrigan to James Gibbons, New York,
November 28, 1887.

work was begun, would be less disastrous than now, though it would be always felt.[10]

To this plea for his return Archbishop Corrigan told the cardinal he would "make the suggestion of Your Eminence the subject of attentive and careful consideration," [11] but about ten days later he wrote again and told him that his decision to resign was final. "I have calmly considered the question of remaining in the University Board, and regret, for your sake particularly, that I cannot withdraw my resignation." [12] The Cardinal of Baltimore received this intelligence in a resigned manner.

> Your letter is rec'd definitely expressing your determination to resign as a member of the University Board. Fiat Voluntas Dei.
> Since I wrote you before, the President sent me a beautifully engrossed & handsomely bound copy of the Constitution for the Holy Father.
> I forwarded it without delay to Rome.
> I wish Your Grace a happy Christmas & many returns of the joyous Festival.[13]

Corrigan's resignation caused something of a sensation when the news got out. Despite the efforts to keep the matter quiet the rumor began to travel that the Archbishop of New York had quit the university committee.

---

[10] NYAA, C–15, James Gibbons to M. A. Corrigan, Baltimore, December 3, 1887.

[11] BCA, 83–U–6, M. A. Corrigan to James Gibbons, New York, December 6, 1887.

[12] BCA, 83–V–4, M. A. Corrigan to James Gibbons, New York, December 17, 1887.

[13] NYAA, C–15, James Gibbons to M. A. Corrigan, Baltimore, December 23, 1887.

Late in January, in answer to a letter of John Ireland asking for permission to address a temperance group in New
York, Corrigan stated: "As to the University, I have studi-
ously avoided a rupture and simply and quietly withdrawn,
so much so that if any one learn of my resignation, the
knowledge will come first from others." [14] Despite the archbishop's desire to keep the matter out of the public press,
the effort proved unavailing and by the last of January the
papers were carrying the story. McQuaid writing to Gilmour stated, "the newspapers have the story of Archbp.
Corrigan's resignation as trustee of the University. Ordinary
self-respect required him to do so after the treatment he received from Baltimore." [15] An interesting example of the
interest shown during this period in Catholic questions by
the large metropolitan dailies is seen in a sharp editorial
of the Chicago *Tribune* in which it dealt harshly with New
York's archbishop and the motives for his action in withdrawing from the university committee:

It is probably true that Archbishop Corrigan of New
York resigned his position as a trustee of the new Roman
Catholic University of America through jealousy of Card-
inal Gibbons and Bishops Ireland and Keane. Archbishop
Corrigan is a small man intellectually. The three other
prelates mentioned are considered the ablest men of the
Church on this side of the Atlantic. The New York prelate
suffers by comparison with them. He is an accident, owing
his promotion to the personal favor of the late Cardinal
McCloskey. It is entirely in keeping with his record to

[14] NYAA, C–39, M. A. Corrigan to John Ireland, New York, January 23, 1888, copy.

[15] Rochester Diocesan Archives, Bernard J. McQuaid to Richard
Gilmour, Rochester, January 31, 1888, copy from Archives of the
Diocese of Cleveland.

resign his university trusteeship, through jealousy, as it is for him to quarrel with Father McDowell, one of his ablest priests, because the latter wears whiskers.[16]

The writer of the *Tribune* editorial could, of course, be accused of being unduly severe on the Archbishop of New York and of charging him without proof with an unworthy motive. Moreover, his claim for the other three prelates might well be charged to exaggeration. Nonetheless, the archbishop's action from the beginning in regard to the university had not been entirely above the suspicion of double-dealing. The *Church News* for February 5 carried a front page story on the resignation in which Ireland and Keane were quoted as expressing surprise at Corrigan's action since, as it was said, such matters were usually the business of a committee meeting, but the Archbishop of New York had attended the meeting on September 7 with no word of his intention to withdraw from the ranks. The explanation given in some of the papers, namely, that he had withdrawn because he found a clique in control of the university, was repudiated by Ireland and Keane, and as a refutation of that charge the two bishops were quoted as having cited Archbishops Williams and Ryan as two of the most active committee members, "men whom it would be ridiculous to suppose capable of either being enrolled in a clique or being swayed by one." The subject continued to furnish considerable material for newspaper comment

---

[16] Chicago *Tribune*, February 1, 1888. Actually Corrigan was the third choice of McCloskey for his successor in New York. Patrick N. Lynch, Bishop of Charleston, was his first choice for the co-adjutorship of New York, Bishop James F. Loughlin of Brooklyn was second, and Corrigan of Newark was third. Cf. BCA, 75–H–2, John McCloskey to James Gibbons, New York, July 14, 1880.

for some weeks to come and the over-all effect on the university's future was, of course, detrimental. However, the damage done to the cause was, fortunately, only temporary and it was in good measure forgotten when Archbishop Corrigan agreed to reconsider his action and to reverse it a year later.

In the meantime the episcopal collectors were preparing for their work. The Boston *Pilot* of December 24, 1887, carried a lengthy circular letter from St. Paul under date of December 5 in which Bishops Ireland, Keane, and Spalding made an appeal to the priests of the United States for financial aid to the university. They stated that during January and February they intended to visit a few of the larger cities but that their home obligations would not permit them to travel more than this. "We place our reliance upon the reverend clergy and ask them to petition, in their several districts, subscriptions to our fund." The bishops repeated what Gibbons had said in his circular to the hierarchy, namely, that the design was to solicit money from the more well-to-do and not from the poor, and they made, of course, a special point of stating that they felt the priests themselves should be generous to this cause. "Is it too much to expect from each priest in America for this purpose one hundred dollars? Will you, Rev. and dear Sir, be pleased to do your share?" In closing their appeal the three bishops remarked that the work had now advanced to the point where immediate preparation for the erection of a building and for forming a faculty made it necessary to have cash, and, therefore, "promises of subscriptions are not of much avail. We need at once money, as we cannot assume responsibilities unless the means to meet expenses are in the hands of the treasurer." Other

Catholic papers carried the same circular to the different dioceses so that through this medium the priests of the country were made aware of developments in the university project.

These were especially busy months for Bishop Keane as he began in November, 1887, his series of articles on the European Catholic universities for the *Catholic World*. The second article was on the Roman universities and, as in previous writings of Keane, it revealed from quotations and comments that he had made a careful study of John Henry Newman's *Idea of a University*.[17] Keane returned to Richmond for Christmas since he had not yet been relieved by the Holy See of responsibilities for his diocese. The day after Christmas he wrote Cardinal Gibbons, enclosing a letter from John Ireland in which the Bishop of St. Paul told him he could not come east early in January. This disappointed Keane since he felt the time for collecting before Lent was short enough. He, therefore, suggested that they proceed to arrange for two meetings in Baltimore, the one on January 12 for a small group of the wealthier persons and a general meeting on January 15. Keane remarked that the flaw in the title of the Washington property "still hangs fire," but that he was pushing Waggaman to get it settled. Until it was adjusted finally the architect "can do nothing toward finishing plans, making specifications & getting bids,—as nothing of all this can be done till the location is *secured* & *ready* for action, which it is not as yet." [18] He closed by saying that the bishops "are not very

---

[17] John J. Keane, "The Roman Universities," in *Catholic World,* XLVI (Dec. 1887), 313–321.

[18] BCA, 83–W–1, John J. Keane to James Gibbons, Richmond,

enthusiastic in their response to Your Eminence's letter."

Certainly the Bishop of Rochester was not enthusiastic, for he wrote Gibbons on December 28 a long letter in which he said that an unfinished cathedral, collections for a diocesan seminary, and special collections for the Pope, the Propagation of the Faith, and for the Negroes in the South and Indians in the West would prevent any more collections from his people. McQuaid did not lose a chance to repeat that the bishops in the Third Plenary Council had been given to understand the university would be paid for by the wealthy Catholics but now they found that all the Catholic faithful were to be solicited. Referring to the language of the cardinal's circular, McQuaid asserted, "a responsibility which we did not assume cannot be forced on us. It is not wise to claim as the act of Divine Providence what may admit of another explanation." Bishop McQuaid felt that the sending of the circular to his priests by the three bishops without the permission of the local ordinary was entirely unwarranted. "To say the least of it, this mode of superseding diocesan management is extremely indelicate." In order that his part in the whole affair would be known to posterity McQuaid closed his letter by stating:

I expect your Eminence to place this letter together with that of June 11, on record, as part of the history of the founding of the University, so that my reasons for withholding cooperation shall appear in after years. These are official answers to official letters, and are therefore matter of record.[19]

December 26, 1887. Cf. Note 65 of Chapter VI for settlement of the flaw in the title.

[19] BCA, 83–W–6, Bernard J. McQuaid to James Gibbons, Rochester, December 28, 1887.

The care with which the archives of the Archdiocese of
Baltimore have been preserved proves that, at least on this
score, the Bishop of Rochester had nothing to fear from
historians of a later date. How deeply agitated Bishop
McQuaid became over the circular to the priests of the
nation is patent from the letter he wrote to Archbishop
Corrigan in which he said, "was it not very cool for Keane
and Co. to send their joint letter to our priests. They are
determined to override us in our dioceses." He went on to
remark that he had written Gibbons in a frank manner.
"The little man at B. has simply lost his head." He alluded
sarcastically to the story in the press about Gibbons acting
as the intermediary for President Cleveland's letter and
gift of the Constitution to Pope Leo XIII. "If only Mc-
Master or Brownson were living there would be a howl." [20]

In the midst of his travels to collect money Bishop
Keane found time to continue his writing and the January,
1888, issue of the *Catholic World* contained an article by
him on the University of Louvain. He noted that Louvain
had reopened in November, 1834, with only a school of
theology at first and this, said the bishop, offered American
Catholics a good precedent for what they intended at
Washington. He found much to admire in Louvain and he
especially emphasized the Belgian university's care to admit
lay students very soon after the ecclesiastical schools had
been established. This was a favorite theme with Keane in
these formative years and he was at pains to enlarge upon
it at every possible opportunity, namely, that the university
was intended ultimately to serve both the lay and clerical

---

[20] NYAA, C–16, Bernard J. McQuaid to M. A. Corrigan, Rochester, December 26, 1887.

Catholic body. To the question as to why the American university would aim so high in the beginning as to start as a graduate institution, he returned what was equivalent to a negative answer, "plainly because the simpler forms already exist in abundance, and an addition to their number is not called for; nay rather, the establishment of another institution in college or seminary form would be rightly considered an unwelcome intrusion . . ." [21] Keane found authority for his position not only in Louvain but in the ideas of President Gilman of John Hopkins University. Although he thought Louvain had much to teach the American university yet he would have it no slavish imitator, for as he wrote, "we are well assured indeed that neither it nor any other institution can serve as a model to be copied by us in all details; for each nation and each generation has its own special character, to which its university must be adapted." [22] Bishop Keane followed up this article by one the next month on the University of Strassburg, the main ideas of which we have already summarized. [23]

The two Catholic weekly papers of the Archdiocese of Baltimore, the *Catholic Mirror* of Baltimore and the *Church News* of Washington, were meanwhile doing all they could to insure the success of the campaign for funds in their respective cities. The *Mirror* published a lengthy editorial in its issue of January 14, 1888, in which it exhorted the Catholics to be generous to the collectors.

[21] John J. Keane, "The Catholic University of Louvain," in *Catholic World*, XLVI (Jan. 1888), 530.

[22] *Ibid.*, p. 526.

[23] John J. Keane, "The University of Strassburg," in *Catholic World*, XLVI (Feb. 1888), 643–652.

"Though the cost of the projected institution will be great, its importance and the vital necessity that calls it into existence insures its ultimate establishment and completion on the scale outlined in the prospectus." The *Church News* of January 15 reported the meeting in Baltimore on the previous Thursday evening and quoted Keane as having said the object of their present campaign was to endow all the professorial chairs at $50,000 apiece, and that to fully endow the school of theology would take a million dollars. An enthusiastic meeting in Baltimore on Tuesday evening, January 17, was addressed by Keane and Ireland at which Keane reported his Baltimore effort capped by $10,000 from two ladies who promised to leave $40,000 more in their wills. Bishop Ireland said he had received $50,000 in Chicago during a short visit. Keane reported, as well, generous offers from groups of the Polish and German clergy. This Baltimore meeting was given generous space in the Boston *Pilot* of January 28, 1888, and the *Church News* of January 29 stated there was a good attendance at the meeting in Washington the previous Thursday evening held in the Masonic Temple with Cardinal Gibbons presiding. On February 7, Gibbons wrote in his diary:

Bps. Ireland & Keane after spending about two weeks in the diocess [*sic*] left for Philadelphia. They have been collecting for the Catholic University & their appeal has met with a hearty response from our people. The diocess [*sic*] has already subscribed $100,000—including about $12,000 from the clergy & there is the assurance that the subscriptions will be increased to $150,000. The success is largely due to the zealous efforts of the two bishops.[24]

---

[24] BCA, Cardinal Gibbons' Diary, p. 222.

These large meetings in the great centers of population helped to arouse enthusiasm for the undertaking and by early February the building committee felt justified in beginning construction. Archbishop Williams of Boston, who was chairman of this committee, recorded in the episcopal register that he had attended a meeting in Baltimore on February 2 and they had "decided to commence work at once in Washington." [25] While benefactions such as those of the Caldwell sisters, Eugene Kelly, and Patrick Quinn naturally received the major notice, yet small donors, too, were becoming more numerous. Sarah L. Keyes wrote Archbishop Corrigan to say that if the university was sufficiently under way to be assisted by small donations, "I am in the way of getting $500.00 for that institution and can send that amount to you now or at a later date if you wish." [26] Corrigan sent this on to Baltimore and Gibbons thanked him for the gift which had come "through your kind offices." The cardinal told the Archbishop of New York that he had promised Williams he would preach in Boston on March 11 and he hoped, therefore, to call on Corrigan on his way through New York. "Please not to mention it as I want to escape the annoying reporters." [27]

Although the Bishop of Cleveland had been kept informed of most of Bishop McQuaid's moves against the university he had never become a complete convert to the latter's opposition. Writing Cardinal Gibbons in mid-February he still regretted the university had not gone to

[25] Boston Diocesan Archives, Episcopal Register, February 2, 1888.

[26] NYAA, C–20, Sarah L. Keyes to M. A. Corrigan, New York, February 2, 1888.

[27] NYAA, C–15, James Gibbons to M. A. Corrigan, Baltimore, February 4, 1888.

Philadelphia, "but I sincerely pray for its success." [28] While
Bishop Edgar P. Wadhams of Ogdenburg felt the need for
establishing Catholic schools in his diocese was too great to
permit a general campaign for the university he did tell
the cardinal that he would soon send him a list of a few
pastors in the diocese, "that I think could absolutely give
some donation to the University." [29] William G. McCloskey, Bishop of Louisville, wrote Keane and Bishop Maes
of Covington to tell them they were welcome to collect in
his diocese, but he hoped they could help him with confirmation on the Sundays of their stay.[30] Maes did not think
he could arrange to be with Keane in Louisville which was
a disappointment, but as Keane said, "I know well that you
would help me out if you could . . ." [31] Ireland wrote from
St. Paul that Gibbons should try to have President Cleveland at the laying of the cornerstone and he believed if the
cardinal was firm the President would yield. "His presence
will in the eyes of Rome add wondrous prestige to the
ceremony." Ireland went on to say:

The West remains enthusiastic for the University. The
withdrawal of Apb. Corrigan has not done a particle of
harm. The Chicago Tribune said editorially that this withdrawal surprises no one, as Apb. Corrigan is a small man,

---

[28] BCA, 84–C–7, Richard Gilmour to James Gibbons, Cleveland,
February 15, 1888.

[29] BCA, 84–C–11, Edgar P. Wadhams to James Gibbons, Ogdens-
burg, February 20, 1888.

[30] Covington Diocesan Archives, William G. McCloskey to Camillus
P. Maes, Louisville, February 24, 1888; William G. McCloskey to
John J. Keane, Louisville, February 26, 1888. Hereafter these archives
will be referred to as CDA.

[31] CDA, John J. Keane to Camillus P. Maes, Richmond, March
10, 1888.

foolishing [*sic*] jealous of the towering position occupied by Card. Gibbons.

Mgr. Farley, whom I saw, remains steadfast in his allegiance to us.[32]

Five days later the *Freeman's Journal* of March 3, 1888, reported that Ireland and Keane had secured an appointment with the President and that Cleveland had shown considerable interest in the university and had expressed the hope that he would be able to be present for the cornerstone laying.

The news of Archbishop Corrigan's resignation was, of course, sent to Rome. That and other stories apparently disturbed Leo XIII since Denis O'Connell wrote Gibbons that he had been received in audience by the Pope the previous Wednesday and, "the Holy Father spoke to me most seriously, recommending unity & energy among the Bishops in pushing forward the work of the University. I felt it my duty to inform you because he evidently thinks the dignity of the Holy See is involved. He is very much in earnest." [33] Two days later O'Connell wrote again enclosing a clipping from the *Moniteur de Rome* and in this letter he commented, "I think too you will soon find N. Y. much more favorably disposed to the University. Some did

---

[32] BCA, 84–D–6, John Ireland to James Gibbons, St. Paul, February 26, 1888.

[33] BCA, 84–F–7, D. J. O'Connell to James Gibbons, Rome, March 25, 1888. News of the university's progress was followed closely by interested Canadians, too, and Cardinal Taschereau of Quebec wrote Gibbons to say that, "Les journaux m'annoncent que les affaires de votre Université Catholique progressent rapidement. Je vous en félicite cordialement et je bénis le Seigneur d'avoir ainsi donné sa bénediction à cette oeuvre importante." BCA, 84–H–8, Eleazar A. Taschereau to James Gibbons, Quebec, April 6, 1888.

not see the prudence of his last proceedings in that regard.
You still rule." [34] Whatever information the rector of the
American College had that made him optimistic about
Archbishop Corrigan's attitude, he did not reveal it. Kathleen O'Meara wrote Gibbons about the same time from
Paris, thanking him for his note of sympathy on her
mother's death. She told the cardinal they were watching
the news about the university with interest and she hoped,
"the ill news we hear is only gossip—that many wise prelates are opposed to it, & that Gwendolyn Caldwell threat-
ens to go to law to get back her gift because her views are
not being carried out!" She thought the latter story a
fabrication and said she had risked denying it in Paris,
"still, la donna e mobile quel 'al vento [sic], and she is a
strange girl." [35] Bishop Keane, who was in Richmond at this
time, was making preparations for his trip to Louisville.
Bishop McCloskey had written to say he believed the priests
of his diocese were so different in type from those of Baltimore that a meeting of the kind held there would not gain
much. He suggested instead a sermon at the high Mass in
the cathedral on Sunday where Keane could meet the
people and several priests could help him with the collecting. McCloskey himself would have to be out of town, "but
you will be in good hands and every effort will be made to
make your call on the people of Louisville as successful as
possible." [36] Keane had apparently persuaded Bishop Maes

---

[34] BCA, 84–G–2, D. J. O'Connell to James Gibbons, Rome, March
27, 1888.

[35] BCA, 84–G–5, Kathleen O'Meara to James Gibbons, Paris,
March 29, 1888.

[36] CDA, William G. McCloskey to John J. Keane, Louisville,
April 6, 1888.

of Covington to join him in the collecting tour in Louisville on weekdays, for he wrote Maes he would meet him there on Monday and "we will do good work together all the week." In this same letter Keane told Maes he had word from Monsignor O'Connell the day before that the Pope had poured out his heart on the subject of the university in a serious and earnest way. Speaking of Leo XIII, Keane told Maes, "he was evidently displeased at the withdrawal of N. York from a work with which the Pope has so identified himself. Let us work hard all together." [37] Anyone reading the correspondence of Bishop Keane in these years cannot help but admire the courage and persistence which he displayed in this assignment. The job of traveling hundreds of miles on the uncomfortable trains of the 1880's, giving dozens of talks, and then often meeting with meager financial returns was, indeed, no pleasant task. He showed signs now and then of discouragement as, for example, when the Archbishop of New York became so cool to the university work, but he must have possessed a great amount of resiliency since he invariably returned to the routine with a good heart.

· The spring of 1888 found the members of the university committee busy with plans for laying of the cornerstone of the new building which was scheduled for May 24. They were anxious, of course, to have the event celebrated with as much ceremony as possible. It was their belief that a good showing before the public on this occasion would help in spreading interest in the university. Cardinal Gibbons called at the White House on April 9 to urge President

---

[37] CDA, John J. Keane to Camillus P. Maes, Richmond, April 9, 1888.

Cleveland to appoint Frederic R. Coudert (1832-1903) of New York, a distinguished Catholic lawyer, to the position of chief justice of the Supreme Court which had been vacated by the death of Morrison H. Waite on March 23. While the cardinal reported the President as friendly, although non-committal, the intervention of Gibbons in Coudert's behalf did not secure the position. Cleveland appointed Melville W. Fuller. Gibbons used the opportunity of his call on the President to request his attendance at the university ceremony. Concerning this he wrote Archbishop Corrigan, "the President is as yet undecided about attending the laying of the cornerstone of the University. I suppose he must feel his way. He was much pleased with the Pope's letter." [38] The unusual prestige enjoyed by Cardinal Gibbons with public officials was a factor on which the university committee was anxious to capitalize for the benefit of the new institution. Keane was glad to hear the cardinal had taken up the matter at the White House and he wrote to thank Gibbons, "for the admirable seige [sic] which you have laid to the President and the two Houses of Congress. May God prosper your endeavors in that direction." [39] The cardinal had passed on to Keane the remarks of Leo XIII on the need for unity among the bishops on the university question and Keane thought the statements made by the Pope to Denis O'Connell "surely *very significant*." He said he hoped and prayed that Archbishop Corrigan might hear of them and "take them to heart. His loyal adhesion to the cause at last would be a real joy &

---

[38] NYAA, C–15, James Gibbons to M. A. Corrigan, Baltimore, April 10, 1888.

[39] BCA, 84–I–3, John J. Keane to James Gibbons, Richmond, April 11, 1888.

blessing." Gibbons had invited Archbishop Patrick W. Riordan of San Francisco to membership on the university committee and Riordan wrote the rector, telling him he was devoted to the work and believed strongly in its essential importance, but since he was so far away he could not promise to attend the meetings and, therefore, he believed he had better decline. But Keane felt the cardinal should take the opportunity of Riordan's anticipated visit to the East to "insist on his taking the position. His name & influence will be a power, & he can give his views in writing when not able to attend meetings." The rector urged the cardinal to give every possible personal attention to the arrangements for May 24 so that they would go off successfully, and he asked Gibbons if he believed it would be wise to make plans for a banquet on the evening of the cornerstone laying. He recognized that many might not wish to remain over for it and consequently there would be the danger of a small attendance, "and it would be a dismal thing to have the banquet unless we could have a grand civic & ecclesiastical gathering at it. What does your Eminence think about it?"

The Archbishop of Baltimore tried to fulfill the expectations of the rector in giving his personal attention to the ceremony in Washington. He wrote the bishops of the United States, urging their attendance, and he did not fail to stress the fact that Leo XIII was showing a close interest in the university. He told Archbishop Elder that he hoped he would be there as "the H. Father has recently urged all the Bishops to take a warm interest in the great undertaking." [40] Elder replied that this was the first time he had

---

[40] AAC, Letters, Jan. 1, 1888–June 30, 1888, James Gibbons to William H. Elder, Baltimore, April 15, 1888.

heard of the cornerstone laying and he had made "engagements for that week," [41] but the Archbishop of Cincinnati
wanted to speak personally with Gibbons about the difficulties of the Church in New Orleans at the time and he
decided to rearrange his schedule of appointments so that
he could be in Washington for May 24, "if I can count on
having an hour or at least a half hour of conversation—
I will try to be present." [42] The *Church News* of April 22,
1888, announced that construction on the new building had
been begun during the previous week, "and the work will
be pressed forward as rapidly as the nature of the building
will permit." Other replies to Gibbons' invitation continued
to reach Baltimore in these weeks. Louis M. Fink, O.S.B.,
Bishop of Leavenworth, wrote to say that previous appointments would prevent his being present in person, "but not
in spiritu. I pray that God may send fair weather, ex-
pressive of the future history of the Church of Catholic
Learning." [43] Bishop McQuaid, of course, refused to be
present and told Archbishop Corrigan that he had written
Gibbons to that effect, "because I am more strongly convinced than ever of the inevitable failure of the projected
institution." [44] While the Archbishop of New York would
have preferred to remain away he confessed to McQuaid,
"on account of circumstances, it will be more prudent, or
at least more expedient to attend the ceremony at Wash-

---

[41] BCA, 84–J–2, William H. Elder to James Gibbons, Cincinnati,
April 18, 1888.

[42] BCA, 84–L–2, William H. Elder to James Gibbons, New Orleans, May 13, 1888.

[43] BCA, 84–J–14, Louis M. Fink to James Gibbons, Leavenworth,
April 27, 1888.

[44] NYAA, C–16, Bernard J. McQuaid to M. A. Corrigan, Rochester, April 28, 1888.

ington, although it will not be convenient at all to do so." [45]
A throat ailment which had kept him in his bed for a week
would prevent Bishop Flasch of La Crosse from being in
Washington and, "I must beg, therefore, to be excused." [46]

When it came time for the laying of the cornerstone
there were some Jesuits who wished to attend the ceremony. The New York-Maryland provincial, Robert Fulton,
who had made a strong speech against the university in the
Third Plenary Council, was asked by some of his men for
permission to be present. Father Fulton wrote to Cardinal
Gibbons ten days before the event to explain his attitude.
He said that he had thought the matter over and he believed that his course "about the University is plain. To
prevent the risk of any influence against, if there should be
any." Fulton explained his views towards collections in
Jesuit parishes for the university and towards the attendance
of the Jesuits at the laying of the cornerstone. He said:

. . . the superiors subscribe as much as they wish, and as
much as the secular clergy in the locality generally give.
Every one who has asked permission to attend the laying
of the corner stone has received it, except one who was,
I thought, too far off. Between enthusiasm and indifference
there are many degrees, and although my views might not
satisfy Bp. Kane, [*sic*] I think they would satisfy a moderate
and impartial man. I have obtained all I aimed at in my
audience that Your Eminence would understand my position.[47]

---

[45] RDA, M. A. Corrigan to Bernard J. McQuaid, New York, May 4, 1888.

[46] BCA, 84–L–1, Kilian C. Flasch to James Gibbons, La Crosse, May 12, 1888.

[47] BCA, 84–L–5, Robert Fulton, S.J., to James Gibbons, New York, May 14, 1888.

Judge Edouard E. Bermudez of the Supreme Court of
Louisiana wrote to thank Gibbons for inviting him but he
regretted that the court's being in session would prevent
his acceptance.[48] Previous engagements would likewise prevent Bishop William O'Hara of Scranton from being present[49] and the same was true of Archbishop Feehan of Chicago.[50] Old Bishop Grace, who had championed the idea
of a university long before most of the American bishops,
found himself unable to attend because of ill health. He
told the cardinal he had delayed answering in the hope
that he could be there, but "the condition of my health is
so uncertain I have concluded it would be imprudent for
me to leave home." Grace said he was glad to hear so many
bishops were coming to encourage by their presence "an
undertaking which I consider the most momentous for the
interests of religion and the Church in this country." [51]
Bishop Joseph Rademacher of Nashville stated that the
pressure of work would keep him at home, but "I beg to
assure you that this important undertaking shall ever enlist my sincere and active interest, as I intend to prove as

---

[48] BCA, 84–L–3, Edouard E. Bermudez, to James Gibbons, New
Orleans, May 14, 1888. Judge Bermudez took the opportunity to tell
the cardinal that as a representative of the Latin population of New
Orleans he should like to see Placide L. Chapelle, or as second
choice, Bishop Francis S. Chatard of Vincennes, fill the vacancy
created by the death of Archbishop Leray of New Orleans.

[49] BCA, 84–L–6, William O'Hara to James Gibbons, Scranton,
May 15, 1888.

[50] BCA, 84–M–1, P. A. Feehan to James Gibbons, Chicago, May 18,
1888.

[51] BCA, 84–L–8, Thomas L. Grace to James Gibbons, St. Paul,
May 16, 1888.

soon as my circumstances shall permit." [52] A letter in the same vein was received from John Hennessy, Bishop of Dubuque, who said he had deliberately delayed answering in the hope he could be in Washington, but since he now found that impossible, "I beg to assure you that I feel a deep interest in the success of the grand undertaking which will, I hope, be the means of advancing the interests of religion in this country even beyond our most sanguine expectations." [53] While, to be sure, the cardinal would have wished to have the entire American hierarchy in attendance, yet letters of this kind were a source of encouragement and joy to himself and Bishop Keane.

The Boston *Pilot* hailed the beginning of construction on the building at Washington in its issue of May 5 and, recalling the glory of the universities of medieval Europe which had flourished under the Church's auspices, the writer concluded:

Why, since the conditions are immeasurably more favorable to her best development, should not the American University yet renew the glories of the golden days of Oxford and Alcala, when there were 30,000 students within their respective boundaries; or, of Paris, when every known nationality was represented within its walls.

The *Church News* for May 6 published a lengthy and glowing editorial on the significance of the approaching event and the enthusiasm of the editorial writer almost ran away with him when he wrote:

[52] BCA, 84–M–2, Joseph Rademacher to James Gibbons, Nashville, May 19, 1888.

[53] BCA, 84–M–6, John Hennessy to James Gibbons, Dubuque, May 20, 1888.

The 24th of May, 1888, will, in the future, be regarded as
a memorable epoch in the history of the Catholic Church
in America. It is to be the dividing line between two great
periods of the permanent existence of the Church in the
New World. The first began when Columbus raised the
cross in the home of the Indian; and the second is to be
ushered in by the laying of the corner-stone of the great
National university.

It was the suggestion of Bishop Keane that a meeting
of the university committee be held at the time of the
ceremony. He instructed John Farley, secretary of the committee, to notify the members to that effect, and Farley
called the meeting for the evening of May 24 at St. Matthew's Rectory, the residence of Dr. Chapelle. In informing Gibbons of this meeting Farley stated that he had been
told that John Gilmary Shea, the church historian, would
appreciate an invitation to the Washington celebration.
"May I ask Your Eminence to whom shall I apply in the
case." [54] Farley congratulated Gibbons that the prospects of
the university were so promising and he assured the cardinal
that he would regard it always as "my sacred duty" to pray
and work for its success. Keane himself had continued his
collecting in the meanwhile and in Philadelphia he succeeded in getting the Misses Drexel to pledge $50,000, the
endowment for a professorial chair in the university. He
told Cardinal Gibbons that the Drexel gift brought Philadelphia's contributions to nearly $80,000 with Bernard
Farren and others yet to be approached. It gave Keane a
chance to say, "Your Eminence will have to rouse Michael
Jenkins & the family to the founding of a chair, or Balti-

---

[54] BCA, 84-K-8, John M. Farley to James Gibbons, New York,
May 10, 1888.

more will be far passed in the race by Phila." [55] While out
collecting Keane had to give attention to details for the
ceremony of May 24 and he remarked to the cardinal that
Father Edward A. McGurk, S.J., president of Gonzaga
College, had told him that he could take it for granted that
Georgetown College would furnish a choir for the event.
On this he said he would write to Father James A. Doonan,
S.J., president of Georgetown. Keane was puzzled by the
question of the Pope's medal for Miss Caldwell. He told
the cardinal:

I feel quite relieved at learning that Miss Caldwell pre-
fers to be her own guest. Archbishop Ryan seems very
unwilling that she should be made prominent in the public
ceremony. I understood Bp. Ireland to feel quite differently
on that point. Just how & when & where to present the
medal to her is a delicate question, which your Eminence
can decide after conferring with others on the 24th.

As the date of the cornerstone laying neared the Catholic
press gave further details on the program. The Boston
Pilot for May 12 reported that the ceremonies would begin
at four in the afternoon with Cardinal Gibbons presiding
and the address was to be given by Bishop Spalding. A
parade would be formed of societies and representatives
from all the parishes in Washington at Brook's Station to
which trains would run every ten minutes from the Baltimore and Ohio depot. The marshal of the parade would
be Major-General William S. Rosecrans with Major Ed-
mond Mallet as aide and the Marine Band would play.
Moreover, three choirs had been engaged for the occasion,

---

[55] BCA, 84–K–10, John J. Keane to James Gibbons, Philadelphia,
May 11, 1888.

namely, those of St. Mary's Seminary, Baltimore, Georgetown College, and a third group under the direction of
Professor L. E. Gannon of Washington. About ten thousand
invitations had been sent out for the event, one of the features of which would be the presentation to Miss Caldwell
of the papal medal. As yet President Cleveland had not
stated definitely that he would be present, although he told
Dr. Chapelle who visited the White House on May 13, that
he would submit the question to his cabinet on the following day and if a majority agreed to accompany him he
would be there. Cleveland remarked to Chapelle that since
he had an appointment to meet a Presbyterian group on
May 23, "he feels less scruple in encouraging us . . ."[56]
Chapelle assured Cardinal Gibbons that he could entertain
all the bishops at St. Matthew's. He had given orders to
have "the table set in the basement of the Church & as we
will have plenty of room you may extend [a] good many
invitations." He said he had received many letters of
acceptances from members of both houses of Congress
and other officials, among them Secretary of State Thomas
F. Bayard. The charges of the Baltimore & Ohio
Railroad irked Chapelle since the company insisted on
charging the full 15¢ fare for the round-trip ticket. The
pastor of St. Matthew's said many in Washington were
saying the railroad should show as much liberality with
them as "they show at the time of the races & that the
charge should be only ten cents. Could you not have some
pressure brought upon them?" About a week later Chapelle
wrote Gibbons again, enclosing a note sent to him by Secre-

---

[56] BCA, 84–L–4, P. L. Chapelle to James Gibbons, Washington,
May 14, 1888.

tary of the Treasury Charles S. Fairchild, which indicated the President had concluded to be present. "I will try to see his Excellency to-morrow & ascertain beyond peradventure what he intends doing." [57] He assured the cardinal he would have accommodations for any bishops who cared to remain overnight. "Matters are in very good shape, details have been looked into & every effort will be made to make the occasion a grand success the weather permitting." Three days before the ceremony old Bishop Conroy wrote from New York that he would be there. "I greatly rejoice at the beginning of the great work and shall constantly pray for its bright and prosperous future." [58]

The scepticism which Archbishop Ryan of Philadelphia had displayed toward the university almost from the beginning had not appreciably changed up to the time of the laying of the cornerstone. Three days before the Washington ceremony he wrote to Archbishop Corrigan of New York to inquire if the latter were going to Washington. He said that since several members of the board of the American College in Rome were to be present he "thought of consulting them in relation to our finances . . ." He went on to remark that Keane had been in Philadelphia and secured promises of over $80,000, and he added:

I told him very frankly that I could not see how he is going to succeed except by making the Divinity School a regular Seminary with the full course of philosophy & theology & not a mere postgraduate course, as I was satisfied he could not get students enough under our present cir-

---

[57] BCA, 84–M–4, P. L. Chapelle to James Gibbons, Washington, May 20, 1888.

[58] BCA, 84–M–7, John J. Conroy to James Gibbons, New York, May 21, 1888.

cumstances, for such a course. He said that on reflection, he believed so himself & asked me to propose this to the Board. Of course this is a change from what is contemplated in the "Seminarium Principale" of the Baltimore Council (pages 93 & 94—No. 185) but it is the only thing to be done now.[59]

The suggestion of Ryan would, of course, have radically changed the character of the new institution. Whether the matter was ever followed up in the meeting of the committee, there is no way of knowing. Keane must have succeeded in convincing others, or they him, that such a change as the opening of another seminary was not advisable, for when it came November, 1889, the university opened as a graduate school and the introduction of undergraduate courses in theology did not follow for many years. Archbishop Ryan in the same letter told Corrigan that Keane "thinks me not 'enthused' on the university question, & I cannot be until it will be possible to see my way toward its success. What do you think? A first class Seminary under the direction of the Sulpitians with very distinguished professors has a mission here, but an 'American Dunboyne' will do little good & cost an enormous amount of money." Just what Archbishop Corrigan thought of the proposal there is no way of knowing, but it is very unlikely that he would have favored it, considering his attitude towards the university in general, and particularly that he was at this very time making the preliminary arrangements for St. Joseph's Seminary at Dunwoodie.

The architect's design for the new building had been submitted and adopted by the university committee in its

---

[59] NYAA, C–17, P. J. Ryan to M. A. Corrigan, Philadelphia, May 21, 1888.

meeting of September, 1887. E. F. Baldwin of Baltimore drew the plans which called for a central building 55x57 feet, five stories in height, with wings on either side 105x45 feet which would be four stories in height. The total frontage was to be 265 feet with provision made for a chapel in the rear of the central building, classrooms, reception rooms, a library to accommodate 10,000 volumes, refectory, kitchen, recreation room, and prayer hall. The upper floors were designed as living quarters for professors, and sixty-four double rooms for students were made with three double rooms for guests. The building was to be in the Romanesque style of architecture and to be built of brown sandstone.[60] The deed to the property had been recorded on April 21, 1887, with James M. Trotter, Recorder of Deeds of the District of Columbia, and copies certifying that it corresponded exactly with the original were signed on June 4, 1888.[61]

The orator chosen for the ceremony of May 24 was John Lancaster Spalding, Bishop of Peoria, who through his addresses and writings had for the previous years agitated for the opening of an institution of higher studies for priests in the United States. In his address, which was delivered before President Cleveland and his cabinet, some thirty bishops,[62] and a large gathering of people, Spalding reviewed the progress of the Catholic Church in America from the puny status of colonial days to the impressive organization which it had attained by the late nineteenth century. Spalding paid special tribute to American democ-

[60] Boston *Pilot*, September 24, 1887.

[61] NYAA, E–u, Certified copy of deed from James M. Trotter of April 21, 1887, compared with original and signed June 4, 1888.

[62] BDA, Episcopal Register, May 24, 1888.

racy which had created an atmosphere wherein the Church
could prosper without hindrance from the state. He said:

And the special significance of our American Catholic history is not found in the phases of our life which attract attention and are a common theme for declamation; but it
lies in the fact that our example proves that the Church can
thrive, where it is neither protected nor persecuted, but is
simply left to itself to manage its own affairs and to do its
work. Such an experiment had never been made, when we
became an independent people, and its success is of world
wide import, because this is the modern tendency and the
position towards the Church which all the nations will
sooner or later assume; just as they all will be forced finally
to accept popular rule. The great underlying principle of
democracy—that men are brothers and have equal rights,
and that God clothes the soul with freedom, is a truth
taught by Christ, is a truth proclaimed by the Church.[63]

The Bishop of Peoria maintained that the United States
did not owe its position among the nations to numbers and
wealth but rather to the respect for law as being compatible
with civil and religious liberty, and to Spalding, America
has shown "that the state and the church can move in
separate orbits and still co-operate for the common welfare." [64] The speaker went on to pay a tribute to modern
science and its accomplishments for human welfare, em-
phasizing that progress in science was not due to material
causes alone but was the product of intellect and will. The
Church, said the bishop, had room for respect for both the
old and the new. "If there are Catholics who linger regret-

---

[63] *Address of the Rt. Rev. J. L. Spalding, Bishop of Peoria, delivered at the Laying of the Cornerstone of the Catholic University
of America, May 24, 1888* (Peoria, 1888), pp. 6–7.
[64] *Ibid.*, p. 5.

ful amid glories that have vanished, there are also Catholics, who in the midst of their work, feel a confidence which leaves no place for regret; who well understand that the earthly environment in which the Church lives, is subject to change and decay, and that new surroundings imply new tasks and impose new duties." [65] Spalding contended that the modern age was shorn of sentimentality and, therefore, the Church, too, faced up to the new realities produced by modern science. "The scientific habit of mind is not favorable to childlike and unreasoning faith, and the new views of the physical universe which the modern mind is forced to take, bring us face to face with new problems in religion and morals, in politics and society." [66] The university would, then, be a home for ancient wisdom and new learning. His concept of the university's function came out a bit more clearly in this address than in his former utterances. He now conceived its task to be that,

. . . it will teach the best that is known and encourage research; it will be at once a scientific institute, a school of culture and a training ground for the business of life; it will educate the minds that give direction to the age; it will be a nursery of ideas, a center of influence.[67]

Spalding made a defense of religion in education as necessary for the completeness of mental discipline, and he ended his address in tribute to the chief donor in the list of university benefactors:

And now how shall I more fittingly conclude than with

---

[65] *Ibid.*, p. 11.
[66] *Ibid.*, p. 13.
[67] *Ibid.*, pp. 17–18.

the name of her, whose generous heart and enlightened mind were the impulse which has given to what had long been hope deferred and a dreamlike vision, existence and a dwelling place—Mary Gweldolen Caldwell.[68]

Bishop Spalding's address was carried in full text or in extracts in most of the leading Catholic and daily papers in the East. The *Freeman's Journal* of May 26 reprinted parts of it and stated that it had been "pronounced to be brilliant." The *Church News* for May 27 gave the full text, and the *Catholic Mirror* of May 26 spoke of it as a "masterly oration," and said that Spalding's words would not soon be forgotten "by those who were fortunate enough to be present to hear them."

While the American press generally wrote in a tone of high appreciation of Spalding's speech, apparently one of Rome's American correspondents had reported its contents to the Congregation of the Propaganda in an unfavorable light. Nearly a year after it had been delivered, Cardinal Simeoni, Prefect of Propaganda, wrote Archbishop Corrigan to say that there had been referred to the congregation a statement that the address delivered at the cornerstone laying contained, "idee singolare, e poco sane." Simeoni said he understood there were copies of Spalding's talk available and he would, therefore, appreciate having one sent to him. "Prego quindi la S. V. a valersi occupare di questo delicato affare, in quel modo prudente *segreto* e riservato, che la S. V. ben comprende." [69]

---

[68] *Ibid.*, p. 25.

[69] NYAA, I–42, Giovanni Cardinal Simeoni to M. A. Corrigan, Rome, April 8, 1889. Gibbons' diary comment on the event was confined to the following: "The corner stone of the Catholic University was laid today in the presence of the President of the U. States &

The program on May 24 was conducted in the midst of a downpour of rain. The cornerstone of the building was blessed by Cardinal Gibbons. It contained copies of Pope Leo XIII's letter to Gibbons approving the university, of the Constitution of the United States, of the *Congressional Directory,* of the *Catholic Directory* for 1888, of the current issue of the *Catholic Mirror* and other newspapers of the day, of the decrees of the Third Plenary Council; also included were an inscription on parchment giving an historical sketch of the university's founding, a number of coins, pictures of all the presidents from Washington to Cleveland, and a souvenir program of the laying of the cornerstone. During the course of the ceremonies the letter of Leo XIII of May 7, 1887, to Bishop Keane was read in which he spoke of the splendid benefaction of Miss Caldwell and of the desire the Holy Father had to render public thanks to her for her service to the Church. "To exercise liberality in the cause of Christian education at a time when the dangers of false intellectuality are so numerous and so great is surely the most excellent use to which wealth can be put." [70] Bishop Keane also read a letter written by himself in the name of the trustees of the university in which they expressed their gratitude to Miss Caldwell for her gift. Among the guests present for the occasion were the Abbé J. E. Marcoux, vice rector of Laval University

his cabinet, about 25 Bishops, seminarians and about 5,000 people. The weather was most inclement, rain having fallen without interruption for nearly 48 hours previous to the ceremony and continuing during it. Bp. Spalding delivered a scholarly discourse of about an hour's length." BCA, Cardinal Gibbons' Diary, p. 224.

[70] *Catholic Mirror,* May 26, 1888.

and Robert Fulton, S.J., Provincial of the New York-Maryland Province of the Society of Jesus.

Following the ceremony the university board held a meeting at St. Matthew's Rectory in the city. In addition to the regular members, the cardinal invited all the archbishops and bishops present at the cornerstone laying to sit in at this meeting. The resignation of the Archbishop of New York was submitted but the trustees unanimously voted against accepting it and the matter was ordered to be held over until the next meeting.[71] It was moved and voted at this meeting that when a vacancy occurred among the laymen on the board, the place should be filled by a layman. The rector reported that over and above Miss Caldwell's donation there was at the time $600,000 "in good subscriptions." This would be enough to endow six chairs, leaving only two to be endowed. Bishop Keane expressed the opinion that he believed all the funds of the university could be invested in the District of Columbia at six per cent interest. At this meeting Eugene Kelly, treasurer of the board, gave his promise of an additional gift of $50,000 in the name of Mrs. Kelly which raised the Kelly benefaction to $100,000 for which Cardinal Gibbons moved a vote of thanks from the trustees. On the day of the cornerstone laying Miss Lina Caldwell likewise ratified her promise to give $50,000 for the erection of the chapel. It was decided to empower the treasurer to meet the expenses of Edward

---

[71] Keane Memorial, p. 15. While the finances of the university at the time were fairly sound, they were not quite as promising as was indicated that fall in a letter of James Driscoll to Henri Hyvernat from Issy on September 9, 1888, when he said: "The University is being built up and M. Hogan told us that financially there is no difficulty whatever." Hyvernat Collection, Catholic University of America.

A. Pace, a priest of the Diocese of St. Augustine, who was then studying in Europe in preparation for the chair of philosophy. The minutes stated that funds should likewise be advanced to Dr. (blank) who was in the East pursuing studies preparatory to taking the chair of (blank). This was probably meant for Henri Hyvernat who was scheduled to give courses in Assyriology and Egyptology. The trustees decided it would be desirable to have the grounds of the university campus ornamented with statues of great men who had rendered distinguished service to the Church in the United States, and they instructed Keane to open negotiations "with a view of securing the statue of Dr. Brownson for the University." The proposal of Cardinal Gibbons, made at the close of the meeting, to make the formal opening of the university a feature of the centennial celebration of the American hierarchy which would come in the autumn of 1889, was accepted by the members of the trustees "and all the Prelates present with enthusiasm." [72]

In the month following the laying of the cornerstone Bishop Keane published another in his series of articles on the Catholic universities of Europe. This one was devoted to those of France, and we have already seen that he felt the French hierarchy's attempt to start five universities within a very brief time was a mistake. Keane stated that the number of theological students at the Catholic Institute of Paris, "has probably never exceeded fifty." [73] The Church of the United States, he wrote, would in time need more colleges and universities and, therefore, more trained

---

[72] Archives of the Catholic University of America, Minutes of the Meeting of the Board of Trustees, Washington, D. C., May 24, 1888.

[73] John J. Keane, "The Catholic Universities of France," in *Catholic World*, XLVII (June, 1888), 294.

people to staff these institutions. Here was a service which
the university could render to other institutions. As the
Church of America came more fully under the norms of
canon law the bishops would also need men "specially
trained in this important branch of practical learning." The
Boston *Pilot* for May 19, 1888, printed a lengthy article
based on Keane's essay in the *Catholic World* and called
the attention of its readers to the lessons to be learned by
American Catholics from French experience, particularly
in not trying to have too many universities and in not depending on the favor of the state. This same month brought
the article of the ex-president of Cornell University, Andrew D. White, in which he strongly advocated Washington
as the ideal location for a university.[74]

The *Freeman's Journal* of June 2 published an editorial
on the university which reflected the critical attitude of
that leading Catholic weekly. It was written by Maurice
Francis Egan, who was serving the paper as editor after
the death of James McMaster and who later became a professor of English at the Washington university. It read:

The Catholic University, the corner-stone of which was
laid with solemn and imposing ceremonies on May 24th,
will in time perhaps realize the hopes of its projectors. But
this realization will take time, and men's strength and zeal,
and money and students. Just now the question of students
is hardly very important. Why Washington was chosen as
the site remains a mystery, and why the particular place
in which the corner-stone was laid should have been marked
out for a great future edifice is a greater mystery. A more
eligible site could easily have been found.

[74] Andrew D. White, "The Next American University," in *The
Forum*, V (June, 1888), 371–382.

The handsome building of Georgetown College, with magnificent grounds, a site scarcely equaled in the country, and for which, it is said, Princeton once offered to exchange its present position with a large sum to boot, stands in the very territory over which the not-impossible Catholic University will scholastically dominate. The Georgetown structure cannot be wasted. With such grounds, such walks, such a river for boating, such a library, such an observatory, and every other advantage that a college can have, a university seems ready-made. Are we to have two rival colleges in Washington, when, in the fullness of time, the corner-stone laid on May 24th shall be covered by a great building, over which that scholarly serenity described by the Right Rev. Bishop Spalding, in his oration, shall brood? No answer to this question has been yet vouchsafed.

The function last week was very fine, in spite of the rain. Miss Caldwell received the Holy Father's medal—not the golden rose—with beautiful humility. Bishop Spalding filled all expectations, and His Eminence Cardinal Gibbons lent his dignified presence to the occasion. But somehow or other the Catholic University being still a vision of the future, does not excite the enthusiasm it ought to. It must be made a success, if possible. Yet there is a feeling that it will take many years before an efficient corps of professors and a sufficient number of students will make a university at Washington. It seems to have been forgotten that it is men, not buildings, that make a college.

A few days after the appearance of this editorial Egan wrote to Archbishop Corrigan to say that it had "raised a storm." He stated that he did not object at all to the chorus of opposition but he did not wish to carry the matter further until he had learned that the archbishop did not object. "I do not see why I should not give an honest opinion on the subject, and I think that the Washington site is excellent for—a castle in Spain." [75] The *Catholic Mirror* of Baltimore was quick to defend the university in its issue of June 9 in a long editorial entitled, "The Site of the University." The *Mirror* admitted it would be a long time until a full university had been developed but it was at pains to distinguish between a university and a college in this regard. Washington was preferred as the site since it was intended that the university should be a national institution, not a local one. "Where, then, could it be more fittingly or advantageously located than in Washington, the common property of the Union, the common meeting place of the States, where, lifted above local and sectional influences, its growth and greatness shall become the pride of all Catholics and all Americans?" In much the same vein the *Church News* of June 10 made answer to the *Freeman's Journal* and the Washington editor believed that with all due respect to the New York paper, "we must say that the mystery to which it alludes has an existence, if at all, in a very limited circle." Another New York paper, the *Catholic Review,* in its issue of July 13, 1888, defended New York's attitude towards the university and the question of a site. The item, published under "Topics of the Hour," stated:

Some Western writers seem to think that New York has been disappointed in not being selected as the site of the new Catholic University. This is not the fact. Quite the contrary. The ecclesiastical authorities of New York, neither now, nor at any past time, desired to have this city chosen for the purpose. It will be well to have it generally known that so far from New York feeling any special anxiety for its own selection as the site of the new university, it took

[75] NYAA, C–20, Maurice Francis Egan to M. A. Corrigan, New York, June 4, 1888.

very effective steps to have it located elsewhere. It has ample work of its own to do. We believe it is a fact that the only instruction given by the late Cardinal Archbishop to his Coadjutor, on starting for the Council of Baltimore, was to say that he did not wish the university in his diocese, and that was so stated from the very beginning of the consideration of the project by the committee of the Plenary Council, so that New York always was ruled out of the question of the site. It has, however, shown its interest in the work in another way. One of its citizens has subscribed twice as much as any other gentleman, and the young lady whose charity and generosity gave the first impetus to the movement is most assuredly of New York, "born and bred." We may add that no other Catholic project has received such warm, constant and effective advocacy from the New York Catholic press.

Early June found Keane in New England for a tour in behalf of university finances. He arrived in Boston on June 2,[76] and wrote Bishop Maes of Covington two days later to thank him for sending on a contribution of $100 from a Father Elsen of that diocese.[77] On June 5 he preached at St. John's Seminary, Brighton, at the Mass where the annual renewal of clerical promises took place. Following the Mass about eighty priests and the Bishops of Springfield, Hartford, Manchester, and Providence joined Archbishop Williams in the prayer hall to hear Keane's talk on the university.[78] The bishop stayed on through a good part of June in Boston, preaching on June 15 in the Cathedral of the Holy Cross on the Church and higher education,[79] and addressing the Catholic Union and other groups of laymen

---

[76] BDA, Episcopal Register, June 2, 1888.
[77] CDA, John J. Keane to Camillus P. Maes, Boston, June 4, 1888.
[78] BDA, Episcopal Register, June 5, 1888.
[79] Boston *Pilot,* June 16, 1888.

assembled at Williams' invitation. Keane was encouraged
by the response and he wrote Cardinal Gibbons: "Boston
is waking up to the great work slowly, but, I hope surely.
The Archbishop made a *powerful* appeal at the meeting
of the clergy, and they are responding very satisfactorily." [80]
While in Boston the rector thought of a bit of unfinished
business from the day of the cornerstone laying. In the
course of the ceremonies it had happened that the site of
the chapel had not been blessed due to the storm which
was raging. Keane now wrote Chapelle to get authorization
from Cardinal Gibbons to have that done.[81] He further instructed Chapelle about the payment of a number of small
bills. "I wish to be square with all parties,—and when we
meet I will square up with you." Chapelle in turn consulted
the cardinal, saying he felt Gibbons or Keane should do
the blessing, but if Gibbons wished him to do it he would
be glad to comply. He wished to know, however, if it
should be done quietly, "sine strepitu, or would it be advisable to have some public announcement made in reference to it?" [82]

Denis O'Connell had meanwhile been following the
progress of university events in America with close interest.
He informed Gibbons that Leo XIII "brightened up all
over" when he summarized the cardinal's letter about the
pleasure President Cleveland had shown over the solemn
reception given him at the ceremony in Washington on

[80] BCA, 84–P–4, John J. Keane to James Gibbons, Boston, June
16, 1888.

[81] BCA, 84–O–10, John J. Keane to P. L. Chapelle, Boston, June
10, 1888.

[82] BCA, 84–P–1, P. L. Chapelle to James Gibbons, Washington,
June 12, 1888.

May 24, and the Pope replied to O'Connell, "And why not? He is President Cleveland, who made me that *stupendo dono* of the Constitution." Roman opposition to the university had not died out and O'Connell told Gibbons that "opinion here about that institution is divided about as before, maybe intensified." [83] Three weeks later O'Connell wrote again to say he had seen Leo XIII the previous evening and that the Holy Father was delighted with the news of the university. "There will be no difficulty about Bp. Keane's resignation." [84] In an audience granted to Father Benjamin Keiley of Atlanta about the same time the Pope spoke the praises of the university and of Bishop Keane.[85]

John Farley, secretary of the university trustees, was likewise able in these weeks to give Cardinal Gibbons and Bishop Keane some encouraging news. He suggested to the cardinal that the university's corporate title be inserted in the current *Catholic Directory* and Gibbons agreed to carry out this detail.[86] Three weeks later Farley wrote again to say he had received the resignation of Bishop Flasch of La Crosse from the university trustees due to his health and the work of his diocese. In this same letter Farley conveyed information which gladdened the cardinal's heart.

The enclosed extract from to-day's *Catholic Review* sug-

---

[83] BCA, 84–P–7, D. J. O'Connell to James Gibbons, Rome, June 17, 1888.

[84] BCA, 84–R–11, D. J. O'Connell to James Gibbons, Rome, July 8, 1888.

[85] BCA, 84–S–1, D. J. O'Connell to James Gibbons, Rome, July 10, 1888.

[86] NYAA, I–4, James Gibbons to John M. Farley, Baltimore, June 19, 1888.

gests to me the prudence of telling your Eminence a secret.
It is that I am in a position to say that our good Archbishop
will return to the Board of Trustees. He very kindly entertained Mr. Kelly's representations and those of your humble
servant on the subject. But he asked me not to say anything
about it until next meeting, or until he would so inform
your Eminence himself. His Grace has good reasons for
keeping the matter quiet which I may tell you when I have
the honor to meet you. I would not consider myself free
to make it known to you now but that I wish your Em.
to use your influence to stop any such remarks on the matter
as those referred to in the enclosed article. Such things
irritate sometimes & may undo all the good intentions the
Archbishop entertains. His Grace knows nothing of what
I write you, and I pray you *to keep the matter to yourself,
even from Bishop Kean. [sic]* [87]

The Archbishop of Baltimore answered immediately and
revealed how happy he was at the news.

I have barely time to thank you cordially for the good
news contained in your letter just recd. Thank God! Many
thanks also to Mr. Kelly & you. I am delighted at his
Grace's return to us. . . .
Bp. Flasch's unwillingness to serve is all the better, as it
enables us to make one or two desirable [selections?] I will
carefully keep the secret as you request. [88]

The return of the Archbishop of New York to the board of
trustees of the university was, of course, a major event in
the history of these formative years. It would have been
difficult, indeed, to win very widespread support for the

[87] BCA, 84–R–10, John M. Farley to James Gibbons, New York,
July 8, 1888.
[88] NYAA, I–4, James Gibbons to John M. Farley, Baltimore, July
9, 1888.

institution had so important a member of the American hierarchy continued to remain aloof. Denis O'Connell had hinted some months before that he believed Corrigan would return and when, therefore, Gibbons informed him of the fact he stated that the news did not surprise him. "In a late audience with the Holy Father I said the University was getting on well, but of course it had its enemies. 'Si,' he replied, 'quello Corrigan.' " [89]

Mid-July found Bishop Keane in the Diocese of Springfield where Bishop Patrick O'Reilly had invited him to address the clergy on the university at their annual retreat at the College of the Holy Cross in Worcester, and from there he was to go to Providence at the invitation of Bishop Matthew Harkins and to Hartford where Bishop Lawrence McMahon had invited the priests of that diocese to meet Keane on August 10, the Bishop of Hartford's feast day. [90] The work was accumulating to such an extent that Keane felt the need of assistance and before he left for New England Gibbons had suggested that he look for a vice rector in that section. The rector made inquiries among the bishops and clergy and found that the choice of a great many of them was Philip J. Garrigan, pastor of St. Bernard's Church in Fitchburg, Massachusetts. Father Garrigan had been born in Ireland in September, 1840. After finishing St. Charles College in Maryland and St. Joseph's Seminary in Troy, he was ordained in June, 1870. For three years this first priest received into the new Diocese of Springfield was director of the seminary at Troy. The news of his selection

[89] BCA, 84–T–7, D. J. O'Connell to James Gibbons, Rome, July 25, 1888.
[90] Boston *Pilot,* July 14, 1888.

was published in the Boston *Pilot* as early as July 21, 1888, although it was still unofficial. About a month later Keane wrote John Farley from Notre Dame to say that, "through his [Garrigan's] advisers' indiscretion, the press got hold of my preliminary advances to him & gave it forth that he was appointed." Keane stated that, of course, only the board of trustees could appoint Garrigan, and that Archbishop Williams had suggested he get their votes in the matter. So far Williams, Gibbons, Ireland, and Spalding had cast their votes for Garrigan and he now asked Farley for his vote. Keane believed Garrigan was the best man the university could find for the position since he was "a model priest, a polished gentleman, an earnest student, an excellent administrator." The salary agreed on for the vice rector was to be fixed at $1,500 a year and board and he inquired if that figure was agreeable to Farley. Keane was doubtful whether he should approach Archbishop Corrigan in the matter—not yet having heard of Corrigan's change of heart on the university—so he asked Farley to find out if Corrigan would care to cast his vote for the vice rector.[91] As the majority of the board of trustees was agreeable to the selection of Father Garrigan, he was elected and, after winding up his affairs in Fitchburg, he was able to give assistance to Keane in the remaining months before the opening of the university.

Bishop Keane spent the remainder of the month of July, 1888, in New England in behalf of the university's endowment and left in early August for the Middle West. The university was attracting considerable attention in circles outside the Church and the weekly *Jewish Messenger* of

---

[91] NYAA, I–4, John J. Keane to John M. Farley, Notre Dame, August 18, 1888.

New York for July 27, 1888, carried a complimentary
editorial.

> The new Catholic University at Washington has already
> $700,000 in funds, with $100,000 more subscribed, 656
> acres of property paid for, the Divinity building ($175,000)
> ready to be paid for as the contracts call for payment,
> chapel and library provided for by a donor, and eight
> Divinity chairs endowed in perpetuity.
> Our Catholic brethren have made a brilliant beginning,
> and they are to be congratulated. They set an example of
> educational and religious zeal which some plausible people
> criticise as behind the age in free and enlightened America;
> but as the dynamite, not the Messianic, era is apparently
> dawning on free and enlightened America, a well-equipped
> university and a creed that upholds personal morality are
> influences surely not to be despised.

But there were inquisitive and sometimes unfriendly voices,
too. Senator John J. Ingalls of Kansas wrote from Washington to Gibbons inquiring from whom the land was obtained on which the university was being built and whether
or not it was purchased by private funds or from funds
belonging to the Church and devoted to such purposes. The
senator said that he had been requested by a correspondent
to get this information and he would be obliged if the
cardinal felt he could communicate this information.[92] The
Independent, a leading Protestant weekly, carried in its
issues of August 16 and 30, 1888, a long communication
from "a Catholic layman," in which the writer bitterly
criticized the university project. He cited the failure of the
Catholic University of Ireland and said one difference be-

---

[92] BCA, 84–V–5, John J. Ingalls to James Gibbons, Washington,
August 13, 1888.

tween the two universities would be that the Irish school
was intended for the laity and the American for the clergy.
He saw in this attempt to erect an American Maynooth
"the secret object of the Catholic University in Washington." He grew sarcastic about the fact that the endowment
originally sought from the rich would ultimately fall on
the poor, and he was critical of Spalding and Keane, the
latter being characterized as "the divinely appointed President" of the university. The letter ran on in the same vein
with aspersions cast on the Archbishops of Baltimore and
New York for their rivalry as well as the clashing ambitions
of the Bishops of Peoria and Richmond. At the time these
communications appeared Bishop Keane was at Notre
Dame working on the statutes for the university. He wrote
the cardinal that he had sent an answer to the *Independent,*
"in reply to a couple of *vile* articles from a 'Catholic layman' that were sent to me (they sounded very like Mc-
Glynn) . . ." [93] Keane's letter to the editor of the *Independent* was given the front page in the issue of September
20. Keane stated that, "it could hardly be expected that I
should try to follow up our good friend in all his flounder-
ings," but he did take the pains to answer the writer on
the matter of the Church's perennial interest in education
—an interest which even many Protestants appreciated
since they sent their children to Catholic schools—and to
explain the difficulties over the university's site. The university rector remarked that although a measure of failure
had befallen the Dublin and French universities no one
could maintain that the one American foundation would
fail because of the troubles of its European counterparts,

[93] BCA, 85–A–5, John J. Keane to James Gibbons, Notre Dame,
September 6, 1888.

any more than one could hold that "the stability of Harvard or Princeton is endangered by the recent failure of the Queen's University at Glasgow."

The *Catholic World* for August, 1888, published an anonymous article in praise of the university's progress and the writer made a special point of the generous response in money which had been made up to that time. To him it was irrefutable evidence of the fact that the critics of the university were quite wrong in believing that the endowment would not be forthcoming for the project. He covered a good deal of ground about the selection of the site and he used White's article in the *Forum* of two months before as the judgment of a university expert in suggesting Washington as the location for such an institution.[94] On August 5 there occurred the death of General Philip H. Sheridan of Civil War fame. The funeral was held in Washington and Cardinal Gibbons preached at the imposing rites which drew most of official society. Keane was glad to hear that the cardinal had consented to preach since, as he said, "the Christian scenes of his death bed is [*sic*] a noble & opportune theme,—and you have, beyond all others, the tact as well as the influence needed to make the lesson efficacious." In the same letter the rector said he was not surprised to learn of Cardinal Simeoni's hesitancy about his resignation of the Diocese of Richmond "& the University business in general." It was, so Keane thought, in harmony with "the over-cautious and timorous policy which always characterizes him." He said he believed the most convincing evidence for Simeoni in these matters would be a letter from Gibbons

---

[94] Andrew D. White, "The Next American University," in *The Forum,* V (June, 1888), 371–382.

himself. Keane urged Gibbons to recommend Denis O'Connell as his successor in Richmond and to take the opportunity to assure Simeoni of his [Gibbons'] interest and confidence in the university and of his belief that Keane should be relieved without delay of all duties save those pertaining to the university. Writing from Hartford, Bishop Keane told Gibbons he was starting for the West the next night via New York where "I shall spend Sunday with the Paulists, so as to have *one* Sunday free from preaching." [95]

The matter of Rome's acceptance of his resignation of the Diocese of Richmond naturally fretted Keane since he found himself so preoccupied with university business that he was forced to neglect his diocesan administration. He was soon, however, to be set free from that responsibility. Denis O'Connell wrote Gibbons in early August that the matter of the resignation was settled. Leo XIII had accepted it *motu proprio* without awaiting any *relatio* on the subject from the Propaganda. O'Connell refrained from cabling the news since Propaganda wished it kept quiet until they had selected another title for Keane. O'Connell said that Canon Sbarretti had asked him if Keane would bring the constitutions of the university to Rome for approval and he reminded the Archbishop of Baltimore that this was necessary before the university could open. In that case a meeting of the board of trustees should be held before Keane's departure from America, "and New York could fall into line very nicely." [96] Keane confided to his diary that in early June he had sent his resignation from

---

[95] BCA, 84–V–1, John J. Keane to James Gibbons, Hartford, August 9, 1888.

[96] BCA, 84–V–2, D. J. O'Connell to James Gibbons, Grottaferrata, August 9, 1888.

the Diocese of Richmond to Rome after consulting Cardinal Gibbons "& several Bishops." [97] It was not until August 28 that word reached him of Leo XIII's action in the case. He then immediately notified the vicar general of Richmond, Augustine Van de Vyver, that he should assume responsibility as diocesan administrator during the interregnum.[98]

At a meeting of the Catholic Total Abstinence Union of America held in Boston in August the suggestion was made by Father Egan of Tarrytown, New York, that the C.T.A.U. raise a fund sufficient to endow a chair in the new university in honor of the approaching centenary of the birth of Father Theobald Mathew, O.F.M.Cap. (1790–1856), the great Irish apostle of temperance. Bishop Keane was present at a dinner at the Waverly House in Charlestown, Massachusetts, which the Union gave during its convention and he took the occasion to thank the members for their generous impulse in regard to the university chair.[99] Later in the month the *Freeman's Journal* of August 25 took up the suggestion and, although not friendly to the university, the editor gave his strong backing to the proposal. "The *Freeman* is always glad to see men stand by their principles, when they are sound, and we are particularly pleased in this instance to see the Father Mathew men show their colors." *Freeman's* offered to help in any way they could by throwing open their columns to contributors to the cause. The President of the C.T.A.U. that year was the Reverend Thomas J. Conaty of the Diocese

---

[97] Richmond Diocesan Archives, Bishops' Diary, p. 152.

[98] *Ibid.*, p. 152.

[99] Boston *Pilot*, August 11, 1888.

of Springfield who was destined to be Keane's successor as rector of the university.

During this same month of August, Bishop McQuaid of Rochester made the annual report to his people with the customary covering letter. Explaining the provisions which he had made to endow professorships in his diocesan seminary, he remarked that since he had inaugurated the plan, "the bishops in charge of the building of the *Seminarium Principale* . . . are wisely doing the same." McQuaid conceded that this institution might in time "grow into something great." He then added that the university did not propose to open its theological and philosophical instruction until its professorial chairs were well endowed. McQuaid gave this decision his approval and "we wish its managers all success." However, he did not hold out much hope to the people of the Diocese of Rochester that the university would make a mark in the field of higher education for a long time to come.

Necessarily, there cannot be many students in the latter seminary. The longer course in the preparatory seminary, and the multiplied studies in a six years' course of science, philosophy and theology, in diocesan seminaries will leave but few to follow a prolonged course of three or four years more in the Seminarium Principale. Besides, many will prefer Rome, Louvain, or Innspruck. [*sic*].[100]

---

[100] RDA, Pastoral letter of Bernard J. McQuaid, Rochester, August 20, 1888. It was probably this pastoral of McQuaid's which drew from Ireland a comment to the effect that, "the most puerile document I have perused for a long time is that letter from Rochester, in which our 'Seminarium Principale,' is the object of his 'telum imbelle.' " BCA, 85–F–13, John Ireland to James Gibbons, St. Paul, October 12, 1888.

During the late summer of 1888, John Keane was chiefly preoccupied in preparing the statutes of the university for presentation to the Holy See. To do this work he took up his residence at the University of Notre Dame where he made a careful study of the constitutions of universities like Louvain, Laval, Paris, Lille, Strassburg, "and other non-Catholic institutions." He drew up two sets of statutes, one for the general governance of the university and the other for the faculty of theology in particular. He wrote Cardinal Gibbons on August 29 that he had about finished the general statutes and was beginning that day the rules to govern the theology school. He said he would submit them for a preliminary examination to Ireland and Spalding and then send them on to the cardinal. He had just received the news of his release from the Diocese of Richmond, "where I was truly the happiest bishop in America," but he was glad the suspense was over and that "the Diocese can now soon have a bishop who can stay home & attend to it." He agreed with Gibbons that there should be a meeting of the board in November before he sailed for Europe and he felt the consecration of John S. Foley as Bishop of Detroit might afford a good opportunity for the bishops to assemble in Baltimore, and it would give, "as you say, an opportunity to Abp. C. to return gracefully." He asked the cardinal, therefore, to instruct Farley to call the meeting for the day following Foley's consecration. He was planning on soliciting for funds in Chicago through the next month and on September 27 he was scheduled to preach at the conferring of the pallium on John Ireland as first Archbishop of St. Paul.[101]

---

[101] BCA, 84–Y–2, John J. Keane to James Gibbons, Notre Dame, August 29, 1888.

It was in early September that Cardinal Gibbons opened the negotiations with Father J. H. Icard, the Superior General of the Sulpicians in Paris, to have the discipline of the students of the university placed under the charge of this community. Gibbons wrote Icard on September 2, 1888, to place before him the formal invitation of the board of trustees for his men in the United States to assume this work.[102] Archbishop Ireland, who had been promoted to the newly-erected Archdiocese of St. Paul the previous May, was busy in these weeks with speaking engagements in the East and preparing for his own reception of the pallium. He wrote Gibbons that he had passed through Baltimore the previous week but that he did not have time to stop off as he was hurrying on to preach for Bishop John A. Watterson of Columbus at the Ohio centennial. He told the cardinal:

When in New York I called on Abp. Corrigan and found him in every respect a changed man. He is determined, he says, to show himself in harmony with his brother-bishops on all important questions, & he will be present as a director at the next meeting of the University Board. This return to the fold is not at all a matter for secrecy.[103]

The consecration of John Foley was scheduled for November 4 at Baltimore but Archbishop Williams wrote that he could not be there on that day, and, furthermore, he thought it a bad time for bishops to be traveling when the

---

[102] BCA, 85–A–1, James Gibbons to J. H. Icard, S.S., Baltimore, September 2, 1888, copy.

[103] BCA, 85–B–6, John Ireland to James Gibbons, St. Paul, September 14, 1888.

country was astir over the presidential election which would
fall that week. Since Keane believed Williams' presence
at the meeting "is of great importance," he suggested to
Gibbons that they fix on November 13 as a more suitable
date.[104] Denis O'Connell wrote from Rome that he was
glad to hear the university's constitution was in course of
preparation and he hoped "you will have N. Y.'s name to
it. The Pope is determined." He added that Archbishop
Ireland's new province was being shaped "according to
his wishes." [105]

Bishop Keane finished his labors on the statutes by the
middle of October. He had been delayed by side trips
to Chicago to preach in some of the larger churches on
Sundays in the interest of the university endowment. He
had the draft of the statutes printed and sent a copy to
each member of the trustees with the request that they
in turn submit any suggestions to the committee as soon
as possible so that the changes could be made in time for
the meeting of the trustees in November. After the November meeting the statutes would then be printed in final
form for presentation to the Holy See. In the preliminary
draft of the statutes which Keane had drawn up at Notre
Dame after study of the constitutions of a number of other

---

[104] BCA, 85–E–5, John J. Keane to James Gibbons, Chicago,
October 5, 1888.

[105] BCA, 85–F–4, D. J. O'Connell to James Gibbons, Grottaferrata,
October 8, 1888. O'Connell's letters to Gibbons contain frequent
references to the cardinal sending snuff to various Roman dignitaries.
In this letter the rector of the American College wrote: "The snuff
has not come yet. Please don't send any more unless you cannot help
it, because the duties here are in excess of the value. The last snuff
you sent me cost $17.00 to get it to the College."

universities, he had outlined first the general aim and organization of the university. It would be the purpose of the new university to offer to the American people "the highest learning in all its branches, illumined by the fulness of Catholic truth." The university would recognize always the voice of the Catholic Church in the voice of the successor of St. Peter and faithfully follow his authority as a guide. In pursuance of Leo XIII's brief of April 10, 1887, the university would always remain under the authority of the hierarchy of the United States, "in their collective capacity," and their authority would ordinarily be exercised through a board of trustees appointed by a plenary council or other general assembly of the bishops of the whole country. The government of the university under the trustees would be entrusted to a rector, assisted by a university senate. There would likewise be a vice rector, and other officials might be added as the trustees thought necessary. The university would begin with a school of theology, but it "shall comprise in its ultimate scope all the Faculties which constitute a complete University." Professors might be chosen from all religious orders and congregations as well as from the diocesan clergy and the laity, but the control of the university was never to pass to any one religious order in particular.

The bishops of the United States in their collective capacity were to have plenary authority over whatever concerned faith and morals, laws of discipline, and programs and methods of studies. The trustees, through whom this authority would ordinarily be exercised, were to hold office from one plenary council, "or similar assembly," until the next, or until successors had been appointed to replace them. Meanwhile the trustees would have authority to fill vacancies and to increase their number if they thought it advisable. They were to meet at least once a year and whenever summoned by the president of the board. To them belonged, as well, the "definite appointment" of the professors and chief officers of the university, as also the definite suspension or removal of the same. In all such matters the trustees were to confer with the university senate. The trustees, too, were to supervise all investments of money, expenditures, accounts, and records, and to receive from the rector an annual report. The board of trustees might, if they chose, appoint an executive committee of their own members, distinct from the university senate, to see to the execution of its decisions. A majority of the trustees would constitute a quorum for business, provided that all the members had been summoned.

The statutes laid down that the rector was to be a priest and a "Doctor of Divinity." He was to be appointed by the trustees with the approbation of the Holy See and no specific term of years was mentioned for the office. The rector was to govern the university in accordance with the statutes and to be, *ex-officio,* a member of the trustees and president of the university senate. He had the right to preside and to vote at all faculty meetings, and all decisions, other than those of the trustees, would need his signature to be binding. He was to have power to appoint to all positions not reserved in the statutes and, with the advice of the senate, he would enjoy the right to decree a provisional suspension of a professor. The rector, likewise, was to have final authority in matters of student entrance or expulsion and in dispensation from the rules of the university. The vice rector, too, was to be a priest and a doctor of divinity; he was to be nominated by the rector and the university senate and appointed by the trustees. He was to aid the rector in all his duties, "and, in his absence, shall represent him and be vested in his authority." The vice rector was to attend to the faithful discharge of the duties of other officials, professors, and students of the university and to exercise "superintendence over the duties of the Treasurer and the Steward." He was to present a financial statement quarterly to the senate and annually to the trustees. The university senate was to consist of the rector, vice rector, general secretary, "the Presidents of the Colleges," the deans of faculties, and two professors elected by each faculty for two years who would retire at the end of their term and not be eligible for re-election. The senate was to meet monthly and at other times if summoned by the rector. The senate's duties were to correct defects, improve methods, and advance the prosperity and efficiency of the university within the limits of the statutes. A record of their meetings was to be kept by one of their number who would be chosen as secretary.

The deans "and Vice-Deans" were to be nominated by their respective faculties and appointed by the senate to a term of two years with eligibility to be re-elected indefinitely. The deans were to exercise general supervision over the faculties and preside at meetings which should be held once a month; in their absence the vice-deans would substitute for them. Each faculty would choose a secretary who was to keep a record of its meetings. The teaching staff was to consist of professors, associate professors, and tutors. The professors must be practical Catholics and would be appointed by the trustees after consultation with the senate which, in turn, would have consulted the faculty concerned. The same authority was to be exercised in the case of a definitive suspension or removal of a professor. Associate professors were to be appointed by the senate with the advice of the pertinent faculty and were to teach "secondary branches and may, in the case of necessity, occupy chairs provisionally." The tutors were to be employed "to give private lessons or to otherwise assist in teaching." A full professor in one faculty could hold only the rank of an associate professor in another. Nothing contrary to Catholic faith or the decisions of the Holy See was ever to be permitted in the teaching of the university.

In the matter of the program of studies, the statutes as drawn up by Bishop Keane were specific in that they provided for graduate instruction. They were to be throughout the university "of a superior or 'post-graduate' order" and to presuppose that the students would have already finished the ordinary studies pursued in college and seminary. Every student before entrance was to give satisfactory evidence of having completed this training. The statutes stated that the officials of the university were to "assiduously cultivate" friendly relations with the Catholic colleges and seminaries of the United States and these institutions might be affiliated with the university by the board of trustees. In case of affiliation the certificates of the students of such institutions would be regarded as equivalent to entrance examinations to the university. The students were to live at the university unless otherwise arranged by their bishops, or by their parents in the case of lay students, and each residence hall was to be governed by rules laid down by the board of trustees. Provision was made for day students to live at home but they were to abide by regulations concerning such things as "resorts dangerous to morals." Students who presented themselves for examinations for degrees would have to show by their studies and their integrity of life that they were worthy of the honor. The examinations would be oral and written as laid down by rules of the university senate and no student would be judged worthy of graduation except he had shown "solid and distinguished merit." Transfer students from other institutions who applied for degrees might be admitted to the examinations if they showed proper credentials and in that case they would be dealt with on the same terms as students of the university.

To give encouragement to promising students whose means were not adequate, the statutes made provision for free fellowships and scholarships. In assigning these scholarships preference was to be shown to students of the university who had already manifested outstanding merit. Endowed fellowships were also mentioned, the revenues of which would enable men of special ability to continue after graduation and "even to devote their lives to the advancement of learning." No mention was made in the statutes as to the exact number of such scholarships and fellowships, nor were any specific regulations laid down for them. Mary Immaculate, the heavenly patroness of the Church of the United States, was chosen as the patroness of the university and December 8 designated as the patronal feast day. Likewise, in accordance with Leo XIII's brief of August 4, 1880, St. Thomas Aquinas was to be considered a patron of the university. The trustees, the senate, and the rector, "in their respective provinces," were to have power to enact regulations calculated to carry out the provisions of the statutes, and no change in the fundamental law of the university was to be made without the approbation of the Holy See.[106]

When Keane finished the original draft of the statutes he deposited it in the archives at Notre Dame. Speaking of his time there during the summer of 1888, the rector remarked, "This institution has always shown itself very friendly, and has expressed the desire that its best graduates should come to our University and finish their studies." [107] The committee on the statutes suggested a few changes in their wording and the board of trustees at their meeting of November 13 in Baltimore made other minor changes. When these had been incorporated the final draft was submitted to James A. Corcoran, professor of theology in St. Charles Borromeo Seminary at Overbrook, to be translated into Latin for the Roman officials.[108]

Bishop Keane meanwhile returned to Richmond where on Sunday, October 16, he bade farewell to his people in a sermon in the cathedral. His final entry in the diocesan diary read:

I thank God that I leave the Diocese in a healthy & prosperous condition, both religiously & financially. Poverty is still its honorable portion, but it has no debts to crush it & no scandals to deplore, & priests & people are marching on bravely & hopefully. I have been very happy as the Bishop of Richmond, and I leave for new work as a soldier ever ready to obey, & caring not what or where be my task, provided only that God's holy will be done.[109]

[106] NYAA, E–u, Printed copy of the provisional statutes of the Catholic University of America with covering letter of John J. Keane to the committee, Notre Dame, October 15, 1888.

[107] Keane Memorial, p. 16.

[108] *Ibid.*, p. 17.

[109] Richmond Diocesan Archives, Bishops' Diary, p. 152.

Monsignor Farley notified the members of the board of trustees on October 17 of the next meeting fixed for November 13 at the cardinal's residence in Baltimore. He wrote Gibbons, "I saw our good Archbishop yesterday, and he promises to be present, and has postponed two engagements on this account." Farley was able to relay other good news on the university from New York in telling Gibbons that, "the laity here seem to take warmly to the University." Two men had recently called on Farley, he said, to get the legal title of the university as they intended to make substantial gifts to the institution, the one his residence which Farley estimated to be worth at least $30,000 and the other a collection of rare and valuable books. But he confessed, "the clergy here do not seem to be as enthusiastic on the subject as I would wish. But they will come round in time I am convinced. If the Bishops work together harmoniously the clergy will be sure to follow." [110] John Ireland wrote from St. Paul that he would not be able to be in Baltimore for November 13 but he saw no necessity of it since he had "such complete confidence in Bp. Keane's practical judgment, that I have no suggestions to make as to his European tour; my views, also, are well known to him, and coincide with his own." [111]

Since the minutes of the meeting of November 13 were not to be found, the historian must depend on the Catholic press for the business of that particular gathering. The *Catholic Mirror* of November 17 reported that the main consideration was the approval of the statutes drawn up

---

[110] BCA, 85–G–3, John M. Farley to James Gibbons, New York, October 18, 1888.

[111] BCA, 85–G–9, John Ireland to James Gibbons, St. Paul, October 27, 1888.

by Keane and other instructions to be given the rector in preparation for his European trip. During Keane's absence the vice rector, Philip J. Garrigan, would be in charge of all matters relating to the university and would be in residence at St. Matthew's Rectory in Washington with Father Chapelle. Announcement was likewise made that the university would be formally opened at the time of the celebration of the centennial of the American hierarchy in November, 1889. Before he sailed for Europe the rector published another article in the *Catholic World* entitled, "A Chat about the Catholic University." In this article Keane sought to meet all the objections that had been raised by critics in the form of a dialogue between himself and two gentlemen he met on a train. To the objection that a "magnificent" institution was being built, the rector replied that it was not of such proportions as to deserve that adjective. He surprised them by saying that the first eight or ten professors would all be engaged in teaching theology and he explained the many ramifications of theological science which made this necessary. One of the men, a non-Catholic, stated that he had heard the charge made that if the Catholics got in power they would "try to force your convictions on your fellow-citizens who differ with you." To this Keane gave assurance that it need never be feared. The objection that the university committee had gone beyond the mind of the Third Plenary Council in the matter of the university was met by Keane by saying he did not know where the idea had arisen; by explaining the language of the decree he demonstrated that the council had, indeed, provided that the initial school of theology should be in time a full university. Asked if the bishops were not divided about Washington, Keane replied they were, but

the great majority had favored the national capital in their
votes on the question. To the question would the university
not injure Georgetown, the rector replied that the bishops
would not think of injuring "dear old Georgetown." The
purposes of the two institutions were different, and, therefore, there would be no conflict. Asked if the university
might not have been set up in one of the existing colleges
and under the Jesuits whose long tradition in higher education might seem to recommend them, Keane replied it was
the wish of the hierarchy that the university be under no
one religious order. He went on to say that "only a few
weeks ago I received from the Late Provincial of the Eastern Province, himself one of the most distinguished men of
the order, a letter in which he denounced as a calumny the
assertion made by some silly people that the Jesuits have
been in opposition to the University, and he declared that
any possible individual act having such an appearance
ought to be explained, or be punished." [112] Keane likewise
answered the objection that the university would be a southern institution and the charge of the "Catholic layman" in
the *Independent* which had appeared several months previous. The final question was directed by the rector's com-
panions to whether or not he thought his university would
rival such institutions as Harvard and Yale in excellence
and prestige. To which Keane replied that it would, of
course, be quite unreasonable to expect that anything of
that kind would happen for some time, for Harvard itself
was a long time in building its reputation. But the rector
hoped the day would come when the new university would

---

[112] John J. Keane, "A Chat about the Catholic University," in
Catholic World, XLVIII (Nov. 1888), 224.

give instruction as good as that of Harvard, "and give a great deal more besides, which we, from our standpoint of theology and philosophy, can well give, but which they, from theirs, cannot give possibly." [113]

Bishop Keane made reservations to sail on the *Gascoigne* from New York on November 17. While waiting to sail he met Bishop James O'Connor of Omaha who told him he had made the long trip to New York to try to persuade him of the need for the university to exercise some sort of supervision over the instruction given in the Catholic colleges and seminaries of the country. O'Connor deplored their low academic standards and he told Keane he felt that unless coercion of some kind came from the outside the situation was almost hopeless in many of these institutions. Keane endeavored to show the Bishop of Omaha the practical difficulties in the way of his suggestion and the resistance it would meet from some of the institutions themselves, but he promised to use his influence in Rome to at least plant the germ of the idea by recommending affiliation of other institutions with the university. He later wrote, "this explains a sentence to that effect in the Holy Father's Brief of March 7th, '89." [114] O'Connor had been a seminary professor at St. Michael's in Pittsburgh and later at Overbrook where he also served for a time as rector. He was the same Bishop O'Connor who had shown at the beginning such a sceptical attitude toward the university;[115] the interval of several years had apparently convinced him of the service which the new university might render to the Catholic colleges and seminaries of the United States.

---

[113] *Ibid.*, p. 226.
[114] Keane Memorial, pp. 17–18.
[115] Cf. p. 130 of this study.

VI
Final Preparations

WHEN JOHN J. KEANE sailed for Europe on the *Gascoigne*
on November 17, 1888, it was principally with two objects
in mind. First, to seek the approval of the Holy See for the
university statutes which had been accepted by the board
of trustees at its Baltimore meeting on November 13, and
secondly, to secure the professors to whom would be entrusted the instruction of the university's first students. One
of the most gratifying features of the meeting on November
13 had been the presence of Archbishop Corrigan. His return to the university board was, naturally, a source of
deep and sincere satisfaction to all those who had in hand
the difficult task of launching the university. The continued
absence of the Archbishop of New York would have been
a crippling circumstance in the university's formative stage
and it was reassuring to find that Corrigan not only attended the meeting but that he agreed to serve as the chairman of a committee for gathering books for the library.
Bishop Keane learned after reaching Rome that someone
had spread the rumor there that he had brought pressure

on Pope Leo XIII to have the archbishop return to the board. Whoever the party was he represented it as a humiliation which Archbishop Corrigan was compelled to suffer at Keane's hands. The rector repudiated the insinuation and, writing of the unpleasant episode later, he said, "I never did anything of the kind, never in any way invoked the action of the Holy See in regard to it." [1] Keane stated that his action was confined solely to urging those archbishops who he thought had the most influence with the Archbishop of New York to persuade him to return to the board in the interests of harmony.

While Keane was absent in Europe work on the building was pushed in Washington under the general supervision of Father Garrigan, the vice rector. A correspondent of the Boston *Pilot* visited the grounds in early November and reported to his paper the progress that was being made. He said he found 160 men at work on the structure which was up to the fourth story and about ready for the roof. In a long article to the *Pilot* the correspondent described the highways leading to the university through Bunker Hill Road, the firs, cedars, and poplars that grew on the property, and the fine view which was to be gained from the high elevation on which the building was rising.

We were looking down on the beautiful city. The Capitol and Washington's Monument glowed in the sunset. The Potomac ran a river of molten gold. The first century of the Catholic Church's life in free America was epitomized in the dimly deserted [sic] towers of Georgetown College of the Jesuits on the one hand; the second century was prophesied in the University from which we had turned away. More Catholics were gathered together on the Uni-

---

[1] Keane Memorial, p. 17.

versity grounds for the laying of the corner-stone last May than were in the whole country when Georgetown was founded. What estimate of Catholic strength will the chronicler of a hundred years hence be making on the first centenary of the American Catholic University?" [2]

If the writer's estimate of the crowd on May 24 was exaggerated in comparison with the number of Catholics in the United States in 1789, his readers were probably not too aware of the discrepancy. He had a chat with Edward Brady of Baltimore who was superintending the construction. Brady had already performed a like service for St. Martin's and St. Leo's Churches in Baltimore and for St. Mary's Industrial School and Jenkins Memorial Church in that city.

At the meeting in Baltimore on November 13, John M. Farley had submitted his resignation as secretary of the board, in the thought that Bishop Keane might prefer to have Philip Garrigan, the vice rector, in that capacity. Farley wrote to Gibbons to explain the motive behind his action, saying he did it to free Keane from embarrassment, since the rector might wish it that way, "but that out of delicacy he did not say so." [3] Gibbons was relieved to know that Farley did not insist on withdrawing from the board. He told him that his request to resign, "came to me like a thunderclap, & I am delighted that you did not insist in demanding it." The cardinal assured Farley of the high value

---

[2] Boston *Pilot,* November 7, 1888.

[3] Baltimore Cathedral Archives, 85–I–3, John M. Farley to James Gibbons, New York, November 22, 1888. Gibbons had recently issued a circular urging the Catholics to participate in the celebration of Thanksgiving Day by having religious services. Farley complimented him on the suggestion of "a Catholic Celebration of Thanksgiving day. It will have a most excellent effect."

CALDWELL HALL, ORIGINAL BUILDING OF THE UNIVERSITY

which the members of the board placed on his services and he said, "You must continue one of us unless Providence should call you from the diocese at any future time." [4] Archbishop Ireland wrote Gibbons just at this time to say that he felt the presence of Archbishop Corrigan was an important gain. "All now is right. I trust you now pardon me for having when in Rome with you insisted that you should not abandon the project. Nothing now remains, but to prepare magnificent celebrations in Baltimore and Washington for November, 1889." [5] The skies seemed to be brightening in Rome, too, in these late days of 1888, for O'Connell wrote the cardinal to tell him that "Bp. Keane will receive a royal welcome here. The influence of the opposition is not much now." [6]

Before sailing on November 17 the rector gave an interview to the press. He explained the main objects of his mission and he told the reporters he expected to be gone about four months. At the moment the university had $750,000 with large sums promised in California, Min-

---

[4] New York Archdiocesan Archives, I–4, James Gibbons to John M. Farley, Baltimore, November 23, 1888. The cardinal was gratified at the compliment concerning his Thanksgiving circular and he told Farley, "I was informed that such a message would do good in the present juncture of our political affairs."

[5] BCA, 85–I–6, John Ireland to James Gibbons, St. Paul, November 23, 1888. Just at this time there was considerable agitation in the Catholic world over the spoliation of papal properties in Rome by the Italian government. The suggestion had been made that the American hierarchy issue a protest. They decided to confine the matter to a letter. Ireland told Gibbons: "I am most pleased that we are to have no popular protest against the spoliation of the Papal temporalities. The letter will not do much; but it is all that we can reasonably send."

[6] BCA, 85–I–7, D. J. O'Connell to James Gibbons, Rome, November 23, 1888.

nesota, Wisconsin, and Michigan which, Keane believed, would in a few more months swell the endowment fund to $1,000,000. That sum would be sufficient for the immediate purposes of the institution. He gave the reporters an account of the progress of construction and he felt confident that the building would be ready by a year from that time. But to the question as to when the university would be ready to open all its faculties, the rector replied that it might not come "in your day or mine. Our idea is to go step by step . . . We cannot hope to endow all the other professorships for years to come." Keane informed the press that he would be accompanied to Europe by the Reverend Thomas J. Shahan who for the past five years had been chancellor of the Diocese of Hartford. He announced that Shahan would remain in Europe to study and that he would be appointed "the assistant professor of canon law in the university." Finally, he stated that he and Shahan would visit a number of European universities while they were abroad, "to make a thorough study of such details as will be of help to us in the management of the American university." [7] Before sailing Bishop Keane preached at the triduum in honor of Blessed John Baptist de la Salle in St. Patrick's Cathedral, New York, and he took the occasion to pay a public compliment to Archbishop Corrigan for his part in the university foundation.

I thank God, then, that I have the privilege, as rector of the University, of speaking this tribute to the founder of the Brothers of the Christian Schools; that I have the privilege of saying it here to-day at the Cathedral of New York, whose Archbishop has ever been, and is to-day, one

[7] *Catholic American*, November 24, 1888.

of the foremost organizers and directors of the Catholic University.[8]

While Keane allowed himself a bit of the orator's license in his sermon, he doubtless felt that he should not let the opportunity pass of dispelling from the public mind the impression that Archbishop Corrigan was unfriendly toward the university.

An annoying circumstance arose shortly before Keane left America from the contract labor law enacted by Congress in 1885. In the scarcity of labor incident to the Civil War, Congress had passed in 1864 a law which made alien labor contracts valid and enforceable in the courts. In the intervening twenty years, however, the great increase in the number of immigrants alarmed the American labor interests with the result that through the agitation of forces like those of Powderly and his Knights of Labor a law was passed in 1885 which forbade giving assistance or encouragement to immigrants coming to the United States under contract to labor. The law had not been specific as to just what constituted labor. For that reason it was found that certain legal authorities held it pertained, as well, to professional men. This threw the contracts which Keane had intended to offer the European professors into serious question. The rector knew he would have to be cautious and, he confessed, ". . . that ridiculous law, or rather construction placed upon it, will prevent me from entering upon any contract with the professors." [9] The matter dragged on without a definite settlement for nearly a year. Archbishop Ryan wrote Gibbons in early June, 1889, stating he hoped

---

[8] *Church News,* November 25, 1888.
[9] *Ibid.*

something could be done, "to repeal the absurd law which excludes the University professors so that there may be no delay in opening the Institution in November." [10] Richard H. Clarke, a New York Catholic lawyer, counseled Gibbons that if the attorney general upheld the opinion of the Solicitor of the Treasury in barring the professors as professional men under the law, the contracts with these men should "be absolutely annulled by mutual consent & in writing." Clarke suggested that the professors could then "come to America and sign their contracts." [11] On June 4, William P. Hepburn, Solicitor of the Treasury, had given a decision in answer to an inquiry of Martin F. Morris, a Washington attorney, to the effect that the contract labor law did embrace foreign lecturers and professors whose contracts had been signed abroad. The Catholic press took up the matter in editorials severely critical of Hepburn's interpretation of the law.[12] The outcome was that Morris informed Cardinal Gibbons on July 5 that he had succeeded in reaching an agreement with the Secretary of the Treasury by which the professors would be admitted, although the secretary wished it kept confidential for the time being. He gave his word of honor to Morris that the European

---

[10] BCA, 86–C–5, P. J. Ryan to James Gibbons, Philadelphia, June 9, 1889.

[11] BCA, 86–C–6, Richard H. Clarke to James Gibbons, New York, June 10, 1889. Clarke had some years before published a biographical dictionary of the American bishops. In this letter to Gibbons he said: "You kindly lent me a small Ms. Journal of Bishop Bayley of his trip to Europe. Professor Edwards of the University of Notre Dame has set his longing eyes upon it for the Bishops' Memorial Hall at Notre Dame. Shall I give it to Notre Dame in your name or return it to you?"

[12] Boston *Pilot*, June 15, 1889; *Church News*, June 16, 1889.

scholars would not be turned back, "but that, on the contrary, if I would notify him when they were expected, he would give special directions that they should not be interfered with." [13] Morris told the cardinal he had already telegraphed Garrigan and Keane that they could proceed to advise the professors, therefore, that they might come whenever they pleased.

During the absence of the rector in Europe the Archbishop of New York took steps to carry out the task assigned him as chairman of the university committee on the library. Corrigan wrote Gibbons to ask if he was free to purchase books immediately and to draw on the treasurer for their payment, or if he should first submit to the cardinal as chairman of the university board a list of the books desired. He added that he proposed to associate with himself Alphonse Magnien, S.S., John B. Hogan, S.S., Ignatius F. Horstmann, and Sebastian G. Messmer as seminary men who would know best the needs of a library for a school of theology.[14] Gibbons answered the archbishop and told him to go ahead at once and to draw on the treasurer for payment. "As I value your own judgment far more than my own in making the selection, there is no need whatever of submitting the list to me." [15] Corrigan wrote, then, to

---

[13] BCA, 86–E–3, M. F. Morris to James Gibbons, Washington, July 5, 1889.

[14] BCA, 85–J–13, M. A. Corrigan to James Gibbons, New York, November 30, 1888.

[15] NYAA, E–7, James Gibbons to M. A. Corrigan, Baltimore, December 1, 1888. Gibbons likewise told Corrigan that, "all the archbishops who have written to me agree with us that a public agitation of the Temporal Power would be out of place. Abp. Kenrick said he would not sign any letter expressly recommending the restoration of the Temporal Power."

Horstmann of Overbrook, Magnien of St. Mary's, Baltimore, Hogan of Brighton, and Messmer of Seton Hall, asking them to submit lists of books to him and telling them
that the university board had set aside $5,000 as the
amount they could spend, ". . . consequently we can only
think of standard and really useful works that may serve
as the foundation for a good theological collection." [16] The
archbishop told Cardinal Gibbons some days later that he
had begun the work with these professors of theology and
"from present indications I think there will be no difficulty
in carrying out the wishes of the Board, and having the
Library ready by the first of next October." [17] The library
committee received a boon in the handsome gift of Bishop
Michael J. O'Farrell of Trenton. O'Farrell wrote the
cardinal an enthusiastic letter about the university in which
he said:

As I wish very much to be able to contribute my share to
promote that great work, I have thought that your Eminence would kindly accept from me a number of volumes
to begin the library. I think I can send you about a thousand volumes, comprising old editions of the Fathers, Ec-

[16] NYAA, C-39, M. A. Corrigan to Ignatius Horstmann, New
York, December 1, 1888, copy; M. A. Corrigan to A. Magnien,
December, 1888, copy; M. A. Corrigan to S. G. Messmer, New York,
December 3, 1888, copy; M. A. Corrigan to John B. Hogan, New
York, March 8, 1889, copy. Just at this time Archbishop Corrigan
wrote Miss Ella Edes in Rome a long letter on various subjects.
Among other things he said, "I must congratulate you again on your
skill in diplomacy, and I certainly think you are entitled to be one
of the first competitors for the chair in that delicate science to be
erected in the Catholic University," NYAA, C-39, December, 1888,
copy.

[17] BCA, 85-K-7, M. A. Corrigan to James Gibbons, New York,
December 5, 1888.

clesiastical Historians in Greek and Latin, many works
somewhat rare on Theology and Canon Law, and also several editions of the Holy Scriptures in the original languages
& eastern dialects; also various works in Hebrew, Syriac,
Arabic, Armenian and other languages.

Presuming on your consent I have been engaged for some
time in putting these works aside, and in having them
packed in cases. I have already over seven cases filled, and
ready to be sent as soon as your Eminence will inform me
where I may send them.[18]

One of those chosen by Archbishop Corrigan to assist him
in getting books was able, as well, to help with the endowment fund. Ignatius Horstmann forwarded to Gibbons the
check of Martin Maloney of Philadelphia for $1,000 for
the university and he asked the cardinal to acknowledge
it personally. Maloney was a comparatively young man
of forty-two at the time, a practical Catholic, and a man
from whom Horstmann expected "the greatest things in
future for the Church and for charity." [19]

About the same time that the rector of the university
left America, Bishop McQuaid of Rochester sailed for
Rome in an effort to secure a decision in the case of Louis
A. Lambert, a priest of his diocese who had served as pastor at Waterloo, New York, for about twenty years and with
whom the bishop was having a serious controversy. The
Lambert case grew out of the priest's indiscreet utterances
as editor of the Waterloo weekly, *Catholic Times,* and from
a difference on the Irish question and the manner of handling it in the paper the quarrel widened to other issues until

---

[18] BCA, 85–Y–3, Michael J. O'Farrell to James Gibbons, Trenton,
April 22, 1889.

[19] BCA, 85–N–3, Ignatius F. Horstmann to James Gibbons, Philadelphia, January 2, 1889.

the whole case was called to Rome for adjudication.[20]
When McQuaid arrived in Rome he found Bishop Keane
ahead of him; both American bishops were guests of the
American College during their stay in the Eternal City.
The Bishop of Rochester kept his friend, Archbishop Corri-
gan, informed of the developments taking place in Rome.
On December 8 he wrote Corrigan that Keane was there
and he went on to say:

We are very friendly of course, but the University question
is tabooed. I manage however to give him some sly hints,
in speaking of your proposed seminary and of mine. What
a craze the poor man has for knowing grand dignitaries!
. . . Last evening I had a long talk with Dr. Smith, the
most interesting ever held with him. It was on Burtsell,
Lambert and the University. The last subject interested him
most. He was astonished to hear that the Archbishops and
bishops of the U. S. had not been consulted except as to the
location of the University; that the statutes had not been
submitted to their consideration; that there was any thought
of including in its classes the study of elementary theology.
This is a confession in advance of complete defeat. How
far the Holy Father will give me an opportunity of speaking
on this and other pressing subjects I do not know. I have
asked for an audience, and it may be given any day.

Dr. O'Connell was not feeling well, and so he and Bp.
Keane went to Porto D'Anzio for the air, and *possibly* for
the preparation of the University Statutes, etc. I admire
their innocence when they told me of the importance of a
change of air. The Abbot told me that the Cardinals are
quite disturbed by some of Keane's utterances, and they

---

[20] For a complete and documented account of this episode in the
life of Bishop McQuaid, cf. Frederick J. Zwierlein, *The Life and
Letters of Bishop McQuaid*, III, 84–149.

begin to fear that a mistake has been made in naming him as Rector.[21]

Ten days later Keane wrote Gibbons a long letter which was devoted mainly to the candidacy of Denis O'Connell for Richmond, but Keane stated that since arriving in Rome he had been besieged from all sides to withdraw the recommendation. Archbishop Riordan of San Francisco and Bishop Maes of Covington, both of whom were in Rome, joined Cardinals Simeoni and Rampolla and Archbishop Jacobini of the Propaganda in urging that O'Connell be left at his important post as rector of the American College. Keane had given serious consideration to these requests and he then told the Prefect of Propaganda to consider the recommendation of Gibbons and himself as withdrawn. Meanwhile Jacobini was said to have been given instructions by the cardinals of Propaganda to proceed with the appointment of O'Connell to Richmond and to take it to Leo XIII, "considering how often his name had been presented for a mitre." Keane hurried to the Vatican and laid the whole question before the Pope with the result that Leo XIII informed Jacobini that evening that the matter was settled and Denis O'Connell was to remain in Rome, and, added Keane, *"it is well for several important interests in America that he does."* The rector had an audi-

---

[21] NYAA, C–16, Bernard J. McQuaid to M. A. Corrigan, Rome, December 8, 1888. Abbot Bernard Smith, O.S.B., mentioned by McQuaid, was pro-rector of the American College, Rome, from December, 1859, to March, 1860. For many years he was professor of theology in the College of the Propaganda. Richard L. Burtsell, a priest of the Archdiocese of New York, was an outstanding canon lawyer and a friend and supporter of Edward McGlynn in the latter's troubles with Archbishop Corrigan.

ence of Leo XIII on December 18 and he presented the letter of the board of trustees. The Latin translation of the statutes had, unfortunately, not yet arrived from Corcoran and that had caused delay, although Archbishop Ryan had cabled the previous day that they were on the way. "When they come, I will lose no time in having them printed & presented to the Holy Father & the Congregation." [22]

While preoccupied with the unpleasant details of the Lambert case, Bishop McQuaid seemed to find relaxation during this Roman winter in teasing Bishop Keane about the university. He wrote Corrigan that he was having "great fun about the University." When Keane "let out before the boys" that he expected to have Edward Pace and Edward Hanna as professors, McQuaid immediately let it be known he would not get Hanna.

And then in the same presence [I] rapped him unmercifully, especially by telling him that in endowing his professorships he was only copying my example; that I too was preparing my professors for their work; that he might have Pace but I would have Hanna; that I had others nearly as talented who after some years abroad would fill creditably the chairs in my diocesan seminary; that I hoped in time to have honorable competition between Rochester and Washington, etc. and plenty more in the same sense. The

---

[22] BCA, 85–L–9, John J. Keane to James Gibbons, Rome, December 18, 1888. The question of the spoliation of papal properties entered much into the correspondence of the American bishops in these months. Keane told Gibbons he hoped that if a protest had to be made the archbishops together, rather than Gibbons singly, would make it. He advised delaying its publication but if it had to be published then they should stress the Pope's need for "independence & freedom of action without mentioning the *temporal power* at all. I am assured here that such declarations would be acceptable & useful."

boys roared so loud that the Rector heard them in his
own room.

My audience with the Holy Father was exceedingly
pleasant. I introduced [Charles A.] Dana of the Sun, who
spoke warmly in commendation of your course.[23]

Apparently Bishop McQuaid had been given no opportunity to air his views on the university during the audience or he would have informed his friend of it. A month
later he was still having "great fun over the University.
I touch up the Rector every now and then. He is wonder-
fully good-natured." One detects here a slight mellowing
of McQuaid's attitude toward Keane, but if there was a
change in his attitude toward the person there was none
in his views on the institution. He was obviously piqued
that his opinions on the university were not asked for by
the Roman officials. In the same letter he told Archbishop
Corrigan:

I handed Jacobini a short statement in relation to the
Statutes, pointing out some of its dangers. I could not do
more as no one here asked my opinion. The Statutes have
been printed and given in to the Propaganda, but my eyes
have not seen them. Hence I cannot say much. I find that
many people here really believe in its success and are
anticipating grand results. They are astonished when I tell
them that there are two sides to this question. They really
believe that all the American bishops are enthusiastic over
the affair, and are looking forward to wonderful results.
What a disillusion is in store for them![24]

23 NYAA, C–16, Bernard J. McQuaid to M. A. Corrigan, Rome,
December 20, 1888.

24 NYAA, C–16, Bernard J. McQuaid to M. A. Corrigan, Rome,
January 22, 1889.

A good deal of Bishop Keane's time was wasted when
he first got to Rome waiting for the arrival of the Corcoran
translations of the statutes, and when they did come after
a lapse of five weeks it was found that Corcoran had sent
only the regulations governing the theological faculty but
not the general statutes. In order to save time Keane secured the services of a Father Laurenti who was recommended to him as a good latinist and he had Laurenti
translate the general constitutions.[25] When the translations
were handed in to Leo XIII the Pope entrusted their examination to a commission of the Propaganda under the
chairmanship of Cardinal Mazzella. Keane held a number
of conferences with Mazzella and found that the two points
on which the latter chiefly demurred were, first, the requirement of graduation from a college or seminary for
entrance to the university, the cardinal hesitating about approval of the university as exclusively a graduate institution, and, secondly, the requirements for graduation in the
university itself. Keane explained that it was the mind of
the Third Plenary Council that the students should have
already finished the ordinary seminary course and that
such, too, had been the view of the board of trustees. But
Mazzella held his ground and told Keane that his view
was likewise that of Pope Leo XIII and Cardinal Simeoni.
Consequently, Keane finally told him that the bishops of
the board would "be thankful for permission from the Holy
See to derogate from the Council in this matter, and would
see, according to circumstances, whether it would be wise
for them to do so." [26] Keane's loss of this little contest with

[25] Keane Memorial, p. 18.
[26] *Ibid.*, pp. 18–19.

Mazzella was made the subject of sharp rebuke from Bishop McQuaid who "assailed quite violently" the rector and accused him of having secured this concession from the Propaganda so that he could bring the university into competition with the seminaries of the country. McQuaid came close to charging Keane with raising money under false pretenses in that the collectors had said the university would be on a higher level than existing colleges and seminaries. Now he found that it would admit students studying for the priesthood.[27] In this whole affair the misunderstanding which arose by virtue of Rome's insistence on leaving open the university for students who had not completed their theology was unfortunate, since the position of Keane and the other American bishops of the board had been quite clear on the point from the beginning. It naturally aroused fears and misgivings that the university competition would harm the provincial and diocesan seminaries. Fortunately, the university was able to open on the original plan and to continue on it for some years, thus allaying the suspicions of competition.

The other major difference set forth by Cardinal Mazzella on the statutes as they had come from America was the requirements for graduation. The cardinal stated that it was the desire of the Propaganda commission that the requirements should be the same as those in vogue in the colleges of Rome. Keane explained that since the instruction contemplated in Washington would be more advanced than that given in Rome, the requirements for degrees were to be higher. "But less [sic] this might seem presumptuous, I concluded that our conditions for graduation

[27] *Ibid.*, p. 19.

should be at least equal to those demanded in Rome." [28]
Beyond a few other minor changes in expression the
statutes were approved as they stood in a document signed
on March 7, 1889, the same day that the Pope issued
his brief giving the university full pontifical approval. In
his dealings with the Roman officials the rector stated later
that he detected a difference between the attitude at the
Vatican and that at the Propaganda. While he had always
been treated courteously at the Propaganda, he did not
feel the same friendliness there as he did with the Pope.
"To put it plainly, I could always see and feel there the
influence of New York." [29] A case in point was Keane's insistence with Jacobini that the petition of the trustees that
no other university be given approval by the Holy See until
the next plenary council, should appear in the brief which
Jacobini was drawing up. To avoid any difficulty Keane
asked to see the brief before it was submitted to Leo XIII.
The limitation asked for was not in the document. Keane
called the omission to Jacobini's attention and the Secretary
of Propaganda promised to have it inserted, but his phras-
ing was so general that it did not suit Keane and he, therefore, told him it would not do. After some further persuasion he at last got a separate letter from Simeoni covering this point.[30]

While conducting these negotiations with the officials of
Propaganda, Bishop Keane was considering, too, the ques-
tion of professors. News had reached him that a Judge
O'Connor of San Jose, California, had given $50,000.
However, he was concerned about scholarships for deserv-

---

[28] *Ibid.*, p. 20.
[29] *Ibid.*, p. 21.
[30] *Ibid.*

ing and promising students and he wrote Cardinal Gibbons that for this he believed diocesan collections would be the best medium. Keane, too, detected a change in McQuaid's attitude toward himself and he told the cardinal that he hoped that the weeks in Rome would "remove somewhat of his *animosities*. He is evidently growing more tolerant towards both the University & its Rector." He reported a long letter from Bishop O'Connor of Omaha in which the latter was following up their New York conversation on making the university a medium for raising the standards of American seminaries. "This indicates a change of front on his part towards the University which quite astonishes all who hear of it. I don't know how such an idea will be entertained here." [31]

At a dinner given at the American College on January 16 in celebration of Pope Leo XIII's gift of his portrait to that institution and of the forty-first anniversary of Bishop McQuaid's ordination, the latter made a speech in which the *Freeman's Journal* reported him as saying:

But I do not consider the picture a gift from the Holy Father to this college alone; it is his gift to the educational institutions of the United States; it is a gift to the proposed University, to our colleges, academies and seminaries counting by the hundred, and it is also a gift to our parochial schools, in which are to-day over 600,000 children, and in which the standard of education is of a high order. [32]

This passing gesture towards the university was probably

---

[31] BCA, 85–P–9, John J. Keane to James Gibbons, Rome, January 22, 1889.

[32] *Freeman's Journal*, February 9, 1889.

not lost on Keane, Denis O'Connell, and Francesco Satolli who were guests at the dinner. But the Bishop of Rochester had not entirely given up the fight. He wrote Archbishop Corrigan on February 16 that he had held a conversation that day with Denis O'Connell to whom he had rarely spoken on the subject of the university. "In his heart he knows it is destined to failure. Yet he feels bound to keep up the delusion." He had reached the point of referring to it only humorously with Bishop Keane, suggesting to the rector that he hire Lambert as a professor of theology, with Quigley of Toledo, Smith of New Jersey, and Burtsell as "adjunct Professors of Canon Law," under Shahan. All these priests were men with whom their bishops were having some trouble. He told O'Connell the American bishops should have been permitted to see the statutes before they were submitted to the Holy See. "I complained that I had not been allowed to see them long as I had been here." When O'Connell replied that Propaganda had told Keane not to allow anyone to see them, McQuaid countered that the prohibition could not apply to him since, as he wrote Corrigan, he had "an absolute right to see and study them according to the Baltimore Council, calling his [O'Connell's] attention to the passage [of the decrees]. He thought the Council had a great deal in it. I said it had for those who meant to be governed by it." McQuaid informed Corrigan that the statutes had been placed before Propaganda and "all evidently is not plain sailing." Abbot Smith had told him they would not pass unless the Pope overrode the decision of the commission of six cardinals. "Bp. Keane has been busy visiting Cardinals, one after another and writing to Baltimore, etc. I have kept quiet, but never fail to insinuate that the U. will ultimately fail, and for sound reasons." [33]

Another matter of business relating to the university which came before Rome during Bishop Keane's second visit was that of the first house of studies for religious at the Washington foundation. In the middle of February, Father Augustine F. Hewit, C.S.P., Superior General of the Congregation of St. Paul the Apostle, wrote Cardinal Gibbons to say that ever since the formal approval of the university his community had contemplated asking permission to open a house of studies for their men in the neighborhood. Hewit explained that Archbishop Corrigan and Bishop Keane had given their permission and he was writing the cardinal to seek his approval. "The plan in view supposes a Paulist House and community in the vicinity of the University Theological College, distinct but affiliated, in the expectation that the ordinary seminary course will be carried on under the direction of the rector, but hoping to engage the services of University professors for instruction, and to give young priests and alumni who are prepared, the benefit of the higher course in the University." [34] Gibbons answered that it was his impression that the board of trustees had the intention not only of permitting but of inviting religious orders "to establish around the University houses for their communities, & therefore far from opposing I am disposed to give you a cordial welcome." The cardinal said that at the next meeting of the board the matter of inviting the religious orders would be formally considered

[33] NYAA, C–16, Bernard J. McQuaid to M. A. Corrigan, Rome, February 16, 1889.

[34] BCA, 85–R–1, Augustine F. Hewit to James Gibbons, New York, February 13, 1889.

but meanwhile Hewit might make application to the Cardinal Prefect of Propaganda.[35] Following the receipt of Hewit's application, Cardinal Simeoni wrote Gibbons asking if the latter consented before he would answer the Paulist superior. The Archbishop of Baltimore replied that he would not only give his consent but that he would be very pleased to have the Paulist house of studies in his diocese.[36] Hewit was grateful for this warm reception given to his request and he stated that only the matter of money would hold them up as the decorations of the mother church of the community and the need for parochial schools were absorbing a great deal of the Paulists' funds just at the moment.[37]

P. L. Connellan, the Rome correspondent of the Boston *Pilot,* reported on February 1 to his paper a conversation he had with Bishop Keane. The rector told him of the O'Connor gift of $50,000 and also that he had received several burses ranging from $6,000 to $7,000 for scholarships for promising students. Keane stated that $5,000 would furnish enough for board and tuition and sums above that would be devoted to helping these students to purchase books and clothes. The rector told Connellan that negotiations had been opened with Henri Hyvernat, the distinguished authority in Assyriology and Egyptology who at the

---

[35] BCA, 85–R–3, James Gibbons to Augustine F. Hewit, Baltimore, February 18, 1889, copy.

[36] BCA, 85–U–12, Joannes Simeoni to James Gibbons, Rome, March 28, 1889; 85–W–7, James Gibbons to Joannes Simeoni, Baltimore, April 12, 1889, copy.

[37] BCA, 85–W–8, Augustine F. Hewit to James Gibbons, New York, April 13, 1889. Hewit told Gibbons: "Bishop Spalding's address at the laying of the corner stone has made a great sensation in Boston and Cambridge."

time was traveling in the Near East under the auspices of the French government. It was proposed to bring Hyvernat to Washington to teach courses in biblical archaeology and Semitic languages in the new university.[38] During February, Bishop Keane preached a series of sermons in the Church of San Silvestro which were reported as making "a great impression in Roman ecclesiastical circles." [39] In the same month there was held in Washington the centennial of Georgetown College. The event was celebrated on

---

[38] Boston *Pilot,* February 23, 1889.

[39] *Catholic Mirror,* March 9, 1889, in a report from its Roman correspondent, "Luigi," dated February 16, 1889. While the statutes were pending in Rome Bishop Keane was submitted to a close examination by Jacobini on the French translation of his article written in honor of Leo XIII's golden jubilee, entitled "The Providential Mission of Pope Leo XIII." The French translation was printed on the Propaganda press without the *imprimatur* of the Master of the Sacred Palace. Jacobini told Keane he should discuss certain passages in it with Thomas Cardinal Zigliara; the cardinal told him he thought he recalled that portions favored the views of Henry George and McGlynn. Keane denied this and went over the article page by page with Zigliara and convinced the cardinal that the charge was unjustified. Keane found Zigliara opposed to the strong endorsement he had given in the article to the democratic tendencies of the age. When Keane saw Leo XIII he explained the episode and the Pope told him he was certain of his devotedness to the teachings of the Church but to satisfy the cardinal he had suggested the conference with Zigliara. Denis O'Connell informed Keane that he knew for certain that the trouble had arisen when a carefully annotated copy of the article had been sent from New York through Ella Edes and placed in the hands of Cardinal Mazzella, "who was the chief actor in the matter." Keane Memorial, pp. 22–24. This controversial pronouncement of Keane's was first delivered as a lecture in Washington and then printed as a brochure by John Murphy Company under the title, *The Providential Mission of Leo XIII. A Lecture* (Baltimore, 1888). I. T. Hecker made it the basis of a complimentary article in the *Catholic World,* XLVIII (Oct., 1888), 1–13, which he called "The Mission of Leo XIII."

February 20–22. The emphasis on Georgetown as a univer-sity rather than a college attracted some attention and Archbishop Ryan of Philadelphia wrote Cardinal Gibbons to say, "I see that Georgetown is putting forward its *university* character with great energy. However there will be room for both institutions in our wonderful future." George-town, to be sure, had every right to use the name of uni-versity according to its charter. Ryan went on to comment that he had seen in the newspapers that His Holiness had "approved of our University statutes." [40] Cardinal Gibbons had presided at the opening festivities of the Georgetown celebration and was the celebrant of the pontifical Mass on February 20. The cardinal gained the impression during the ceremonies that there was nothing in Georgetown's re-cent moves which would prove inimical to the new uni-versity. He wrote this view to Keane in Rome. The rector answered that he was "thankful indeed that the impression gathered by your Eminence from the Georgetown celebra-tion has been so favorable to the Catholic University. No doubt, other people will draw different conclusions but I am happy to accept the one which you have arrived at. It shall certainly be my constant study to maintain friendly relations with *all*. May God deliver us from the spirit of narrow self-seeking and antagonism." [41]

One of the major objectives of Keane's second Roman trip had by now been attained. On March 7, 1889, Pope

---

[40] BCA, 85–S–6, P. J. Ryan to James Gibbons, Philadelphia, March 4, 1889. In this letter Ryan told Gibbons he would not oppose Igna-tius Horstmann's promotion to the Diocese of Richmond, although he would be sorry to lose him.

[41] BCA, 85–T–3, John J. Keane to James Gibbons, Rome, March 12, 1889.

Leo XIII issued his apostolic letter to Cardinal Gibbons and the American hierarchy in which he placed his final approval on the university at Washington. In this document the Pope expressed his pleasure at the realization of the university project and he stated that the constitutions, submitted to the cardinals of the Congregation of the Propaganda, had been examined. The Pope, therefore, stated that he approved, "by these present letters the statutes and laws of your University, and endow it with the rights proper to a lawfully-constituted University." The right to confer all academic degrees in theology, philosophy, and canon law was granted, "and in those other studies in which the different degrees and the doctorates are usually conferred, whenever the teaching of these branches shall have been established." To Cardinal Gibbons and his successors as Archbishop of Baltimore was given the right to hold the office of chancellor of the university. The Pope asked that the course of studies, "especially in so far as they relate to philosophy and theology," be submitted to the Holy See for approval, and he further requested that there be established in the university a "school of Pontifical law." Leo XIII urged that seminaries and colleges, "and other Catholic institutions," be affiliated with the university according to the plan suggested in the statutes, but in such a way, "as not to destroy their autonomy." This provision of the papal letter was as close as the document came to carrying out the suggestion given to Keane by Bishop O'Connor of Omaha just before the former left the United States. The Holy Father inserted in his letter a suggestion which, had it been adopted immediately by the board of trustees, would have meant a change in the university's character as exclusively a graduate school. The Pope said:

In order that a greater number may enjoy more abundantly the benefits of the teaching of the University in its various departments, let these schools, and especially the Schools of Philosophy and Theology, be thrown open, not only to those who have completed their studies according to the decrees of the Third Plenary Council of Baltimore, but also those who wish to begin or continue their studies.

This was the provision which Cardinal Mazzella had urged on Keane in their discussion of the statutes. The rector had protested the point, only to be charged later by Bishop McQuaid with having introduced it and thus jeopardized the diocesan seminaries. After exhorting the Catholics of America to be generous in their help to the university, the Pope near the end of his letter inserted the sentence which the board of trustees had requested of the Holy See. "And as the University at Washington is established by these our letters, we decree that no other institution of this nature shall be undertaken by anyone without consulting the Apostolic See." [42] This safeguard, as we have seen, did not satisfy Bishop Keane and he, therefore, secured from Cardinal Simeoni a rescript on March 23, 1889, which gave a more specific directive to Leo XIII's sentence. In a letter addressed to Keane the Prefect of Propaganda said:

Now, in order that this declaration may not give opportunity for equivocation or incorrect interpretation, His Holiness has affirmed that this clause must be so understood that there can be no action taken concerning another university in the United States of North America until all the ordinary faculties have been established in the University at

---

[42] Archives of the Catholic University of America, *Constitutions of the Catholic University of America translated from the Latin* (Washington, n.d.), p. 3.

Washington, and unless, before anything whatever has been done in the matter, the Holy See has been consulted.[43]

With the letter of Simeoni in his possession the rector felt more assured.

When the difficult work of the statutes was finished Keane wrote Gibbons that it was "entirely ended, and very satisfactorily." He went on to tell the cardinal that the Pope and the Propaganda *motu proprio* had urged the deviation from the decree of the Third Plenary Council to admit students who had not finished their ordinary course. Since this was the case the bishop was naturally hurt at McQuaid's accusation that he had instigated the charge.

He [McQuaid] spoke of it with the greatest heat & bitterness last Sunday, virtually accusing me of having raised the funds of the University under false pretences of a plan now deliberately abandoned. He says he knows all that was done in that line at the last meeting of the Board! May God grant me patience—and may He deliver us from misrepresentation & treachery.[44]

Keane informed the cardinal that he would have the statutes and the papal documents printed and sent to all the bishops; he expected that visits to some of the European universities and interviewing prospective professors would take about six more weeks of his time after which he would sail for home.

Before leaving Rome the rector of the university was host

---

[43] *Ibid.*, p. 4. The Latin texts of the letters of Leo XIII and Simeoni can be found in *American Ecclesiastical Review*, I (June, 1889), 223–227.

[44] BCA, 85–T–3, John J. Keane to James Gibbons, Rome, March 12, 1889.

at a dinner given at the American College on March 19, the feast of St. Joseph. Accounts of the affair cabled to America were enthusiastic. It was attended by Cardinals Parocchi, Schiaffino, and Bianchi. Cardinal Mazzella, who had been unable to be present, sent a letter to be read. Archbishop Kirby, rector of the Irish College, Bishops McQuaid and Rademacher, Monsignori Robert Seton and Denis O'Connell besides a large group of clergy, and members of the Roman nobility were in attendance. Cardinal Parocchi, the Vicar of Rome, spoke in Latin on the high regard of Leo XIII for the United States and the hope he held out for the university. Archbishop Jacobini of the Propaganda addressed the gathering in his own name and in that of Cardinal Simeoni and contrasted the strong and vigorous Catholic life in America with the painful situation in which the Church found itself in some parts of the old world. Monsignor Paquet, rector of Laval University, spoke in compliment to the sister university in Washington, and Bishop Keane responded to these speeches. The Roman correspondent of the *Catholic Mirror* under date of March 23 described the dinner as, "one of the most successful celebrations that have taken place for a long time, and praise of Bishop Keane, his eloquence, zeal, and enthusiasm in the great work which he is doing is on everybody's lips." [45] At the dinner it was announced that Pope Leo XIII had given the Ugolini portrait of himself which had attracted much attention at the recent Vatican exhibition, to the university as his personal gift. P. L. Connellan writing to the Boston *Pilot* on March 22 with pardonable exaggeration called the dinner, "one of the most significant events

---

[45] *Catholic Mirror,* April 13, 1889.

in the modern history of the Church." [46] One reason why this inaugural dinner received so much attention was, perhaps, because of the presence of a considerable number of newspaper correspondents, there being in attendance representatives of the New York *Herald* and *Sun,* the Boston *Pilot,* the Dublin *Freeman's Journal,* the *Irish Catholic,* the Paris *Union,* and the London *Tablet.* Even the *Freeman's Journal* of New York, which had shown such a begrudging attitude, carried an effusive editorial in its issue of March 23 in which the writer strongly exhorted American Catholics to come behind the project. "The fact that His Holiness, in the midst of his ever-increasing cares, takes such a deep interest in the Washington Catholic University, should, of itself, be an incentive to American Catholics to strain every nerve to make the enterprise worthy of our great Pontiff's interest, to make it the great national university of the United States, a credit to Church and country." [47]

While it was the desire of Bishop Keane that the new institution should be staffed by Americans, he realized that for a while that would prove impossible. For that reason he had, shortly after reaching Europe, begun negotiations with several European professors of distinction. He had

---

[46] Boston *Pilot,* April 13, 1889.

[47] *Freeman's Journal,* March 23, 1889, editorial entitled, "Pope Leo and America." In this editorial the writer referred to an incident which had recently happened at Yale University when some students during the night threw a rope around the statue of Benjamin Silliman and pulled it from its pedestal to the ground. *Freeman's* said in this connection, "Even the most bigoted enemy of the Church must feel the necessity of such an institution in view of the scandals constantly occurring in so-called Protestant colleges." The Yale incident was then recounted. *The Independent* of March 28, 1889, editorialized on the same episode under the title, "The Outrage at Yale."

become acquainted in Rome on his visit in 1886 with Professor Hyvernat, who was then teaching at the Roman Seminary, and on his second trip he entered into a "conditional contract with him which was ratified by the Board, so that he was the first of our Professors chosen." [48] Two young American priests were already in Europe preparing for professorships in the university, namely, Edward A. Pace of the Diocese of St. Augustine and Thomas J. Shahan of the Diocese of Hartford. Pace was to study psychology at the University of Leipzig under the famous Professor Wilhelm Wundt and Shahan was to spend the next three years in the universities of Rome, Germany, and France taking courses in church history, rather than canon law for which he was first destined. Keane tried to secure the services of Professor Checci who taught moral theology at the College of the Propaganda but he was not successful. He had first in mind to secure a Roman for canon law, but he was persuaded to seek Sebastian G. Messmer of Seton Hall

---

[48] Keane Memorial, p. 24. On Professor Hyvernat cf. the memorial sketch of his life and academic attainments by Theodore C. Petersen, C.S.P., "Professor Henry Hyvernat," in *Catholic World*, CLIII (Sept. 1941), 653–666, written some months after Hyvernat's death. Bishop Keane first approached Abbé François Vigoroux, S.S., the famous scripture scholar in Paris, to join the new university but Vigoroux suggested to the rector that he get in touch with his former student, Henri Hyvernat. Evidence of the fact that Keane and Vigoroux discussed Hyvernat for the university is found in the letter of Vigoroux to Hyvernat from Paris, June 28, 1887, in the Hyvernat Collection at the Catholic University of America. In the same collection is a letter from James Driscoll at Issy to Hyvernat written on November 29, 1888, in which he said Keane had been at Issy "the day before yesterday," and he went on to tell Hyvernat: "He is going to use his persuasion to engage the Père Lepidi, and not only do I hope and pray he may succeed, but moreover I have reason to believe that he will."

College for that position. He, therefore, wrote Messmer, a Swiss-born priest who was forty-one years of age at the time. Messmer had been trained at the Seminary of St. George in St. Gall and at the University of Innsbruck. The Seton Hall professor immediately got in touch with Archbishop Corrigan and Cardinal Gibbons upon receipt of Keane's letter, asking them if they thought he should accept and if they considered him fit for the position. As he told Corrigan, "I need not say that the position would just suit my taste & inclination; but then, likes or dislikes are a very poor criterion." [49] Keane had told him that if he accepted he should resign from Seton Hall at the end of the current academic year, attend lectures in civil law during the winter, and then go on to Rome where he would take the degree of doctor of both laws. Gibbons replied that he should accept and Messmer wrote him in thanks and said that he had communicated his assent to Bishop Keane. "I certainly can say one thing before God: that I seek no personal advancement in accepting the position, but only his greater glory." [50]

From Rome, Keane went to Fiesole to interview the general of the Jesuits with a view to securing the famous moral theologian, Father August Lehmkuhl, S.J., but he found that because of impaired health it was doubtful if he could ever teach again. By early April he had reached Germany and at Fulda he got in touch with Professor Joseph Pohle, "one of the first philosophers of Germany," and succeeded

---

[49] NYAA, C–24, S. G. Messmer to M. A. Corrigan, South Orange, April 3, 1889; BCA, 85–W–3, S. G. Messmer to James Gibbons, South Orange, April 7, 1889.

[50] BCA, 85–W–10, S. G. Messmer to James Gibbons, South Orange, April 15, 1889.

in engaging him for the university faculty.[51] From Fulda
the rector traveled on to Bonn, Cologne, Münster, Louvain,
Liège, and Paris. At Louvain he tried unsuccessfully to engage Bernard Jungmann, the dogmatic theologian. He did
enter into a conditional contract with Joseph Schroeder
of the Cologne seminary to teach dogmatic theology.
Thomas Bouquillon of the Catholic Institute of Lille was
engaged to teach moral theology. The following summer
William Byrne, vicar general of the Archdiocese of Boston and former president at Emmitsburg, wrote a strong
letter of recommendation of Charles P. Grannan who
since October, 1881, had taught scripture at Mount Saint
Mary's Seminary in Emmitsburg.[52] Byrne outlined to
Cardinal Gibbons the qualifications of Grannan for sacred
scripture in the new university. But since he was a priest
of the Archdiocese of New York no action could be taken
until Archbishop Corrigan's permission had been secured.
The matter dragged on for some months and Corrigan
finally wrote Keane his assent. However, a misunderstanding had arisen, since the archbishop believed that Grannan
had already been offered the position. Keane was quick
to tell him that *"no invitation whatsoever has thus far*

---

[51] BCA, 85–V–7, John J. Keane to James Gibbons, Fulda, April 5,
1889. Keane confessed to the cardinal that securing the professors
"is a task full of difficulties,—but I push on, trusting in God, whose
work we are trying to do." In the same letter he stated that he felt
compelled to differ from Gibbons' judgment in regard to the suit-
ability of Ignatius Horstmann for the Diocese of Richmond. He expressed himself in that manner to Jacobini before leaving Rome and
instead of Horstmann he favored Devine. George W. Devine was the
chancellor of Baltimore from 1881 to 1885.

[52] BCA, 86–F–5, William Byrne to James Gibbons, Boston, July
25, 1889.

been given him." [53] Knowing the background of Archbishop Corrigan's relations with the university, the rector was at pains to assure him that no thought of engaging Grannan was entertained until they had first learned that the appointment would be pleasing to the archbishop, "both as his Ordinary and as a member of the Board of Directors." Keane stated that Grannan had assured him that he had not meant to convey the idea that he had been formally invited and the rector closed by saying he hoped Archbishop Corrigan would be pleased, however, to give permission for this priest to join the faculty. The Archbishop of New York then wrote to say that the misunderstanding had been cleared and he gave his consent for Grannan to join the faculty and, "in case the University or Mt. St. Mary's do not need Dr. Grannan, abundance of work awaits him at home, where he would be very useful, and very welcome." [54] On receipt of this letter Keane thanked Corrigan for his help in the matter and said that he was inviting Grannan the same day to join the university staff and to prepare himself for the position "by some years of study in Europe." [55]

In addition to the priests mentioned above, Bishop Keane entered into a contract with Charles Warren Stoddard, lecturer and writer, who had been converted to the Catholic Church in 1867 at the age of twenty-four and had taught English for a time at the University of Notre Dame.

---

[53] NYAA, C–16, John J. Keane to M. A. Corrigan, Washington, September 11, 1889.

[54] NYAA, C–16, M. A. Corrigan to John J. Keane, New York, September 16, 1889, copy.

[55] NYAA, C–16, John J. Keane to M. A. Corrigan, Washington, September 20, 1889.

Stoddard was engaged to teach English in Washington. There was considerable rumor through the spring and summer of 1889 about the faculty that would inaugurate the new university. Bishop Foley of Detroit wrote Cardinal Gibbons to say that it had appeared in the papers and had been confirmed in the Dacotah [*sic*] *Catholic* that Bishop Marty of Dakota was to lecture on plain chant, "as one of the grand Professors of the University. Everybody is laughing out in the West and asking if this is the higher education to be given after so much effort and expense. Announcements of this sort coming [from] Washington are injuring." [56] Where the rumor arose it is difficult to say, but at any rate the university opened that fall without benefit of plain chant from Bishop Marty. Another case which drew considerable discussion among the bishops on the university board was that of St. George Mivart. This English convert-biologist had attained a distinguished position in the world of science and had taught at Louvain and Cardinal Manning's Kensington College. Keane wrote the Archbishop of New York saying that Archbishop Ireland and others were urging him to engage Mivart. He said he felt that he would be admirably fitted "to give our Divinity students the scientific knowledge so necessary in our times." The rector stated that Mivart's name would give prestige to the university and that without some such name the faculty, "no matter how learned & eloquent in Latin, will count for very little in the estimation of the American public, whose expectations ought to count for something with us." Keane realized there were suspicions of Mivart's ortho-

---

[56] BCA, 86–E–6, John Foley to James Gibbons, Detroit, July 11, 1889.

doxy from some of his earlier heated controversies but he felt his more recent writings had removed all grounds for such fears.[57] Archbishop Corrigan, however, objected on the grounds that it would be unwise to have the university invite opposition at the start. He acknowledged that Mivart's attainments were high and, therefore, he suggested that the chair of natural science be reserved for him when later on the university would admit lay students. "If I do not mistake, Professor Mybart's [sic] difficulties have occurred chiefly, when he left the field of science for the domain of theology." [58] Archbishop Ryan wrote Gibbons on the same subject, saying he had recently been in Boston where Archbishop Williams had suggested that they first consult Cardinal Manning or someone equally competent to pass judgment on his qualifications.

The Pope's recent recommendation of his new book would not be sufficient in itself, & anything like a suspicion even of unsound philosophy in the new institution might prove a permanent enjury [sic] to its character. I wrote to Bp. Keane ("juxta exposita") to invite Mivart, but it will be well to give the matter serious consideration & consult before doing so.[59]

---

[57] NYAA, C–16, John J. Keane to M. A. Corrigan, Cape May, August 2, 1889.

[58] NYAA, C–39, M. A. Corrigan to John J. Keane, New York, August 5, 1889, copy.

[59] BCA, 86–M–3, P. J. Ryan to James Gibbons, Philadelphia, September 9, 1889. In this letter Ryan told Gibbons that he had the most positive assurances from Archbishop Corrigan that the latter knew nothing whatever of the investigation in Rome of Keane's article on "The Providential Mission of Leo XIII." Ryan said: "He never drew attention to it. As it was published in Rome, some one there must have pointed out the obnoxious passages, which were probably only the expression of American views."

Although Pope Leo XIII's recommendation of Mivart's recent work might seem to have been sufficient guarantee of his orthodoxy for the university's trustees, it did happen that the scientist in later years got into serious trouble on matters dealing with the relation of religion to science and even with points of Catholic teaching, so that at the time of his death he was denied Catholic burial by Cardinal Vaughan.

While these matters affecting the future faculty were under discussion, continued interest both here and abroad was shown in the university. Edward Douglas White, future chief justice of the United States Supreme Court, wrote Cardinal Gibbons from New Orleans in April that a client of his had just expressed a wish to help the university but he did not know exactly in what form to make his bequest. White asked Gibbons for his ideas on the subject and he told the cardinal that, judging from his client's present frame of mind, he believed he would probably give the university in his will "something between a hundred and two hundred thousand dollars, if such practical suggestions can be made as will crystalize the inchoate intention which he now has." [60] In the *Catholic Mirror* for April 20 there appeared an account of an interview given by "an American prelate" to a correspondent of the *Observateur Français*. It contained a glowing, if not always accurate, explanation of the university's progress to date, and it gave expression to views which would at a later day serve those in Europe who chose to see heresy in what came to be called Americanism. Speaking of Spalding's address at the

---

[60] BCA, 85–W–11, E. D. White to James Gibbons, New Orleans, April 17, 1889.

laying of the cornerstone, this American churchman was quoted as saying:

Read the discourse pronounced by the Bishop of Peoria, Mgr. Spalding, at the corner-stone laying at Washington. You will read there what may perhaps astonish you, that the prelate is almost as proud of his title of citizen of a free country as of that of a son of the Catholic Church. This is, after all, our right. Did not St. Paul claim, even before the executioner, his title of Roman citizen? Likewise, outside the New World you will find brilliant minds, who believe that the new political state that we personify will conduce to a higher development of humanity than has been attained in the Old World. This is notably the opinion of Cardinal Manning.

Expanding on the instruction which would be given at Washington, the churchman was quoted to the effect that in time the humanities would be introduced as also the social sciences. "We shall study those, that is to say, we will seek to demonstrate that the new political state, that we personify, is much better adapted to the evangelical precepts and the instructions of our common Father, than your worm-eaten constitutions and your old institutions. Catholics first, yes, but democrats after." With all due allowance for the man's pride in America and her democratic institutions, this was hardly a tactful way of winning Europeans to the American way of life. It was utterances such as these that caused in later years a shadow to fall over some of the men most closely connected with the university. That the vision of the new world and the new Catholic university rising in Washington did give renewed hope to some European Catholics in these years, we know. For example, Father Kenelm Vaughan wrote an enthusiastic article entitled, "The Washington Catholic University and the English Colony at Rome," which appeared in the *Catholic Mirror* of May 4. Vaughan paid high tribute to Keane who, he said, had captured all hearts in Rome, and he traced the relations of the Papacy to the English universities and the sad fate which the Church experienced in those foundations. He continued:

Let us turn from this picture of sorrow and look upon the image of hope that rises beyond the ocean. America will atone for the sin of her mother country and appease the just wrath of heaven. The light of Catholic learning which was driven from our midst is about to receive a new throne in the great republic of the West. The Washington University will teach the descendants of those who learnt at the feet of the old Catholic masters of Oxford and Cambridge. Hence with joy and consolation, that surpass words to express, we hail as a happy omen the Washington University, which is rising up in sight. And with all eagerness we shall watch from afar its career of development.

Bishop Keane returned from Europe on the *Umbria* the first week in May. He had succeeded in attaining all his major objectives in Rome and had gathered together what appeared to be a noteworthy faculty. All this notwithstanding he was soon met with criticism from some circles outside the Church for having engaged European professors. His critics maintained that only Americans should have been chosen to staff the new American university, as their background and training were such as to dispose them to favor monarchical forms of government and the philosophy underlying that system. Keane took the trouble to answer these charges in a communication sent to the Baltimore *Sun* and reprinted in the *Church News* of May 19. The rector contended that it would have been the wish of all to open the university with a corps of professors enlisted entirely from the United States but that they simply were not to be had. "It is no disparagement to American Catholics to say they are not yet ready to take up university teaching, since it is an entirely new thing here, and they could therefore have no training in it." Keane characterized the assertion that the professors were selected for their monarchical tendencies and training as "a contemptible absurdity."

Every one who knows me knows that my opinions are the opposite of monarchical, that I am an out-and-out American, thoroughly imbued with the doctrines of our American democracy and the principles of popular sovereignty established by our American constitution.

He said everyone who had met him in Europe from the Pope down knew this of him and he remarked that Leo XIII had no desire whatever to cultivate monarchical principles on this side of the Atlantic, "for he fully appreciates that the American constitution contains the highest form of government for our country." He noted the fact that Pohle, a German, engaged to teach philosophy, could hardly be said to have been trained in a land where the medieval philosophy held sway. "The political and social tendencies of thought in Germany of to-day is [sic] hardly in that direction." Pohle had, moreover, spent a number of years in England teaching at the seminary of Leeds, and in England "the great liberal tide that is rising and the present condition of public feeling is also at variance with such ideas." As for Bouquillon, he was born and trained in Belgium, "and all know how heartily the Belgians enter into the spirit and republican ideas of our American institutions." Keane did not fail to mention that several Americans were being trained in Europe for the faculty and he concluded by saying, "In all the details of the university it has and always will be our aim to make it thoroughly American in all its characteristics." To the charge made by some Protestants that Americans should not have to apply to the Pope for approval of a purely American institution, Keane answered that the board of trustees had sought its powers as an educational institution from both the State and the Church. "To the one we must prove our ability to teach the requisite limit of letters and science before we can receive a charter to grant degrees. Was there anything wonderful, then, when we intended to bestow the highest honors in theological and divinity studies, that we should prove to the head of the Church that we would be competent to teach in the fullness of Catholic faith and morals?" [61]

Upon his arrival in New York the rector of the university gave an interview to the newspapers in which he covered certain aspects of his European trip. He told how he went from Rome to Vienna with letters of introduction from Monsignor Merry del Val to the latter's father, Spanish ambassador to the court of Emperor Francis Joseph. Through the ambassador he met many of the professors of the University of Vienna, "and I was especially interested in the departments of physiology and laboratory work." From Vienna he went to Munich where he found the department of philosophy widening into "physiological avenues," and Keane commented, "the Johns Hopkins philo-

---

[61] *Catholic Mirror,* May 11, 1889, editorial, "Bishop Keane and the Catholic University." *Church News,* May 19, 1889.

sophical department is organized on this German system."
There followed stops at Bonn, Münster, Fulda, and Cologne
before he left Germany for Belgium. At Louvain he was
given a reception by Monsignor Jean B. Abbeloos, the rector
of the university, and he spent several profitable days in conference with the professors at what he termed "the best organized Catholic university in the world . . ." From Louvain he traveled to Paris to consult the rector of the Catholic Institute; there he met Edward A. Pace, "a young
priest from Florida, who graduated in Rome three years
ago with tremendous éclat." Keane crossed to England
where he met Cardinals Newman and Manning and Bishop
Herbert Vaughan of Salford. He remarked, "I did not go
to Ireland, because when I was in Paris Archbishop Walsh
sent me by letter all the information I desired." Nor did he
visit Oxford or Cambridge since he had been at the latter
place two years before.

Upon his arrival in Washington, Keane was given a dinner at Welcker's Hotel on May 21 by a number of the
prominent Catholics of the capital. At this dinner the
Reverend J. Havens Richards, S.J., president of Georgetown University, spoke and extended a cordial welcome to
the sister institution. Reporting this dinner speech of Richards, the *Church News* for May 26 said the president of
Georgetown had remarked that other universities were said
to look with disfavor and suspicion on the coming of the
Catholic University of America, "but he wished to say
that such a report was utterly without foundation. He then
proceeded to speak of the great need of the educational
institutions of this country for united action." The rector
was also given a reception at the Carroll Institute in Washington on the evening of May 30 at which Keane referred

to the days when he was "scudding around these streets"
as a parish priest and that now he felt he was coming
home.[62] Following his brief visit to Washington, Bishop
Keane set off for the West on another speaking tour.

In the months before the opening of the university its
officials continued to receive applications for positions from
interested parties. John Stephen Martin wrote Cardinal
Gibbons on June 5 recommending a French Dominican of
Toulouse.[63] At about the same time the Canon Salvatore di
Bartolo addressed the cardinal from Palermo to recommend his own *Les Critères théologiques* which he had recently translated into French, and the canon went on to
say in his rather difficult English, "I wish besides to be
appointed among the foreign members of philosophical and
theological faculties; and these institutions will encourage
those who are devoted to scientific pursuits, and at the
same time the latter will hold up institutions." [64] In this
same month Denis O'Connell was able to report that Miss
Edes, the private agent of Archbishop Corrigan in Rome,
"is now entirely on my side, and one of my best friends,
and the Abp. of N. Y. seems to be coming 'round nicely,"
although O'Connell confessed that Miss Edes was as yet
no greater a friend than before "of Baltimore or of the
University, and the possible damage to the American College is now a new argument." [65] A month later O'Connell

---

[62] *Catholic Mirror,* June 1, 1889.

[63] BCA, 86–B–8, John Stephen Martin to James Gibbons, Brooklyn, June 5, 1889.

[64] BCA, 86–B–6, Salvatore di Bartolo to James Gibbons, Palermo,
June 5, 1889.

[65] BCA, 86–C–12, D. J. O'Connell to James Gibbons, Rome, June
14, 1889. O'Connell told the cardinal in this letter: "I arranged with
Father Kenelan [*sic*] Vaughan for a letter in the 'Tablet' on the Uni-

told the cardinal that McQuaid's agenda was quite crowded when he came to Rome, but that in one particular he failed since "he found it useless to speak to the Pope about the University." Bishop McQuaid had remarked to O'Connell that Miss Edes once had great influence in Rome but that now it had evaporated.[66]

The *Catholic World*, which from an early date had displayed a very friendly feeling toward the university, carried in its July, 1889, issue an anonymous article on the conclusion of Keane's Roman visit and the results of his European tour. After describing the approved statutes, the writer sought to allay the fears of the American seminaries

---

versity and for a presentation, and it is working beautifully. Lady Herbert of Lea pours out her admiration to me for America in terms of enthusiasm." Apparently O'Connell had found the Bishop of Rochester a genial fellow on close acquaintance as he told Gibbons: "Bp. McQuaid, when you know him, is an exceedingly kind gentleman, and his dealings with me have been marked with the utmost consideration." It was at this time that the legal difficulties concerning the title to the university property were finally cleared up. The following explanation is given by Reily: "In Oct., 1886, Archbishop Gibbons filed bills in the Washington Courts against Mary Aranton and David Duley *et al.*, to secure a perfect title and lawful conveyance of the new University land. Henry Duley owned the tract in 1802, leaving ten children, and in 1807 Wm. Duley owned two undivided tenths, but in the deed of conveyance by an error conveyed only one tenth to a man named Smith, and the other tenth was conveyed by Wm. and Eleanor Ducker. June 26th, 1889, in the Court in General Term, in the case of Gibbons vs. Duley, Judge Montgomery delivered the opinion, directing a decree in compliance with the prayer of the bill, thus correcting the papers and conveyance and securing a clear title to the site of the Catholic University." *Passing Events in the Life of Cardinal Gibbons* (Martinsburg, West Virginia, 1890), I, 288–289.

66 BCA, 86–E–10, D. J. O'Connell to James Gibbons, Rome, July 16, 1889.

that the university might injure their status. It was his
belief that the seminaries in general would experience "an
immediate benefit from the influence of the University."
It was too early to say just how the relationship between
these institutions would be worked out. "Methods must
be tried, some rejected, others retained, and the experience of all concerned will so shape a policy as to secure the
common end proposed." [67] Referring to Keane's tour of
European universities, the writer stated that the rector's ob-
servations had "resulted in impressing his mind more favorably with the German methods than the English," and in
the new university at Washington the degrees would be
given "on the models of Louvain and the German universities." [68] Since Keane stopped with the Paulists upon
his return to America and was always close to Hecker and
Hewit, the opinions expressed in this and other articles in
the *Catholic World* probably reflected rather accurately the
mind of the bishop on these university questions. Keane
himself contributed a brief article to the July number of the
American Ecclesiastical Review in which he made a direct
appeal to the clergy of the United States for their financial
and moral support, outlining how they could help by
interesting their people in the undertaking and by coming
themselves as students to Washington.[69] The next month
an unsigned article in the same journal, presumably written by Herman Heuser the editor, praised the results which
had been brought about in so short a period of time in the

---

[67] "The Catholic University and Its Constitutions," in *Catholic
World*, XLIX (July, 1889), 429.

[68] *Ibid.*, pp. 429–430.

[69] John J. Keane, "The Clergy and the Catholic University," in
American Ecclesiastical Review, I (July, 1889), 241–245.

university matter. The writer would have the new university act as a general arbiter for all Catholic educational projects in the country. "The University, once that its existence has become a fact, will necessarily act as a regulator and promoter of all other education in the land." [70] He would even have it assume the task of regulating the press! He thought that the abuses of the freedom of the press might easily be corrected by having a center, "whither every eye and mind is turned, and whence proceeds that authoritative impulse which is the prerogative of superior knowledge." [71] He approved the advanced course which would be offered in Washington and he felt the student entrance requirements would raise the academic standards at Washington above that exacted in most European universities, "unless we except Louvain and some of the German Universities." The success in gathering the endowment for the school of theology made the writer confident that its high standards governing admission and examinations would not be jeopardized, "since it has been wisely started upon a financial basis which will not make it dependent for success or failure upon the number of students who may support it." [72]

Another staunch supporter of the university was Father Daniel Hudson, C.S.C., editor for many years of *Ave Maria*, the bi-weekly publication at the University of Notre Dame. In its issue of August 3 the critics of the university were scolded in no uncertain terms.

---

[70] "Present Aspect of the Catholic University," in *American Ecclesiastical Review*, I (August, 1889), 290.

[71] *Ibid.*, p. 292.

[72] *Ibid.*, p. 293.

The most exasperating and fatal critics are those who, while refusing to take an initiative themselves, keep up a fusillade of doubts on men who do take an initiative . . . Now a means of remedying all defects in Catholic educational training is about to be provided. The Catholic University is a fixed fact,—the Holy Father has done everything in his power to make it so. The time for criticism is passed. The "what?" or the "why?" is now a childish impertinence. Enthusiasm in word and act is now demanded.[73]

But if there were critics, there were also friends. Sylvester Johnson of New Haven, Kentucky, died on July 16 and willed $10,000 to the university at a time when the expenses in preparation for the formal opening were running high.[74] The Catholic journals and papers continued in these final months to carry items of news and articles on the university. Philip J. Garrigan, vice rector, contributed such an article in September to the *American Ecclesiastical Review* wherein he gave a sketch of the steps which had been taken since 1884 to bring the university into existence. To those who had feared that there would be no students at the opening, the vice rector replied that the difficulty was removed by the fact that, "there are fully as many applicants for admission to the higher course of Divinity as the present buildings can well accommodate." [75]

---

[73] "A Word Concerning the New University," in *Ave Maria*, XXIX (Aug. 3, 1889), 109.

[74] Boston *Pilot*, August 10, 1889. The *Pilot* in its issue of August 3 reported the engagement of Mary Gwendoline Caldwell to Prince Gioacchino Murat, grandson of the former King of Naples.

[75] "The First Lustrum of the Catholic University," in *American Ecclesiastical Review*, I (Sept. 1889), 345. This article and one on Caldwell Hall were announced as to be written by Garrigan, *Ibid.*, I, 281, although his name was not signed to them.

ORIGINAL FACULTY OF THE UNIVERSITY

Back row left to right: Henri Hyvernat, Charles Warren Stoddard, John B. Hogan, S.S., John J. Keane, Joseph Schroeder. Second row left to right: Thomas Bouquillon, Alexis Orban, S.S., Philip J. Garrigan, Augustine F. Hewit, C.S.P., Joseph Pohle, Joseph Graf.

VII
The Opening of the University

TWO MONTHS before the opening of the university Bishop Keane published a leaflet describing the ceremonies for November 13 and giving the entrance requirements for prospective students. In this official announcement it was stated that students would be expected to have finished in a creditable manner "the usual Seminary course, or at least the philosophical course and three years of Theology." The derogation from the decree of the Third Plenary Council which the Holy See had expressed through the letter of Leo XIII of March 7, 1889, namely, that students might enter who had not finished their college or seminary course, was not to be used for the present. Students entering the university might work for a degree or not as they chose. The annual fee was fixed at $250 payable semi-annually, and it was announced that, "the University hopes this year to bestow ten free scholarships or burses." [1] As the time neared

[1] *Official Announcements of the Catholic University of America, September, 1889* (Baltimore, 1889), Archives of the Catholic University of America. This six-page leaflet has no pagination.

for the celebration of the centennial of the American hierarchy and the formal opening of the university, which were
to be held on consecutive days, considerable rivalry arose
in Rome among officials of the curia to be named as the
delegate of Pope Leo XIII. It constituted a worry to Denis
O'Connell who wrote Cardinal Gibbons four letters on the
subject between July and September. Monsignor O'Connell
told Gibbons that he was trying to avoid showing any
partiality in the matter and he counseled the Archbishop
of Baltimore to beware of making a blunder himself. The
chief contenders for the honor were Satolli, Jacobini, and
Sbarretti. On August 12, Gibbons confided to his diary:
"Wrote to Dr. O'Connell enclosing 25,000 francs for the
Holy Father, and inviting Mgr. Jacobini, Canon Sbarretti,
and Rev. Dr. Satolli to the Catholic Centennial celebration
to [be] held on the 10 of Nov. next." On the same day
he inserted in his diary: "I wrote to the H. Father asking
him to send a delegation to the Catholic Centennial." [2]
Whether Gibbons' invitation to the three ecclesiastics mentioned in the diary entry was in the form of personal letters
or a commission to O'Connell to execute the task, there is
no way of knowing. In the end the Holy Father chose
Francesco Satolli, Archbishop of Lepanto, to represent
him. Satolli wrote Gibbons after receiving the appointment
to say that the Pope,

In his sovereign goodness, . . . has destined me to so noble
an office. Filled with reverence and admiration, I accept

---

[2] Baltimore Cathedral Archives, D. J. O'Connell to James Gibbons,
Rome, July 23, 1889, 86–E–14; July 24, 86–E–3; September 7,
86–L–9; September 13, 1889, 86–M–10; BCA, Cardinal Gibbons'
Diary, p. 235.

this most noble mission and shall be happy to come and see how the Catholic Church shows her divine and ever-lasting vitality where the wisdom and zeal of the bishops recall the most glorious epochs and the most illustrious men of the Catholic apostolate.

The pleasure and honor of assisting at their celebration will be for me the pleasantest event and will remain the happiest remembrance of my life.[3]

The Catholic Total Abstinence Union of America mean-while continued its collection of funds for the Father Mathew chair, and *Freeman's Journal* for September 7 re-ported that the sum had reached $6,523.75 in a year's time. Three weeks later the *Freeman's* for September 28 an-nounced a lecture for the evening of October 10 in the Paulist hall on 60th Street to be given by Walter Elliott, C.S.P., on the subject of "The Saloon," the proceeds of which would go to the fund for the chair. The Ancient Order of Hibernians, which had been under suspicion for a while by some of the bishops as a secret society, was likewise manifesting interest in the university, and Thomas A. E. Weadock, one of its members, wrote Gibbons to in-quire if the order would be allowed to endow a chair. "If you approve I will bring the matter before the officers of the Society at an early day, and I believe the project will succeed." [4] About the same time Archbishop Corrigan wrote the rector to tell him that on his advice J. F. Loubat of New York, who had already founded a burse in the uni-versity, was interested in having erected in America a large

---

[3] BCA, 86–Q–1, Francis Satolli to James Gibbons, Grottaferrata, October 9, 1889.

[4] BCA, 86–M–4, Thomas A. E. Weadock to James Gibbons, Bay City, Michigan, September 9, 1889.

marble statue of Leo XIII. The statue was being executed
by Professor Lucchetti in reproduction of the one shown
at the Vatican exhibition in Leo XIII's year of jubilee. It
would be ready for installation by October, 1890.[5] Corrigan
said he had suggested the university to Loubat as the proper
place for the statue and that the nuncio in Paris had also expressed the hope that it "might eventually be placed in the
Grand Hall of the University in which degrees are to be
conferred."

The rumors about various aspects of the university foundation continued in the public press. One such was that
Miss Caldwell was thinking of withdrawing the gift she had
given five years before. When this story got into the newspapers the young woman was quite irked and she wrote
Cardinal Gibbons:

I have been much annoyed by an article which has appeared in the newspapers to the effect that there was question of my withdrawing the money I gave to found the
University. I trust you will do me the favor to have this
baseless rumor authoritatively contradicted, as it does me
serious injustice.
    It might not seem proper for me to publish a denial un-
der my own name, therefore I hope that Your Eminence
as President of the Board will make known that no thought
of the kind has ever entered my mind.[6]

Bishop McQuaid decided early that he would not go to
Baltimore and Washington for the celebrations. He wrote
Corrigan that he would likely be in Boston the first week

---

[5] New York Archdiocesan Archives, C–18, M. A. Corrigan to John
J. Keane, New York, September 19, 1889, copy.
    [6] BCA, 86–N–12, Mary Gwendoline Caldwell to James Gibbons,
St. Regis Lake, September 21, 1889.

of November to inspect the Brighton seminary. "As I am not to be in Baltimore and Washington for the gorgeous celebration of the ensuing week I will leave for home Friday morning, having to administer Confirmation in two churches the following Sunday." [7] His preparatory seminary of St. Andrew at Rochester was doing well, and it probably made McQuaid chuckle to have Bishop Wigger of Newark write him: "So St. Andrews has 39 students this year! I am inclined to think that our Catholic *University* will scarcely have as many to begin with. Seton Hall is also doing well this year. We have 98 students." [8]

The most complete account of the original faculty of the university to appear up to this time was published in the *American Catholic Quarterly Review* a month before the opening at Washington. After paying tribute to Cardinal Gibbons as chancellor, to Keane and Garrigan as the ranking executive officers of the university, and to various members of the board of trustees, the writer, Charles G. Herbermann, gave brief biographical sketches of the professors. He described Monsignor Joseph Schroeder, the professor of dogmatic theology, as a Roman-trained priest who had been selected by Archbishop Krementz of Cologne to fill the chair of Matthias J. Scheeben in his seminary. Schroeder had been prominent in supporting Cardinal Lavigerie's anti-slavery movement in Africa. He was the author of a volume, *Liberalism in Theology and History,* and a contributor to European periodicals. Schroeder was then about forty years of age. Henri Hyvernat, as we have

---

[7] NYAA, C–16, Bernard J. McQuaid to M. A. Corrigan, Rochester, September 22, 1889.

[8] Rochester Diocesan Archives, Winand M. Wigger to Bernard J. McQuaid, Newark, September 25, 1889.

seen, was appointed to teach scripture and oriental languages. Charles Warren Stoddard, who was forty-six at the time, was a newspaperman, author, and world traveller. He was a convert to the Catholic Church and had taught English at the University of Notre Dame during the year, 1885–1886. The director of the divinity college was Abbé John B. Hogan, S.S., Irish-born and since 1884 superior of St. John's Seminary, Brighton. The professor of philosophy, Joseph Pohle, was thirty-eight and had taken the doctorate in both theology and philosophy at the Gregorian University. He had been kept out of Germany by the *Kulturkampf* and during these years he taught in Switzerland and in the seminary of the Diocese of Leeds in England. When the Falk laws were permitted to lapse he was called back to Germany where he taught in the seminary of Fulda. He was co-editor of the Goerres Society's *Philosophische Jahrbuch*. For canon law the university would have the Swiss-born Sebastian G. Messmer who had been trained at the University of Innsbruck. He had been in America since September, 1871, serving as a professor of dogma at Seton Hall. Thomas Bouquillon, around forty-two years of age at the time, would be the professor of moral theology. He had been trained at the University of Louvain and had been for some time teaching at the Catholic Institute in Lille. For lectures in church history the university had selected Augustine F. Hewit, C.S.P., who had been converted in 1846 and was of the original band who helped Isaac Hecker found the Paulists in 1858. Hewit had graduated from Amherst College at nineteen and then attended the Hartford Theological Seminary. He had done a considerable amount of writing since publishing his autobiography in 1846 and had been one of the editors of the works of Bishop John England. For astronomy and physics the students would have another Paulist, George M. Searle, English-born and Harvard graduate of 1857. He had been assistant professor at the Naval Academy in Annapolis for the years, 1862-1866, and for nearly two years he had served as assistant at the Harvard Observatory. He had become a Catholic in 1862 and six years later joined the Paulists. Searle had published a volume on the *Elements of Geometry* in 1877. Alexis Orban, S.S., assistant to Abbé Hogan, was to fill temporarily the post of librarian. In answer to the charge made in certain circles that the faculty would be mostly foreigners and that this was being done because the Pope did not trust American scholars, Herbermann stated that it was not possible to fill the professorships at once with properly trained Americans. Some of America's best brains were drawn off to the episcopacy as, for example, Kenrick, Spalding, Corrigan, Heiss, and Keane. Moreover, Harvard had attained increased fame through the Swiss-born Agassiz, Johns Hopkins University with the English mathematician, Sylvester, the physiologist, Martin, and the distinguished German Assyriologist, Haupt, and Princeton had just ended the successful presidency of McCosh, brought from Scotland to fill the post. "But what is perhaps a little amusing, some of the very journals that fret and fume because foreigners are going to teach in the Washington University, have been owned and are edited by foreigners—by self-imported foreigners." [9]

Archbishop Ryan of Philadelphia wrote to Archbishop Corrigan a month before the opening to say that he had

---

[9] Charles G. Herbermann, "The Faculty of the Catholic University," in *American Catholic Quarterly Review*, XIV (Oct. 1889), 715.

informed Gibbons that Corrigan had absolutely nothing to
do with complaints made about certain obnoxious passages
in Keane's article on "The Providential Mission of Leo
XIII." He furthermore said he told the cardinal that since
Archbishop Kenrick of St. Louis was not coming to the celebration he had suggested that he, Corrigan, be asked to sing
the pontifical Mass. But Gibbons replied that the Archbishop of New York had declined "because you thought it
would be fatiguing . . . I fear that if you have nothing
to do in either Balto. or Washington, it will be observed.
Card. Gibbons requested me to use my influence with
you to induce you to sing the Mass at Washington. You
know, as well as I do, the situation & I leave the matter,
of course to your own judgment." [10] About two weeks later
Keane wrote Corrigan that he had received word from
Bishop Spalding that the latter's physician had ordered him
to desist for the present from all work and, therefore, he
could not give the inaugural oration on November 13.
Would Archbishop Corrigan be good enough to give the
address? "I can easily understand the many reasons which
make this look like an unreasonable request, considering
the shortness of the time and your Grace's ever crowding
duties. But in this strait, I can only trust to your generosity
and ask almost the impossible." The address need not be
long and it might be confined to a statement of the motives
of the Holy See and the American hierarchy in founding

------

[10] NYAA, C–17, P. J. Ryan to M. A. Corrigan, Philadelphia, October 16, 1889. Ryan informed Corrigan he had written Gibbons also
about a chair in the university for Mivart and about Keane's article
on Leo XIII, and that Gibbons in reply had said the Mivart matter
had been postponed "until further enquiry . . . He said nothing of
Bishop Keane's lecture."

the university. "A thousand pardons for intruding on you with such a request;—and for your charity in the matter you shall have my lasting gratitude." [11] But Archbishop Corrigan was not to be persuaded and as soon as he received Keane's invitation he sent a wire declining. He wrote the same day to say that a provincial meeting the following week, a sermon in the cathedral on Sunday, and a string of guests arriving in New York for the centennial would prevent his preparing a talk for Washington. In this same letter Corrigan called Keane's attention to an attack on the university made recently by Eliphalet N. Potter, president of Hobart College at Geneva, New York. He promised that if Keane could find time to answer it he would have it sent to James Wilton Brooks, nephew of Erastus Brooks, who would see that it got proper publicity. [12] Keane wrote a reply to Potter and sent it to Brooks and he remarked to the Archbishop of New York, "Your declining to give the inaugural discourse was a great disappointment; but surely the reasons were abundantly sufficient, and we must be resigned." [13]

Several months before the festivities in Baltimore and Washington, Cardinal Gibbons had sent invitations to the leading churchmen of the world in the name of the American hierarchy. Cardinal Place of Rennes wrote to say he could not be present but he desired to express his good wishes to the new university with which, he remembered,

---

[11] NYAA, C–16, John J. Keane to M. A. Corrigan, Washington, October 28, 1889.

[12] NYAA, C–39, M. A. Corrigan to John J. Keane, New York, October 30, 1889, copy.

[13] NYAA, C–16, John J. Keane to M. A. Corrigan, Washington, November 3, 1889.

Gibbons had been so preoccupied when they received their
red hats together at Rome.

Je suis heureux que cette gracieuse attention de Votre
Eminence me fournisse l'occasion de vous dire avec quel
intérêt j'avais appris le projet et suivi les préparations de
cette grande oeuvre et avec quel bonheur j'ai salué de loin
la réalisation dont une si grande part revient a Votre Eminence.[14]

Bishop John McLachlan of Galloway wrote to say it would
give him the greatest pleasure to attend so interesting an
event as the opening of the university, "& also to have a
glimpse of your prosperous & wonderful country,—but it is
impossible." [15] When Bishop John Virtue of Portsmouth
wrote Gibbons in early October he did not think he could
be present,[16] but a month later found him on his way
across the Atlantic as the representative of the English
hierarchy. Virtue had been in the United States in 1853
as the secretary to Archbishop Bedini. Cardinal Rampolla,
Secretary of State to Pope Leo XIII, sent Gibbons a letter at the suggestion of Satolli, although as Rampolla said,
the Pope's delegate would need no introduction from him,
for Gibbons knew his reputation as one of the most distinguished of the Roman professors and as president of
the Pontifical Academy of Noble Ecclesiastics. The letter
which Satolli was bearing from the Pope and "la squisita
gentilezza di Vostra Eminenza," would excuse Rampolla

[14] BCA, 86–O–8, Charles Philippe Place to James Gibbons, Rennes,
September 29, 1889.

[15] BCA, 86–P–7, John McLachlan to James Gibbons, Dumfries,
October 5, 1889.

[16] BCA, 86–P–8, John Virtue to James Gibbons, Portsmouth,
October 6, 1889.

from dwelling on the qualifications of the papal delegate to the American celebration.[17] Old Archbishop Kirby, rector of the Irish College in Rome, sent a long and enthusiastic letter of congratulation in which he said the "dreary deserts & gloomy forests" of North America had been converted into a land studded with temples to God, with schools, academies, and colleges, and now it was to receive the crowning perfection "in the erection of your new university."[18] Bishop MacCormack of Galway could not be present but he took the occasion of his reply to recommend the scriptural commentary of the Archbishop of Tuam for use as a textbook in the university.[19] Cardinal Manning, who was eighty-one at the time, could not make the trip but he informed Cardinal Gibbons:

When I wrote the letter in answer to your Telegram, no one of my Colleagues had promised to be present at the centenary of your Episcopate.

But the Bishop of Portsmouth has kindly undertaken to represent the English Bishops & will start for Baltimore on Thursday next. He will convey to you our affectionate congratulations & assure you that the hearts of your English brethren are with you.

I need not add that mine is in the trust [of] brotherly love, for in America I have many more friends than I deserve.[20]

---

[17] BCA, 86–Q–10, Mariano Rampolla to James Gibbons, Rome, October 16, 1889.

[18] BCA, 86–R–4, Thomas Kirby to James Gibbons, Rome, October 19, 1889.

[19] BCA, 86–R–5, F. J. MacCormack to James Gibbons, Galway, October 20, 1889.

[20] BCA, 86–S–6, Henry Edward Manning to James Gibbons, Westminster, October 27, 1889. On October 20, 1889, Cardinal Manning had sent a formal address of congratulations to the American hierarchy from the hierarchy of England, BCA, 86–R–6.

Bishop James L. Patterson, auxiliary of Westminster, stated
that as a convert who owed his faith, under God, to his
days at Oxford University more than to any other factor,
"I hail with the most heartfelt thankfulness this great undertaking, in which I would fain discern the germs of immense good in the future of America." [21]

The most interesting of the letters received by the chancellor of the university from foreign prelates was that of
Bishop Bartholomew Woodlock of the Diocese of Ardagh
and Clonmacnoise. He recalled that as a child he had seen
Bishop Dubois of New York when he [Dubois] visited
Dublin "in the second decade of this century" and his
father had given him hospitality. That was his first contact with the American Church. It was now forty-seven
years since he had joined the original band of Father Hand
and others in founding All Hallows College which had since
given so many priests to the Church of the United States.
Likewise, he was the man chosen to follow "the great
Cardinal Newman" as rector of the Catholic University of
Ireland and, therefore, "I feel special joy in seeing another
great seat of learning added to the numerous Universities,
with which the Church has studded the Old World."
Woodlock went on to recall the difficulties under which the
Irish university operated by reason of restrictions from the
state, which had prompted Archbishop Hughes of New
York to say in his address at the Dublin university's
foundation: *"Woe to you . . . for you have taken away
the key of knowledge; you yourselves have not entered in,
and those that were entering in you have hindered."* The

---

[21] BCA, 86–R–13, James Laird Patterson to James Gibbons, London, October 23, 1889.

bishop quoted Newman on the anxieties which would be
suffered in Dublin before the university would succeed and
he added, "for 18 years I shared largely in those anxieties."
He prayed that the American bishops would be spared like
worries and that the vision of which Newman once wrote
would be theirs: "Thither students are flocking from the
East, West & South . . . all owning one faith, all eager for
one large true wisdom; and thence, when their stay is over,
going back again to carry peace to men of good will over
all the land." [22] Other well-wishers sent their greetings to
Gibbons in these days, among them J. Madison Cutts,
prominent Washington figure and descendant of Dolly
Madison, and the Viscount De Meaux.[23] With the final
details on the building almost complete the Catholic press
carried descriptions of Caldwell Hall to the country in the
weeks before the formal opening.[24]

Bishop Gilmour, who was a close friend of the Bishop of
Rochester and shared many of his views, did not join Mc-
Quaid in his attitude towards the university and a week
before the Washington celebration he wrote to say, "I again
suggest that you attend all meetings of your Episcopal
Brethren where business and position direct such attendance. To stay away is to admit defeat." [25] But Bishop Mc-

---

[22] BCA, 86–S–5, Bartholomew Woodlock to James Gibbons, Long-
ford, October 26, 1889.

[23] BCA, 86–R–11, J. Madison Cutts to James Gibbons, Washington, October 23, 1889; 86–T–3/1, Vicomte de Meaux to James Gibbons, New York, November 4, 1889.

[24] "The Divinity Building of the Washington University," in *American Ecclesiastical Review,* I (Nov.–Dec. 1889), 453–460; Boston
Pilot, October 26, 1889.

[25] RDA, Richard Gilmour to Bernard J. McQuaid, Cleveland,
November 7, 1889.

Quaid was not to be convinced and when the festivities opened in Baltimore and Washington he was absent. Among the details for the formal opening was the choice of a speaker for the overflow crowd who would not be able to find place in the university chapel during the pontifical Mass. For this Bishop Keane, in the name of the chancellor, invited James Kent Stone, or, as he was known in religion, Father Fidelis of the Cross, the Passionist convert-missionary. Stone received word of the assignment only a week in advance since he had been absent from home, but in reply he assured the cardinal, "I am deeply sensible of the honor conferred upon me; & though I feel myself altogether unworthy & incompetent, I will do what I can, with God's help, to fulfill your desire." [26] A week before the opening Archbishop Corrigan as chairman of the library committee drew up his report to the trustees, stating that the contract for purchase of the books had been let out to Benziger Brothers as the lowest bidder and to date eight cases of books had been passed, duty free, through the customhouse and were stored in Benziger's warehouse awaiting shipment to the university. The archbishop himself announced that he was making a gift of a complete set of the Greek and Latin Fathers in the Migne edition.[27]

The *Freeman's Journal* for November 9, 1889, devoted generous space to the celebration of the centennial of the American hierarchy which would take place in Baltimore on November 10–12. In an editorial entitled, "1789—Our Centenary—1889," it devoted a long paragraph to the

---

[26] BCA, 86–T–6, Fidelis of the Cross, C.P., to James Gibbons, West Hoboken, November 7, 1889.

[27] NYAA, C–39, M. A. Corrigan to the Board of Trustees of the Catholic University of America, New York, November 8, 1889, copy.

university and its significance for the future of American
Catholic life. The editorial writer gave his distinction between a college and a university. "Correctly speaking, a
college is only a part of a branch of a university. A university is a school in which the whole round of arts, letters,
sciences, law, medicine, and theology are taught by their
respective faculties, crowned by philosophy, the queen of
all knowledge and learning; and it is empowered to confer degrees in all these branches—we mean *real* degrees,
not *honorary*." The Baltimore ceremony which opened
with solemn pontifical Mass on Sunday, November 10, at
the cathedral, drew almost the entire hierarchy of the
United States as well as representatives of the hierarchies
of other nations. At the evening service in the cathedral
the preacher was the Archbishop of St. Paul whose subject
was "The Mission of Catholics in America." Ireland outlined the characteristics of the age and the manner in which
the Church should greet them. One characteristic of the
late nineteenth century was that it was an intellectual age
and in developing this point the archbishop paid tribute
to the university about to open:

In love, in reverence, in hope I salute thee, Catholic
University of America! Thy birth—happy omen!—is
coeval with the opening of the new century. The destinies
of the Church in America are in thy keeping. May heaven's
light shine over thee and heaven's love guard thee. Be ever
faithful to thy motto, *Deo et Patriae*. Hasten thy work, so
that our youth, whatever be the vocation to which they
aspire, may soon throng thy halls, and by thee be fitted to
be ideal children of Church and country. Meanwhile,
School of our Hopes, nurture well our youthful priesthood!

The priests will be leaders, and as they are, so will the whole army of God's soldiers be amid the battles of life.[28]

The board of trustees of the university took the occasion to hold a meeting on November 12 at the cardinal's residence. All the members were present except Bishop Spalding and Father Lee. Bishop Keane gave a report of his Roman visit for the approval of the statutes and he explained the attitude of the Holy See on the admittance of students before they had completed their seminary or college course. The rector stated that permission had been granted to admit such students but their admittance was not insisted upon. The second point of change suggested in Rome was that the requirements for graduation might well be reduced, but since all that was wanted was that the standards of the Roman universities be met, the board concluded to meet those requirements as a minimum but over and above that to make other requirements so as to maintain a high standard of scholarship. Keane reported on the professors engaged, and $2,000 a year and board was fixed as compensation for them. Since pensions were granted to retired professors elsewhere the board stated that this should be considered later. The rector announced he had a list of forty students for the opening with nine students listed for the Paulist house of studies; the building was ready for occupancy, and $340,000 was out at interest and would yield an annual income of $19,000. A committee was appointed to work out details concerning the program of studies and the role of the Sulpicians in the university administration. Archbishop Corrigan's report on the library

---

[28] John Ireland, *The Church and Modern Society* (St. Paul, 1905), I, 92–93.

was read and accepted with a vote of thanks to him for his gift of the Migne collection. It was moved and carried that students pay $25 a semester as a tuition fee and that "priests on mission" be admitted to lectures free of any charge. The matter of a choir master and his salary was delegated to the committee on studies for settlement. Bishop Keane suggested that the university adopt the *American Catholic Quarterly Review* as its organ and take over its editorial management, but the board of trustees decided to postpone action in the matter.[29]

Following the close of the centennial ceremonies in Baltimore the bishops and their foreign guests left for the formal opening of the university in Washington on Wednesday, November 13. The day drew weather that was no better than when the cornerstone was laid on May 24, 1888.

A lowering sky, with clouds that hung so low over the earth they seemed to drift through the tree-tops; a steady rain coming in on an east wind, now in fine, misty drizzle, but always in a never-ceasing, pitiless, shower—this was the condition of the weather the people of Washington found upon looking out their windows this morning.[30]

The ceremony of the dedication of the building was scheduled for 10:30 o'clock with the chancellor, Cardinal Gibbons, performing the ceremony. The solemn pontifical Mass was celebrated in the Caldwell Hall chapel by Archbishop Satolli as the papal delegate and the sermon was preached by Bishop Gilmour of Cleveland. Gilmour struck the note that the university was to be the home of religion and he

---

[29] NYAA, F–u, Minutes of the Meeting of the Board of Trustees, Baltimore, November 12, 1889.
[30] *Catholic Mirror,* November 16, 1889.

reminded his listeners that they were not there to witness the dedication of a university merely to the cultivation of the arts and sciences, "valuable though they are." A higher motive had brought them together, namely, to dedicate the building to a cultivation of the "science of sciences—the knowledge of God." The bishop emphasized the two orders of society, the spiritual and the temporal, and the mutual dependence which the Church and the State had on one another.

In this country we have agreed that religion and the state shall exist as distinct and separate departments, each with its separate rights and duties, but this does not mean that the state is independent of religion, or religion independent of the state. God is as necessary for the state as He is necessary for religion.[31]

The Bishop of Cleveland noted that the 650 colleges and academies, the 3,100 parish schools, and the twenty-seven seminaries and two universities [Georgetown and Notre Dame] of the Church in the United States, "are a glorious galaxy amid which to plant this Catholic University." He urged the university, its professors and students, to realize they owed a debt to society and that they should not keep their learning to themselves. "Let generosity mark the spirit of this house of learning . . . But above all, let no narrowness seek to make this the only Catholic University in this country. We have broad lands and eager hearts elsewhere, who in time will need new centers." [32] While

[31] *Solemnities of the Dedication and Opening of the Catholic University of America, November 13th, 1889. Official Report* (Baltimore, 1890), p. 10.

[32] *Ibid.,* p. 17.

Gilmour was preaching in the chapel, Father Fidelis of the Cross was addressing the large crowd who could not be accommodated inside on the subject, "The Vitality of the Church, a Manifestation of God."

Following the Mass a dinner was served for about 250 of the special guests in the hall beneath the chapel while about 1,400 others were served in the refectory. During the course of the toasts President Benjamin Harrison arrived with his suite and was ushered up the hall by Father Garrigan, the vice rector. Amid much applause the President was received—as the New York *Tribune* put it—"by priest and prelate [greeting] with respectful reverence the chief of a Nation of 65,000,000 freemen." [33] Harrison was seated between Cardinal Gibbons and Cardinal Taschereau of Quebec. Others at the main table were Archbishop Satolli, Secretary of State James G. Blaine, Secretary of the Interior John W. Noble, Secretary of Agriculture Jeremiah M. Rusk, the Archbishops of Philadelphia and Montreal, Bishop Keane, the Spanish minister to Washington, De Muruaga, and Judge Leo Knott, ex-assistant Postmaster-General. The New York *Tribune* remarked that despite the rain the occasion, "nevertheless, was one of the deepest interest to all Catholic citizens of the United States, and one which no American citizen can regard with indifference."

The first toast offered at the dinner was to the Pope. To this Archbishop Satolli responded. The second to "Our Country and her President" was given by Secretary Blaine. A third to "Our Sister Universities" was spoken by Cardinal Taschereau, former rector and present chancellor of Laval University. To the toast to "The Press, the Great Co-

---

[33] New York *Tribune,* November 14, 1889.

Educator," John Boyle O'Reilly, editor of the Boston *Pilot,*
responded with a poem. But it was the toast of Archbishop
Ryan of Philadelphia, given in response to the subject of
"The Hierarchy of the United States," which drew most
attention both during and after the banquet. Gibbons was
scheduled for this particular speech but that morning he
asked the Archbishop of Philadelphia to substitute for him.
Ryan had a fine reputation as a public speaker and he
demonstrated the fact that on short notice he could make
a very clever speech. He remarked at the outset that only
on his arrival at the university a few hours before had he
been requested to speak and his preparation, therefore, was
brief. The speaker described the various characteristics
that marked a bishop, saying that our Lord was the great
model Bishop of men's souls. Christ was, indeed, the true
gentleman, for He was gentle, yet manly, and manly yet
gentle. But as no two things in nature were identical, so in
no single bishop would one find all qualities perfectly
delineated. Each was an individual and it was best for him
to act—under the dictates of reason and religion—according to his individuality. That was the reason why the
Church found some bishops who had gentleness as a
"Christian Heritage" coming down with "The Faith of
Our Fathers," an allusion, of course, to Cardinal Gibbons.
Other bishops had a quiet, mossy surface beneath which
was the solid rock and their motto might well be, *Dominus
Petra Mea.* The audience recognized in this Archbishop
Peter R. Kenrick of St. Louis; other bishops stood bravely
at their posts during the peril of yellow fever and though
later promoted to higher places, they went back in the hour
of the pestilence to aid the priests of their former diocese.
"Such men," said Ryan, "would lift their crowns before

the Throne." The reference was to the return of Archbishop Elder of Cincinnati to Natchez during the yellow fever epidemic. Then there were the busy bishops, battling among new surroundings whose zeal was attributable only to the pentecostal inspiration of the apostles and who certainly were not mere "consecrated blizzards" nor men filled with "new wine." Everyone recognized here Archbishop Ireland of St. Paul who had been nicknamed by some, "the consecrated blizzard of the Northwest." Other bishops represented great cities in their physical and intellectual qualities, represented those cities in all but their modesty, for while the bishop was modesty itself the modesty of the city was certainly not visible to the naked eye. This allusion was probably to Archbishop Corrigan of New York. Other bishops were noted for their consummate prudence which, although it was a cardinal virtue, was not to be monopolized by the Sacred College, for prudence regulated all the virtues which, like the spokes of a wheel, move around the hub. The reference was unmistakably to Archbishop Williams of Boston. And then there were the naturally brave bishops, men who, when it was necessary, could be aggressive and could fight the battles of the Church. If they were not always successful, their defeats were triumphant ones, like those of Thermopylae and Waterloo.[34] This last

---

[34] NYAA, C–17, a printed version of Archbishop Ryan's speech at the banquet on November 13, 1889, with a printed notice attached which read: "The Catholic papers will oblige Archbishop Ryan by publishing the enclosed version of his speech at the University Banquet." Bishop McQuaid kept clippings from the press on the episode in a scrapbook. On the opposite side of the page from the clippings of the Philadelphia *Public Ledger* and the Baltimore *Sun* he pasted in Ryan's corrected version of his speech and wrote over it: "The amended version of the same speech. Too late!"

reference was to Bishop McQuaid of Rochester who had
recently had a rough time of it with one of his pastors,
Father Lambert of Waterloo, New York. The press picked
up the reference and gave it in a way which could only
call down the wrath of the Bishop of Rochester. The Baltimore *Sun* of November 14 put Ryan's reference to Mc-
Quaid in these words:

Many manly bishops shows [*sic*] in the beginning a too
manly, perhaps a fighting character, true to his instincts
and individuality, for a man is not another man. It does
a deal of good now and then that they have to meet their
Waterloos.

The Philadelphia *Public Ledger* of the same date emphasized the Ryan speech and said, "He then compared the
characteristics of Bishops present and referred to one who
had met his Waterloo, which was much enjoyed by those
who understood the reference."

   Bishop McQuaid was furious at the speech of Archbishop Ryan. The latter realized the damage which had
been done and he telegraphed McQuaid the next day:
"Proper version of my speech in next issue of Catholic
papers." [35] He also wrote him a letter in which he tried to
explain his reference to Waterloo and Thermopylae as
"triumphant defeats" since Greece gained more by Thermopylae than by Marathon.

   As an unfriendly feeling towards you never entered my
heart, & I trust never shall, I hope you will not misunderstand me. I was speaking at the time of manly fearless

---

[35] RDA, telegram, P. J. Ryan to Bernard J. McQuaid, Philadelphia,
November 15, 1889.

Bishops who were yet gentle at heart, & I confess I had you in my eye with others of your class, as I spoke of the Bishops under certain headings which I announced & not as individuals. The use of the word Waterloo was unfortunate, but in an extempore speech one cannot always possess your perfect coolness in such circumstances.[36]

But McQuaid was not to be pacified. Writing to Corrigan two days after the Washington dinner he said: "And now on the top of all comes the blunder of Archbp. Ryan. No explanations will remove the fact. His allusions to Thermopylae and Waterloo will be whispered from lip to lip, all over the country. It gave me some comfort to know that I had resisted all invitations to go to the festivities." [37] Archbishop Corrigan tried to pour oil on the troubled waters in Rochester by saying that Ryan "assured me he had no thought of your difficulty when he made his unfortunate speech. I was not present at the dinner on account of illness." [38] More than a month later McQuaid received consolation from Bishop Wigger of Newark who told him that Ryan's "imprudent remarks have often since run through my mind. The more I think of them, the more astonished I am that he should have made them." [39] And Bishop McQuaid felt he could now come back at his friend, the Bishop of Cleveland, who had urged him to go to Baltimore and Washington with real justification for his absence.

[36] RDA, P. J. Ryan to Bernard J. McQuaid, Washington, n.d.

[37] NYAA, C–16, Bernard J. McQuaid to M. A. Corrigan, Rochester, November 15, 1889.

[38] RDA, M. A. Corrigan to Bernard J. McQuaid, New York, November 9, 1889.

[39] RDA, Winand M. Wigger to Bernard J. McQuaid, South Orange, December 21, 1889.

I still think that I was wise in not going to Baltimore and Washington. Had I been at the Washington banquet the jocular play on Waterloo, as illustrative of the occasional mishap of a *fighting bishop* might not have gone off without a rebuke. How good some bishops are, and how conscious of their goodness they are! [40]

Upon the completion of the banquet the guests witnessed the presentation to the university of a marble bust of St. Thomas Aquinas presented by Bishop Virtue and Monsignor Gadd as the gift of the Catholics of the British Isles resident in Rome. Bishop Keane read letters from Monsignor d'Hulst, rector of the Catholic Institute of Paris, J. Carray, rector of the Catholic Institute of Lyons, Joseph Cardinal Foulon of Lyons, Monsignor Abeloos, rector of the University of Louvain, Monsignor Mercier of the same university, President James Lemon of St. Cuthbert's College, Ushaw, Thomas Wrennall, rector of St. Bede's College, Manchester, and a letter from the Irish hierarchy. President Celestin Augier of the University of Ottawa and Monsignor Benjamin Paquet, rector of Laval University, spoke for their respective universities. There then ensued an interval during which the Marine Band played. The afternoon ceremony was held at four o'clock when Bishop O'Farrell of Trenton spoke in place of Spalding and a Latin discourse was given by Monsignor Schroeder, professor of dogmatic theology. At the end of the day the students assembled in the chapel for the opening of a retreat which was given by Abbé Hogan and Bishop Keane.

Classes were scheduled to begin on Monday, November 18, following the close of the retreat. The first student

---

[40] RDA, Bernard J. McQuaid to Richard Gilmour, Rochester, December 31, 1889, copy.

body consisted of thirty-seven members in residence in Caldwell Hall and nine in the Paulist house of studies. Among
the diocesan students the Archdiocese of Baltimore led with
four, Boston and Philadelphia three each, New York, Chicago, St. Paul, Buffalo, Cleveland, Hartford, Springfield,
and Trenton having two students each, and one each from
Cincinnati, Milwaukee, St. Louis, San Francisco, Albany,
Brooklyn, Marquette, Providence, Sioux Falls, and Vincennes. There was one Sulpician student and two places
were reserved for students from the Diocese of Detroit who
had "not yet entered." [41]

The formal opening of the university naturally drew attention from many quarters. *Harper's Weekly* for November 16 devoted an extensive account to it and traced the
germ of the idea back to Bishop Spalding. The writer ad-
mired Spalding's idea of a university as giving breadth of
view.

In the Catholic Church the education, or rather the
training and instruction, received by priests in American
seminaries has not been sufficiently liberal, in the intellectual sense. No ministers of religion could be better fitted
to defend the Christian belief from the scholastic point of
view, or for the careful performance of their daily duties.
Their training and knowledge have been—when they came
entirely from the ecclesiastical seminary—professional
rather than liberal. Firmness of Christian faith and deep
reading in the Greek and Latin fathers, profundity in the
rubrics and canon law, skill in the use of time-honored
polemical weapons, do not prevent a man from being one-
sided and narrow-minded, or give that flexibility, grace,
breadth, and culture which the modern defender of Chris-

---

[41] *Solemnities of the Dedication*, p. 83.

tianity needs. Cardinal Newman is revered in the world because he has these qualities.

Harper's referred to the objection raised on the score of the professors being foreigners, but the writer remarked, "Objection might just as well be made to the having of an Oxford man pre-eminent in any way at Princeton, or a Heidelberg man at Johns Hopkins. It would not shock us if Harvard were to import Max Müller, or Yale Professor Dowden. The teachers brought by Bishop Keane to this country are eminent—some of them uniquely eminent—in the various branches of philosophy, theology and the Bible languages." The New York *Examiner* of November 28 said, "Never was gathered in Washington, and perhaps not in America, such a notable assembly of Catholic prelates." After enumerating the principal guests and their accomplishments, the *Examiner* remarked, "to give the dedication a national character President Harrison and most of the Cabinet were present. Mr. Harrison made a sickly speech, and Mr. Blaine responded to the toast, 'Our country and her President.' " During the course of the next month comments continued to appear in the press both here and abroad. John T. Murphy, C.S.Sp., of Holy Ghost College in Pittsburgh wrote an article for the December *Catholic World* which he devoted to the profitable relations which should exist between the university and the existing Catholic colleges. Murphy stated that the university could perform a valuable service by raising the standards of scholarship and making them more uniform throughout the Catholic school system, and he felt there was none who could rightly question the good which the university would do for all Catholic institutions. "There is no one who has Catholic

interests at heart but will wish it God-speed," [42] and he
believed it was morally certain that the "vast majority" of
the Catholic colleges would gladly co-operate with the university in carrying out its program. In an editorial note
accompanying this article J. Havens Richards, S.J., president of Georgetown University, was quoted as having said
in a recent address:

There is, indeed, one other agency which, as I foresee,
will be of decided benefit in aiding us to overcome the fail-
ings I have noted. When the Catholic University of America
opens its doors to all comers and subjects them to a rigid
matriculation *examen* we shall have a test to which we can
appeal . . . I know not what others may feel, but I for
one am impatient for the day when the Catholic University
will open its literary courses.[43]

James F. Loughlin, a professor of theology in St. Charles
Seminary, Overbrook, discussed the university in relation
to the existing seminaries in an article published some six
weeks after the Washington inauguration. He asserted that
he felt there was no reason why the major seminaries could
not give courses equal to those given in the university, although "they may not be denominated as such, and will
possess no independent authority to confer degrees." Loughlin was careful, however, not to be misunderstood and he
said readers who did not follow his thought carefully might
seize on this statement as "a covert fling at the new university so auspiciously inaugurated amongst us." [44] He elabo-

[42] John T. Murphy, C.S.Sp., "The New Catholic University and
the Existing Colleges," in *Catholic World*, L (Dec. 1889), 302.

[43] "Note to Article on the Catholic University," in *Catholic World*,
L (Dec. 1889), 297.

[44] James F. Loughlin, "The Higher and Lower Education of the

rated on the university's disadvantages. To Loughlin its lack
of reputation, the undue optimism of its friends, and the
fact that it was, to him, only a seminary would tell against
it. What advantage of any kind, then, did the university
have? "One, but a great one. It starts out upon its career
with the traditions, the machinery, the approved methods,
the innate dignity of an organized university. It does not
claim a superiority of genius, either as regards its professors or its students; it ought, however, to claim and exhibit
a vast superiority of *system;* for, deprived of this, its days
would be few and evil." [45] Loughlin's final plea was for a
reorganization of seminary methods along university lines
and he felt the time was ripe to inaugurate this change in
the seminary organization.

In the early days of December, 1889, foreign comment
on the new university reached America. *L'Eclair* of Mont-
pellier, France, wrote enthusiastically of it in its issue of
December 7, contrasting the happy beginnings of the Washington university with the state of the Catholic institutes of
France.

Quel contraste, en vérité, avec nos oeuvres de France! A
peine les nobles sacrifices de nos catholiques français ont eu
fait germer du sol fécond de notre chère patrie les Universités catholiques, qu'un gouvernement indigne du nom
de République, et plus autocrate que la pire des monarch-
ies absolues leur enlève, par de basses intrigues et de
honteuses persécutions, leurs moyens d'honorable existence,
fait rayer de leurs documents publics le nom même d'Université et les soumet à des conditions dont le résultat, dans
l'esprit de ceux, qui vous gouvernent, devrait être leur ruine.

American Priesthood," in *American Catholic Quarterly Review,* XV
(Jan. 1890), 117.

[45] *Ibid.,* p. 118.

En Amérique, sur une terre encore protestante, nous pouvons, au nom de la liberté, faire germer et s'épanouir, presque en un clin d'oeil, les plus brillantes oeuvres de notre foi, couvrir ce grand pays de nos nombreuses écoles, garantir a l'élite de notre jeunesse la haute éducation qu'elle désire, et donner à nos esperances pour l'avenir un élan que rien ne vient étouffer.

Two weeks later in a long article on the centennial of the American hierarchy, *Univers* of Paris, in its issue of December 21, spoke of the university.

Il semble que c'était témérité, imprudence, de la part de l'Eglise, de construire son université près du siège du gouvernement de des temples de toutes les sectes. L'Eglise n'agit pas suivant les motifs humains, et ce qui prouve qu'elle a été bien inspirée, c'est que tous les journaux la félicitent d'établir aussi hardiment un nouveau foyer de lumière, d'ouvrir un palais où l'on enseignera les sciences divines et humaines, et où toutes les intelligences pourront s'abreuver et se nourir d'aliments salutaires.

If the French Catholic press saw salutary lessons in the opening of the university, a number of non-Catholic Americans were not so pleased. Senator George F. Edmunds of Vermont made a strong plea for the establishment of a national university in the capital, an idea which the New York *Post* of December 5 characterized as, "expected ever since the scheme of a Catholic University in the same city began to take shape." Senator John J. Ingalls of Kansas had introduced a bill four years before for a national university but it had not been acted upon. According to the *Post*, Edmunds' effort was calculated to be, "a sort of Protestant offset to the Catholic Institution, and expresses the dislike of the various evangelical denominations, especially of the

West, to seeing the national capital made a great centre of Catholic influence." The plan of Edmunds was explained and the *Post* writer stated that a national university might well prove to be "the glory of the country," but he warned against such an institution being made subject to political influence, for "a political college in whose doings every Son of Thunder whom the President or the Governor of a State wished to 'recognize' would have a giner, [*sic*] would be simply in the long run, a national shame." The incident of President Harrison being seated at the left of Cardinal Gibbons instead of at the right at the university dinner also drew critical comment. Letters of protest were written to various papers claiming a slight had been offered to the President of the United States in favor of Cardinal Taschereau. *The Nation* for December 12 contained such letters and the Boston *Herald* of December 16 carried a news article on Justin D. Fulton, an "anti-papist" preacher, trying to rouse the indignation of native Americans of the country at the threat of Romanism in the national capital.

With the university in operation the work of the library committee was completed and Archbishop Corrigan wrote to the rector to say that the matter of books could now be turned over to the professors; he, therefore, asked "to consider myself discharged from the work under consideration." [46] Keane promptly thanked the archbishop for having "so admirably discharged" the task of laying the foundations of the university library. He said the recent list of books from Benziger's would be turned over to Professor Bouquillon, "who is our chief guide in the organization of

---

[46] NYAA, C–39, M. A. Corrigan to John J. Keane, New York, December 16, 1889, copy.

the library." [47] Plans were progressing meanwhile for St. Joseph's Seminary for the Archdiocese of New York and Bishop McQuaid wrote to say that he was happy to hear of its advancement. He remarked that there was a glowing account of the Dunwoodie project in the current issue of the *Catholic Mirror* of Baltimore, "which will not greatly please the Card. or Dr. Keane." He was at a standstill on his own seminary, "owing to the uncertainty of my future." He had not changed his attitude towards the university at Washington and he was beginning to see real possibilities for the Catholics at Cornell University in his own diocese.

The University is lapsing into quietness, and quietness precedes death. Time will tell who was right. My convictions are stronger now than ever. There are now nearly one hundred students in Cornell University at Ithaca. One of the tutors is a Catholic, a convert and much in earnest. He is at the head of a Catholic Union formed of Cath. Students. Some of the careless ones have been brought into it and to church. Some of them lead in their classes, especially in the graduating class. I neither approve nor disapprove, telling them that I look for results which I hope will be favorable. The President is a Congregationalist and very kindly disposed toward us. At one time the tendency among some of the Professors was toward rationalism. This of late years has changed. [48]

When the many preoccupations attendant upon the centenary celebration and the opening of the university had been laid aside, Cardinal Gibbons wrote Pope Leo XIII a long description of these events for the Holy Father's

---

[47] NYAA, C–16, John J. Keane to M. A. Corrigan, Washington, December 18, 1889.

[48] NYAA, C–16, Bernard J. McQuaid to M. A. Corrigan, Rochester, December 30, 1889.

information. The cardinal closed his letter by reference to the university inauguration.

On Wednesday, the 13th, in spite of the bad weather, the bishops, priests, and faithful went en masse to Washington for the inauguration of the University. There, as in Baltimore, everything went well. The President of the United States, the Vice-President, the Secretary of State, and several members of the Cabinet made it a point to honor this festivity with their presence, and the applause which burst forth when Your health was proposed and which followed the answer of Mgr. Satolli to this toast, as well as that which greeted the President, manifest greatly that the love of the Church and the love of the country are indissolubly united in the hearts of the faithful . . .[49]

The Catholic University of America was, then, a reality by the closing days of 1889. Its formal opening on November 13, coinciding almost five years to the day when it had been proposed in the Third Plenary Council of Baltimore, marked the end of a long and often difficult series of negotiations for the bishops, priests, and laymen who stood sponsors at its birth. Considering the obstacles which arose during those five years it was a remarkable accomplishment for them to have pushed the work to so speedy a conclusion. There were times when the life of the entire project hung by a slender thread but the persistence of a few hardy and courageous men succeeded in bridging these trying episodes to bring it to completion. A real break with the past in Catholic educational procedure in America had been made. The university opened as an exclusively graduate school thirteen years after Johns Hopkins had inaugurated that

---

[49] BCA, 86–V–7, James Gibbons to Leo XIII, Baltimore, December 7, 1889, copy in French.

system in the United States and in the same year that Clark University brought the ideal of an exclusively graduate university to New England. There were still trying days ahead for the university, but during the seven years of Bishop Keane's rectorship a goodly number of these problems were met and solved, and when in September, 1896, John J. Keane went out of office there was no further doubt in the minds of reasonable men of the university's ultimate success. If a few diehards still refused their support as the century neared its end, they were in such a decided minority that the university administration did not need to fear seriously that their criticism would endanger the work which had been planned so carefully and so thoroughly by Bishop Keane and his colleagues. The friends of the university could rightly feel that the words written some months before by Daniel Hudson had now received a deeper meaning:

The straight line from one point to another has been drawn by Leo XIII. All we have to do is to follow it, and to hold up the hands of that noble enthusiast who has made the ideal real, and who will save us from our own lack of what the French call *esprit de corps,* but which is better expressed by Christian fellowship.[50]

---

[50] "A Word Concerning the New University," in *Ave Maria,* XXIX (Aug. 3, 1889), 110.

A Note on the Sources

SINCE THERE are no published volumes on the history of the Catholic University of America a formal bibliography would not be in place here. The preponderant amount of material which provided the basis for this study was found in the various diocesan archives of the United States. The following are the most important:

Baltimore Cathedral Archives. These archives, housed in the chancery office of the Archdioceses of Baltimore and Washington at 408 N. Charles Street, Baltimore, are a veritable mine of riches for the history of the Church in the United States. The Gibbons Papers, with which this study was mainly concerned, have been indexed and catalogued down to September, 1902. The Spalding Papers were likewise helpful for the Second Plenary Council and the university question.

New York Archdiocesan Archives. These archives are housed at St. Joseph's Seminary, Dunwoodie. It is an exceedingly important collection for late nineteenth-century church history. The Corrigan and Farley Papers, which are indexed only in part, contain a great deal of information on the subject of this monograph.

Archives of the Archdiocese of Cincinnati. The Cincinnati collection is kept at Mount Saint Mary's Seminary of the West, Norwood. The Elder Papers, with which we were mainly concerned, are filed in chronological order and contain considerable material on the university's formative years.

Archives of the Diocese of Rochester. These archives are kept at St. Bernard's Seminary, Rochester. The McQuaid Papers are classified under headings which make their use relatively easy. These archives also contain copies of the McQuaid-Gilmour correspondence from the archives of the Diocese of Cleveland.

Archives of the Diocese of Richmond. These archives are housed in part in the chancery office and in part in the bishop's residence. The principal items of importance here were the entries of Bishop Keane in the diocesan diary. The Keane correspondence was meager, although it is possible that when the collection is indexed more material may come to light from Keane's days at Richmond.

Other archival materials were made available to the writer from the collections of the Archdiocese of Boston and the Diocese of Covington in the form of copies of letters. A search in the archives of the Archdioceses of Philadelphia and Chicago revealed nothing on the university from the few remainin papers of Archbishops Ryan and Feehan. The loss of the personal papers of Ireland and Spalding likewise deprived the writer of the possibility of finding pertinent documents on the university in the archives of the Archdiocese of St. Paul and the Diocese of Peoria. The rich archives of the University of Notre Dame are, in the main, limited to a period earlier than that of the university's foundation and, therefore, a search in this collection yielded only one or two letters.

The press, both Catholic and secular, of the years covered by this study enabled the writer to fill in many lacunae that would otherwise have been left by the manuscript sources. An effort was made to cover a number of the leading metropolitan papers for episodes in the university's development. The papers examined, mainly for the years 1884–1889, were the following: Baltimore *Sun,* Boston *Pilot, Catholic Advo-*

cate (Louisville), *Catholic Mirror* (Baltimore), *Church News* (Washington), *Freeman's Journal* (New York), New York *Sun,* New York *Times,* and the New York *Tribune.* Other individual items from papers like the Chicago *Tribune,* the Philadelphia *Ledger,* and the *Independent* (New York) were used, but these did not carry the amount of news on the university which characterized those listed above.

The third category of sources for the present study was that of the periodical literature. The following articles will prove of assistance to the student who wishes to investigate the subject further.

Anonymous. "The Catholic University and Its Constitutions," in *Catholic World,* XLIX (July, 1889), 427–432.

——. "Present Aspect of the Catholic University," in *American Ecclesiastical Review,* I (Aug. 1889), 281–298.

——. "A Word Concerning the New University," in *Ave Maria,* XXIX (Aug. 3, 1889), 109–110.

——. "The First Lustrum of the Catholic University," in *American Ecclesiastical Review,* I (Sept. 1889), 338–347.

——. "The Divinity Building of the Washington University," in *American Ecclesiastical Review,* I (Nov.–Dec. 1889), 453–460.

——. "Shall We Have a Catholic Congress?" in *Catholic World,* VIII (Nov. 1868), 224–228.

——. "On the Higher Education," in *Catholic World,* XII (Mar. 1871), 721–731; XIII (Apr. 1871), 115–124.

Azarias, Brother. "The Catholic University Question in Ireland and England," in *American Catholic Quarterly Review,* III (Oct. 1878), 577–594.

Becker, T. A. "Shall We Have a University?" in *American Catholic Quarterly Review,* I (Apr. 1876), 230–253.

——. "A Plan for the Proposed Catholic University," in *American Catholic Quarterly Review,* I (Oct. 1876), 655–679.

Calvet, J. "Catholic University Education in France," in *Catholic University Bulletin,* XIII (Apr. 1907), 191–210.

Guilday, Peter. "The Founding of the Catholic University of America," in *American Ecclesiastical Review,* CIX (Jan. 1944), 2–16.

Herbermann, Charles G. "The Faculty of the Catholic University," in *American Catholic Quarterly Review,* XIV (Oct. 1889), 701–715.

H(euser), H(erman) J. "American Catholics and the Proposed University," in *American Catholic Quarterly Review,* X (Oct. 1885), 634–657.

Hewit, A. F. "The American Catholic University," in *Catholic World,* XLII (Nov. 1885), 223–226.

Keane, John J. "Leo XIII and the Catholic University of America," in *Catholic World,* XLVI (Nov. 1887), 145–153.

——. "The Roman Universities," in *Catholic World,* XLVI (Dec. 1887), 313–321.

——. "The Catholic University of Louvain," in *Catholic World,* XLVI (Jan. 1888), 525–534.

——. "The University of Strassburg," in *Catholic World,* XLVI (Feb. 1888), 643–652.

——. "The Catholic Universities of France," in *Catholic World,* XLVII (June, 1888), 289–297.

——. "A Chat about the Catholic University," in *Catholic World,* XLVIII (Nov. 1888), 216–226.

——. "The Clergy and the Catholic University," in *American Ecclesiastical Review,* I (July, 1889), 241–245.

Loughlin, James F. "The Higher and Lower Education of the American Priesthood," in *American Catholic Quarterly Review,* XV (Jan. 1890), 101–122.

Murphy, John T. "The New Catholic University and the Existing Colleges," in *Catholic World,* L (Dec. 1889), 302–306.

Niedermasser, Andrew. "Malines and Würzburg," in *Catholic World,* II (Dec. 1865), 332–347.

O'Gorman, Thomas. "Leo XIII and the Catholic University," in *Catholic University Bulletin,* I (Jan. 1895), 8–24.

Shea, John Gilmary. "The Rapid Increase of the Dangerous Classes in the United States," in *American Catholic Quarterly Review,* IV (Apr. 1879), 240–268.

——. "The Pastoral Letter of the Third Plenary Council of Baltimore," in *American Catholic Quarterly Review,* X (Jan. 1885), 1–18.

——. "The Proposed American Catholic University," in *American Catholic Quarterly Review,* X (Apr. 1885), 312–325.

Thébaud, A. J. "Superior Instruction in Our Colleges," in *American Catholic Quarterly Review,* VII (Oct. 1882), 673–699.

White, Andrew D. "The Next American University," in *The Forum,* V (June, 1888), 371–382.

Significant Dates

August 23, 1865. Archbishop Martin J. Spalding suggests a Catholic university for the United States to Bishop John Timon.

October, 1866. Second Plenary Council of Baltimore expresses the hope for a university.

April–October, 1876. Articles on a Catholic university by Bishop Thomas A. Becker in the *American Catholic Quarterly Review*.

August 29, 1880. Bishop John Lancaster Spalding suggests a higher school of theology be established by the American hierarchy at Cincinnati.

June 30, 1881. Bishop Spalding preaches a sermon on the need of an institution for advanced training of the clergy at the silver jubilee of St. Francis Seminary, Milwaukee.

November 13, 1884. Miss Mary Gwendoline Caldwell signifies her intention of giving $300,000 for the establishment of an institution for the higher education of the clergy.

November 16, 1884. Bishop Spalding preaches on "The Higher Education of the Priesthood," in the Third Plenary Council of Baltimore.

December 6, 1884. Bishops in council approve committee of hierarchy to begin work for a university and decree its foundation.

January 26, 1885. Preliminary meeting of university committee, New York City.

May 7, 1885. First formal meeting of university committee, Baltimore.

October 22, 1885. Letter of Pope Leo XIII to Archbishop Gibbons approving the idea of a Catholic university for the United States.

November 11, 1885. Meeting of university committee at Baltimore. Appointment of episcopal collectors for university funds; appointment of Archbishop John J. Williams as chairman of university building committee.

May 12, 1886. Meeting of university committee at Baltimore. Selection of Bishop John J. Keane as first rector; decision to lay matter of university formally before the Holy See.

October 27, 1886. Meeting of university committee at Baltimore. Acceptance and signing of letters to Pope Leo XIII and Cardinal Simeoni; Bishops Keane and Ireland commissioned to take letters to Rome.

March 9, 1887. Cardinal Gibbons' letter to Pope Leo XIII giving details of plan for university and meeting objections which had been raised.

April 10, 1887. Brief of Pope Leo XIII giving approval to the plan of the university committee.

September 7, 1887. Meeting of the university committee at Baltimore. Washington finally decided upon as site; formal appointment of Bishop Keane as first rector.

November, 1887. Bishop Keane inaugurates series of articles on Catholic universities in the *Catholic World*.

November 28, 1887. Archbishop Michael A. Corrigan of New York resigns from the university committee.

May 24, 1888. Laying of the cornerstone of Caldwell Hall, original building of the university; Bishop Spalding's address; meeting of the university committee at Washington.

October 15, 1888. Bishop Keane completes draft of original statutes for the university.

November 13, 1888. Meeting of the university committee at

Baltimore. Approval of the statutes as drawn up by Bishop Keane; return to the committee of Archbishop Corrigan.

November 17, 1888. Bishop Keane sails for Rome to secure approval of statutes and to engage professors.

March 7, 1889. Pope Leo XIII issues letter to Cardinal Gibbons giving formal approval to university project and to statutes for the institution.

March 19, 1889. Bishop Keane gives dinner at the American College, Rome, to mark the successful completion of university affairs at the Holy See.

November 13, 1889. Formal opening of the university.

Index

408